Spanish songs for voice and p

Carlos López Galarza

Spanish songs for voice and piano on poems by Lope De Vega

Lope de Vega in the Spanish concert song

ScienciaScripts

Imprint

Cover image: www.ingimage.com

This book is a translation from the original published under ISBN 978-620-2-14044-7.

Publisher:
Sciencia Scripts
is a trademark of
Dodo Books Indian Ocean Ltd. and OmniScriptum S.R.L publishing group

120 High Road, East Finchley, London, N2 9ED, United Kingdom
Str. Armeneasca 28/1, office 1, Chisinau MD-2012, Republic of Moldova, Europe

ISBN: 978-620-7-27703-2

Contents

I know very well that the study of Lope de Vega's Musical Theatre in the 18th century would give rise to a fourth volume and the investigation of Lope's verses set to music in the 19th and 20th centuries would undoubtedly produce a fifth volume. So, with all my love I bid farewell, while offering the younger generations of musicologists the continuation of this Cancionero Musical de Lope de Vega.

(QUEROL, Miquel, *Cancionero musical de Lope de Vega*, vol. *Poesi'as cantadas en las comedias,* CSIC, Barcelona, 1991, p. 7).

Presentation

The musical repertoire, and especially the vocal repertoire, has for years suffered from a certain stagnation as it has focused on a reduced group of works in comparison with the enormous amount of compositions of all periods that can be performed. In recent decades, the expansion of this repertoire has undergone notable progress, especially in terms of discographic recordings, an expansion which has not, however, been transferred in all cases to the field of concerts or the publication of scores, an essential element for the works to be disseminated and widely performed. The situation is no different with regard to the genre of songs with piano by Spanish composers. While recordings have been numerous, public performances and their use in the academic environment have remained restricted, except for a few laudable efforts on the part of the performers, to a handful of works that are repeated ad nauseam and generate a logical loss of interest in the public and in the singers.

The expansion and renewal of the musical repertoire involves, at the same time as creating new works, bringing to light compositions that for various reasons have not reached the concert halls, the record or the classrooms of conservatories and higher education centres. This study discreetly aspires to collaborate in the necessary work of rescuing so many compositions that have been forgotten for various reasons, by focusing on more than a hundred songs for voice and piano by Spanish composers, most of them outside the repertoire of concerts and recordings, taking as a unifying factor the author of all the texts, Felix Lope de Vega Carpio.

The choice of Lope de Vega as the unifying element came after a process of searching for new repertoire in Spanish song. The interest in offering rarely performed compositions for this type of concert put us on the track of a large number of songs written on poems by authors of the Golden Age. In a first approach, after consulting several catalogues, especially those of the Biblioteca Nacional de Espana and the Biblioteca Espanola de Musica y Teatro Contemporaneos of the Fundacion Juan March, we observed that Lope de Vega is one of the writers most frequently chosen by composers to compose songs for piano, and that he also comes close in number to the poems set to music by Gustavo Adolfo Becquer or Federico Garcia Lorca, far surpassing those of Juan Ramon Jimenez, Antonio Machado or Miguel Hernandez[1] . We were also interested in the fact that Lope is the classical writer most used in the musical genre in question, far ahead of Gongora, Cervantes or Quevedo[2] .

In order to assess the importance of the corpus to which we refer, we examined all the catalogues of Spanish archives and libraries with musical collections, searching for references to this type of works in various manuals on the History of Spanish Music, locating 172 compositions that we subsequently filtered by applying the criteria that we will refer to below, finally establishing the catalogue at 109 works. The process was parallel to locating the scores of all the songs, a costly task that has lasted until the closing date of the catalogue in March 2012. Very few of the works that have been published are currently commercially available. Most of the pre-1940s editions are out of print and a large number are unpublished, so we have had to work with the copies found in

---

[1] In order to make these statements we rely on the excellent and very useful work by Tinnell which compiles the musical compositions based on Spanish poets: TINNELL, Roger, *Catalogo anotado de la musica espanola contemporanea basada en la literatura espanola,* Centro de Documentation Musical de Andalucia, Granada, 2001. In it we have counted 140 songs with lyrics by Becquer, 86 by Jimenez, 83 by Machado and 16 by Hernandez. Tinnell does not include Garcia Lorca in his *Catalogo...,* and devotes a separate volume to him in which one can see the great number of songs for voice and piano, among other genres, that Lorca's poetry inspired: TINNELL, Roger, *Federico Garcia Lorca y la musica- catalogo y discografa anotados,* Madrid, Fundacion Juan March, 2ª edition, Madrid, 1998.

[2] Tinnell's catalogue lists 26 songs with lyrics by Gongora, 16 by Cervantes and only 5 by Quevedo. The *Gran Enciclopedia Cervantina* contains annotations of some of the works listed by Tinnell with lyrics by Cervantes, together with other works with different vocal and instrumental combinations. ALVAR, Carlos (dir.), *Gran Enciclopedia Cervantina*, 8 vols., Centro de Estudios Cervantinos, Castalia, Alcala de Henares, 2005- [to date, the first 8 of the 10 volumes have been published].

the archives and libraries consulted. In some cases we have had to locate and ask the heirs for permission to obtain a copy of the manuscript, in others we have had to ask the composers themselves to provide us with a copy of their work.

The comparison of the scores with the data appearing in the catalogues and reference manuals consulted has been fundamental in filtering the catalogue, thus detecting some errors of assignment to the genre of the song with piano and even errors of attribution of the text. Thus, from the first list of works we excluded those composed with instruments other than the piano, as well as songs without accompaniment, those without an original text by Lope de Vega, or those written by non-Spanish composers.

The choice of Lope is therefore due to three reasons. The first is the sufficiently large corpus on which to investigate, more than a hundred songs. Secondly, the songs that will be included in our catalogue cover a time span that coincides, with few exceptions, with the 20th century, the period of splendour of the genre in Spain, especially its first half, which will allow us to study the musical treatment of the texts of the Golden Age in that century. Thirdly, only eight of the songs we present remain with a certain regularity in the vocal repertoire of the singers of our pals[3] , a fact that brings an undoubted novelty to this work.

The works included in our catalogue are limited to the genre of song originally written for voice and piano by Spanish composers who have taken original texts by Lope de Vega, either from his lyrics, from fragments of plays or from works written in prose. We therefore exclude songs composed on adaptations or translations into other languages[4] , as well as vocal works in genres other than songs with piano, such as choral works, symphonic-choral works, or works for voice alone with other types of instrumental accompaniment.

The geographical limits we impose on ourselves are those derived from the expression "canciones espanolas" in the title of this book. In the first phase of the work we contemplated the possibility of including foreign composers and gathering all the existing compositions for voice and piano based on Lope. This first orientation was discarded for several reasons, among them the need to delimit a unitary corpus, and in a practical order, the impossibility of searching in archives and libraries all over the world to offer a real and complete catalogue. Thus, an initial search, which could be extended in works subsequent to this one, has yielded a reduced, but no less interesting, balance. By the Chilean composer Carlos Botto Vallarino we have located his Op. 4, *Doce canciones,* a collection written in 1952, made up of four subgroups: *Canciones de siega, Canciones de boda, Canciones de amor* and *Canciones Sacras*[5] . By the Mexican Manuel Leon Mariscal, *Morenica*[6] , from 1956, is preserved. A particular case is that of the composer Eduardo Grau, based in the Argentinian city of Mendoza, author of a song entitled *Zagalejo deperlas,* from the well-known poem of *Pastores de Belen (Shepherds of Bethlehem).* Grau left his native Barcelona with his parents, as emigrants, at the age of eight, and lived and developed his entire

[3] Although this figure does not objectively reflect the reality of live recital performances, we can assess the situation by looking at the number of recordings of each song presented in the catalogue included in this work. These are Enrique Granados' *No lloivis ojuelos (*13 recordings), Joaquin Rodrigo's *Pastorcito Santo (*37) and *Coplas del pastor enamorado (*18), Eduard Toldra's *Madre unos ojuelos v (*39) and *C'antaicillo* (19), and to a lesser extent the three from Joaquin Turina's *Homenaje a Lope de Vega (*13, 9 and 9 recordings respectively). These eight songs alone account for 79% of the catalogued recordings.

[4] As far as adaptations are concerned, we do not include Joaquin Rodrigo's *Romance del Conde Ocana,* whose text, not entirely original by Lope de Vega, was adapted by Joaquin de Entrambasaguas for this composition in 1947.

[5] Canciones de siega: a. Blanca me era yo, b. Oh, cuan bien segado, c. Esta si que es siega; 2. Canciones de boda: a. Talamo de amor, b. Por un si dulce amoroso, c. Esta novia se lleva flor; 3. Love songs: a. Blancas coge Lucinda, b. Si os partierades al alba, c. Pobres negros ojuelos; 4. Sacred songs: a. Mananitas floridas, b. A la esposa divina, c. Esta es la justicia.) The total length is 16', edited by IEM and premiered in Chile by various singers and pianists between 1953 and 1965. See: GRANDELA DEL RIO, Ines, "Catalogo de las obras musicales de Carlos Botto Vallarino", Revista musical chilena, vol. 51, n° 187, Santiago de Chile, 1997, pp. 92-106.

[6] A copy of this song is preserved in the Fons Conxita Badia of the Biblioteca de Catalunya, call number 2007-4-C 18/47.

musical career in that city, which is why he is not included in the catalogue.
In the German-speaking area, Emanuel Geibel published in 1852, together with Paul Heyse, his *Spanisches Liederbuch,* an anthology which included German translations of poems by Spanish authors from the Middle Ages and the Renaissance, including *No Uoreis, ojuelos, Pues andais en las palmas* and *Madre, unos ojuelos vi,* which became famous in the German-speaking countries in their German translation: *Went nicht, ihr Augelein, Die ihr schwebet* and *Mutter ich hab' zwei Augelein* respectively. The popularity of these translations led to them being set to music, for voice and piano, by famous composers such as Johannes Brahms, who wrote his *Geistliches wiegenlied* (On *Pues andais en las palmas*) for voice, piano and viola, or Hugo Wolf, who composed his *Spanisches Liederbuch* based on the aforementioned translations by Geibel and Heyse, a cycle which includes *Die ihr schwebet.* Lesser-known musicians such as Melchior Diepenbrock (1798-1853), Eduard Lassen (1830-1904), Gustav Flugel (1812-1900) also wrote songs based on the same text. Adolf Jensen (1837-1879) and Friedrich August Naubert (1839- 1839) wrote music for *Mutter, ich hab' zwei Augelein.*
1897). On a Swedish translation of *Pues andais en las palmas,* Ingvar Lindholm (1921-) composed *I anglar, som vandren bland palmer dar ovam.*
The time frame covered by this research covers a period approximately coinciding with the 20th century, with a few works from the end of the 19th century and nine compositions from the 21st century. The authors whose works we catalogue, presented in chronological order of birth, are the following: Manuel del Populo Vicente Garcia, Julio Perez Aguirre, Jose Maria Casares y Espinosa de los Monteros, Bernardino Valle Chinestra, Enrique Granados y Campina, Jose Maria Guervos y Mira, Conrado del Campo y Zabaleta, Angel Larroca Rech, Joan Llongueres Badia, Joaquin Turina Perez, Francisco Cotarelo Romanos, Benito Garcia de la Parra y Tellez, Eduard Toldra i Sabater, Julio Gomez Garcia, Angel Mingote Lorente, Juan Altisent Ceardi, Federico Moreno Torroba, Manuel Palau Boix, Jose Maria Franco Bordons, Juan Maria Thomas Sabater, Salvador Bacarisse Chinoria, Arturo Menendez Aleyxandre, Joaquin Rodrigo Vidre, Angel Martin Pompey, Enrique Truan Alvarez, Gustavo Duran Martinez, Jose Luis Iturralde Perez, Joaquin Nin-Culmell, Enrique Casal Chapi, Fernando Moraleda Bellver, Francisco Escudero Garcia, Mercedes Carol[7] , Miguel Asins Arbo, Matilde Salvador Segarra, Jose Peris Lacasa, Pascual Aldave Rodriguez, Eduardo Rincon Garcia, Felix Lavilla Munarriz, Antonio Barrera Alvarez, Jose Maria Benavente Martinez, Vicente Miguel Peris, Jose Bueno Aguado [Buen Aguado], Fernando Colodro Campos, Antoni Parera Fons, Miquel Ortega i Pujol and Gonzalo Diaz Yerro.
The Spanish song for voice and piano is a section of our musical historiography which is always present in the works of prestigious researchers and of which we have valuable catalogues. However, the task of systematically studying the entire repertoire has yet to be completed, at least as far as 20th century works are concerned. The main contribution to Spanish musical historiography is that of Celsa Alonso, who with her work on Spanish lyric song in the 19th century has not only highlighted the importance of the genre in Spain, but has also made us aware of the enormous number of composers and works that were produced in that century[8] . We have no comparable study of the 20th century. The American singer and teacher Suzanne R. Draayer published in 2009 a much-needed encyclopaedic volume on Spanish song[9] , which, although it covers a wide range of composers, is not exhaustive considering the extent of the subject. A brief but precise and well-structured article by Celsa Alonso, corresponding to the entry "cancion" in the *Diccionario de la musica espanola e hispanoamericana,* published under the direction and

Pseudonym of Mercedes Garcia Lopez.
[8] ALONSO, Celsa: *Cancion lnica espanola en el siglo XIX,* Institute Complutense de Ciencias Musicales, Madrid, 1998. Since this work Alonso has published numerous articles and collaborations of which we will continue to give news.
[9] DRAAYER, Suzanne R., *Art Song Composers of Spain. An Encyclopedia,* Scarecrow Press, Maryland, 2009.

coordination of Emilio Casares Rodicio[10] , presents a complete vision, although evidently centred on the contributions of the composers considered most important. The publications by Antonio Fernandez-Cid[11] on the song in Spain and the specific studies by Federico Sopena[12] on the *Lied,* focus on this group of outstanding composers and represent important approaches, albeit of an informative nature, to the subject that concerns us.

We know, moreover, from the references given by Tomas Marco[13] and Fernandez-Cid[14] , in their respective histories of 20th century Spanish music, and from the catalogues of composers published by the SGAE, of the boost given to the cancion, in quantity and quality, from the beginning of the century until the 1960s, in many cases approaching the model of the *Lied* mentioned above. However, these references to the song only deal with the best known and most performed works, a small number among thousands of works written for voice and piano. But the greatest source of information comes from the valuable collections and catalogues of the Biblioteca Nacional and the Biblioteca Espanola de Musica y Teatro Contemporaneos of the Fundacion Juan March. These two centres hold most of the works of this genre that have been composed in Spain since the beginning of the 20th century[15] .

Although there are studies that address the role of music in the plays of the Golden Age and Lope de Vega in particular, as well as the songs and texts to be sung in his comedies, the relationship between Lope and 20th century music has received little consideration. In the first case, the works of Louise K. Stein, Ingrid Simson, Jose Maria Ruano and Antonio Martin Moreno[16] are of reference. In the case of the works that study the songs in Lope's comedies, the studies of Alin y Barrio, Blecua, Campana and Umpierre[17] stand out.

Lope's influence on twentieth-century music is a subject that has not had the good fortune to be as extensively studied as has been done with other classical writers, as in the case of Cervantes[18] . We

[10] CASARES RODICIO, Emilio (dir. and coord.); FERNANDEZ DE LA CUESTA, Ismael; LOPEZ-CALO, Jose (eds.), *Diccionario de la Musica Espanola e Hispanoamericana*, 10 vols., Fundacion Autor-Sociedad General de Autores y Editores, Madrid, 1999-2002.

[11] FERNANDEZ-CID, Antonio, Lieder y canciones de Espana. Pequena historia contemporanea de la musica nacional 1900-1963, Editora Nacional, Madrid, 1963.

[12] SOPENA, Federico, *El Lied romantico,* Moneda y Credito, Madrid, 1963. SOPENA, Federico, *El Nacionalismo musical y el "iie"",* Real Musical, Madrid, 1979.

[13] MARCO, Tomas, Historia de la Musica espanola. Siglo X, Alianza, Madrid, 1983.

[14] FERNANDEZ-CID, Antonio, *La Musica espanola en el siglo XX*, Madrid, Fundacion Juan March, Rioduero, Madrid, 1973.

[15] In the FJM library alone there are 2,455 records of scores for voice and piano written in the 20th century, each of which may contain several songs. In the BNE there are 4,750 of all periods.

[16] STEIN, Louise K., *Songs of Mortals, Dialogues of the Gods. Music and Theater in Seventh Century Spain,* Oxford, 1993, pp. 336-45. SIMSON, Ingrid, "Calderon as Librettist: Musical Performances in the Golden Age", in Theo Reichenberger (coord.), *Calderon: Eminent Protagonist of the European Baroque,* Edition Reichenberger, Kassel, 2000, pp. 217-43. RUANO DE LA HAZA, Jose Maria, *La puesta en escena en los teatros comerciales del Siglo de Oro,* Editorial Castalia, Madrid, 2000. MARTIN MORENO, Antonio, "Musica, pasion, razon: la teori'a de los afectos en el teatro y la musica del Siglo de Oro", *Edad de oro,* vol. 22, 2003, pp. 321-360. Two doctoral theses have recently been read which approach the subject from different temporal perspectives: MOLINA JIMENEZ, Maria Belen, *Literatura y Musica en el Siglo de Oro Espanol Interrelaciones en el Teatro Lirico,* Universidad de Murcia, Murcia, 2007, CARRILLO GUZMAN, Mercedes del Carmen: *La musica incidental en el Teatro Espanol de Madrid (1942-1952 y 1962-1964)*, Universidad de Murcia, Murcia, 2008.

[17] ALIN, Jose Maria; BARRIO ALONSO, Maria Begona, *Cancionero teatral de Lope de Vega,* Tamesis, London, 1997. ALIN, Jose Maria, "Sobre el "Cancionero" teatral de Lope de Vega: las canciones embebidas y otros problemas", *Lope de Vega y los orgenes del teatro espanol: actas del I Congreso Internacional sobre Lope de Vega*, 1981, pp. 533-40. BLECUA TEIJEIRO, Jose Manuel, "Canciones en el teatro de Lope de Vega", *Anuario Lope de Vega*, IX, 2003, pp. 11-174. CAMPANA, Patrizia, "Las canciones de Lope de Vega. Catalogo y apuntes para su estudio", *Anuario de Lope de Vega*, 5, 1999, pp. 43-72. UMPIERRE, Gustavo, *Songs in the Plays of Lope de Vega: A Study of their Dramatic Function*, Tamesis, London, 1975. For a compilation of musical scores, see: QUEROL, Miquel, *Cancionero musical de Lope de Vega*, 3 vols, CSIC, Barcelona, 1991.

[18] The most relevant studies on Cervantes and music that have been published recently are collected in: LOLO, Begona (ed.), *Cervantes y el Quijote en la musica: estudios sobre la recepcion de un mito*, Centro Estudios Cervantinos, Madrid, 2007, and LOLO, Begona (ed.), *Visiones del Quijote en la musica del siglo XX*, Centro Estudios Cervantinos, Madrid, 2010. Both volumes bring together the papers presented at the I and II Congreso

only have, in the form of a catalogue, the invaluable work of Roger Tinnell[19] , which presents an extensive list of musical productions of all genres, focusing on contemporary Spanish music. This book tries to fill in part the existing gap in the knowledge of the reception of Lope de Vega by the Spanish composers of that century.

The editions of the works are another matter. There is no doubt that for their dissemination and use in the academic or concert environment, performers need accessible materials, preferably adapted to the tessitura of the different vocal categories, as is the case with the songs of the great authors of German and Austrian *Lied*[20] . In the collections of the aforementioned libraries there are many manuscripts and numerous scores published by publishers who have disappeared or whose collections have been acquired by foreign companies with little interest in the commercial reissue of their collections, with abundant out-of-catalogue references or lack of reissues[21] . This situation hinders the study, but above all the dissemination and performance of the works, from which it can be inferred that their inclusion in recitals and discographic recordings is limited to specific cases of performers with the aim of rescuing forgotten songs in archives and libraries, and thus renewing and expanding the repertoire of Spanish song for voice and piano.

In recent decades some publishers have released modern, complete and revised editions of the songs of Granados, Albeniz and Garcia Abril, but the vast majority of works of this genre written in the 20th century remain either unpublished or published in editions that are in need of critical revision of texts and music. Of the 109 songs with texts by Lope, only fourteen are currently available in commercial editions[22] .

In the catalogue of the songs presented in this work, an account is given of the recordings, both discographic and radio, of each of the works. We can see the absence of recordings of many of them, concentrating on only 8 songs[23] , 138 recordings of the 198 that are included in the catalogue.

In the repertoire of Spanish songs with piano, the modern interpretations of songs by Isaac Albeniz, Padre Donostia, Manuel de Falla, Anton Garcia Abril, Roberto Gerhard, Xavier Gols, Julio Gomez, Enrique Granados, Ernesto Halffter, Joaquim Homs, Joan Lamote de Grignon, Frederic Mompou, Xavier Montsalvatge, Joaquin Nin-Culmell, Felipe Pedrell, Eduardo Rincon and Eduard Toldra, from the record labels Columna Musica, Fundacion BBVA, NB, Trito-La ma de Guido and Verso. As for editions and recordings that take the author of the texts as a unifying element, in the style of the concert programmes and recordings so fashionable in the field of German *Lied* in the last decades, monographic programmes with *Lieder* based on poems by

---

Internacional Cervantes y el Quijote en la Musica held in Madrid in 2005 and 2009 respectively.

[19] TINNELL, Roger, *Catalogo anotado..., op. cit.,* pp. 488-508.

[20] Of Spanish composers only the *Siete cancionespopulares espanolas* by Falla (Ediciones Manuel de Falla / Chester Music / Max Eschig) in two keys are available in revision by Miguel Zanetti, the *Cuatro madrigales amatorios* by Rodrigo (Chester Music). The three songs from Joaquin Turina's *Homenaje a Lope de Vega* were transposed by the composer himself for middle voice to a lower minor third, and from *Si con mis deseos* to a lower fourth, but were not published. Catalogue of works by Joaquin Turina [online] <http://www.joaquinturina.com/opus90.html> [accessed: 18-5-2011]. Anton Garcia Abril's liedeiislica works have recently begun to be published by Bolamar, in arrangements for various vocal tessituras.

[21] The most notable case is that of Union Musical Espanola, a company that ended up absorbing more than 70 music publishers. Its enormous music collection was acquired by the multinational Music Sales Group. It is currently held by the Instituto Complutense de Ciencias Musicales (ICCMU), located at the headquarters of the Sociedad General de Autores y Editores (SGAE) in Madrid. The complete catalogue was published in 2000: ACKER, Yolanda; ALFONSO, M.ª de los Angeles; ORTEGA, Judith; PEREZ CASTILLO, Belen, *Archivo historico de la Union Musical Espanola. Partituras, metodos, librettos y libros,* Ediciones y Publicaciones de la Sociedad General de Autores y Editores, Madrid, 2000.

[22] The composers and publishers are as follows: Antonio Barrera, Real Musical; Francisco Escudero, Alpuerto; Manuel Garcia, Institute Complutense de Ciencias Musicales; Enrique Granados, UME/Trito; Felix Lavilla, Real Musical; Joan Llongueres Badia, DINSIC; Manuel Palau, Piles; Joaquin Rodrigo, Ediciones Joaquin Rodrigo; Eduard Toldra, Union Musical Espanola; Joaquin Turina, Union Musical Espanola. In our catalogue we note the details of each edition.

[23] They are: No lloreis ojuelos by Granados, Coplas del pastor enamorado and Pastorcito Santo by Rodrigo, Madre, unos ojuelos vi and Cantarcillo by Toldra, and the three from Homenaje a Lope de Vega, by Turina.

Goethe, Ruckert or Heine, for example, are scarce, with isolated cases such as Garcia Lorca or Becquer, who have been the protagonists of some monographic recital. There are only a couple of records devoted entirely to songs with texts by Tomas Garces[24] or Joan Oliver[25] . As an isolated example, the record dedicated to poets of the Golden Age with songs composed in the 20th century, which includes four with texts by Lope, is remarkable: *Cantar del alma. La poesa del Siglo de Oro en la musica del siglo XX*, recorded by Fernando Latorre and Itziar Barredo[26] .

The sources we have used are of two types: the scores of the songs catalogued and the editions of Lope de Vega's works from which the lyrics of these songs are extracted. In order to compile the catalogue, we have located the scores of all the works we have included, from which we have extracted the data provided. We have preferred the scores of the works that have been published, resorting to the manuscripts in the case that they have not been published.

Many of the published scores are not commercially available today. Some have been found in libraries and archives, as they correspond to old editions that are no longer available from the respective publishers, or from publishers that have disappeared. The manuscripts have been found in both public and private archives. Among the former, of the fourteen consulted, the music collections of the BNE and the Fundacion Juan March stand out. The private ones correspond to those of living composers who still manage them themselves, or those whose heirs keep them personally. An exact list of both cases is given in the following section. The royalties that may accrue on some works have led some archives to request a written statement specifying the purpose for which the copies of the requested works are to be used. In other cases the copies have been kindly provided to us without any requirement.

The sources of the second type have been selected from among the editions considered to be of reference in the academic field for their prestige and rigour. Generally speaking, we have preferred modern, rigorous and well-documented critical editions. In cases where such editions are not available, we have opted for older editions by researchers of recognised academic prestige. In total, we have handled editions of 37 of Lope's works, including comedies, prose works and lyric works.

Documentary research on the 1935 National Music Competition has been difficult and unfortunately not as successful as we would have wished. There is no documentation about the competition in the General Archive of the State Administration (AGA) and the Central Archive of the Ministry of Culture. The databases of both bodies do not contain any documents relating to it. An explicit request to the specialised staff of the AGA did not bear any fruit, and they informed us by letter[27] of the negative result of their enquiries.

---

[24] *A l'ombra del lledoner. Poetry by Tomas Garces,* Ana Ibarra, soprano, Ruben Fernandez, piano, CD, Ensayo, 2001.

[25] *Songs on poems by Joan Oliver*, various performers, CD, Ars Harmonica, 2001.

[26] *Cantar del alma. La poesia del Siglo de Oro en la musica del siglo XX,* Fernando Latorre, bantono, Itziar Barredo, piano, CD, Arsis, 2007. Includes three of the songs with text by Lope de Vega written in 1935, of which we present here a study, edition of the score and sound recording.

[27] Letter addressed to the author of this work by Daniel Gozalbo Gimeno, Head of the Information Section of the AGA on 2-6-2009, in which he indicates that "having exhaustively consulted the inventories and descriptive instruments corresponding to the Culture and Education collection groups, in which the documents produced by the former Ministry of Public Instruction and its Directorate General of Fine Arts are kept, we inform you that no documentary reference has been found relating to the prize that is the subject of your study". Subsequently requesting a new search for which the exact dates and the texts of the *Gaceta de Madrid* in which the announcements and awards of these prizes appear, we received another negative communication on 16-6-2009. The search in the Central Archive of the Ministry of Culture was also negative, the responsible personnel informing us that this ministry was created in 1977, and that therefore they do not have any previous documentation.

Part I

The genre of the piano song

Vocal music, in general, inevitably needs a text to which to set music, although occasionally some musical works have been written in which the voice uses vocal and/or consonant sounds that do not have a textual meaning. Experimental music and the avant-garde of the second half of the 20th century were fertile ground for the use of the voice as an instrumental element in different groups, however, these works are an exception, as the common thing in musical composition is to start from a text that will influence to a greater or lesser extent the sonorous and expressive result. The language used in songs, regardless of their literary quality, is, in essence, different from the common language, and therefore we can assimilate it, if not identify it, with poetic language. The music and the poetic text are, therefore, the two substantial elements in a song[28] , whatever its musical and poetic style and form, the instrumental elements accompanying the voice, or the context in which it is performed.

In the song, taken in its broadest sense, the word acquires a musical dimension by being organised by specifically musical elements. Hugo Riemann, extending the basic concept of song above, defines it as the union of a lyrical poem with music, in which the sung words replace the speech, while the musical elements of rhythm and cadences inherent in the speech are elevated to the rhythm ordered by the melody[29] . This definition considers the poetic text subsidiary to the musical organisation, however, when the music in turn is ordered in function of the meaning and form of the text, the resulting composition is the fruit of a mutual feedback of both elements. In this sense, Steiner, from the point of view of linguistics and literary translation, affirms that the composer who sets a text to music must follow the same sequence of technical intuition that is followed in the translation of a text, and the musical composition must offer a new dimension that neither devalues nor eclipses its linguistic origin[30] . The greater weight of the musical component in some cases, of the literary in others, or the search for balance and mutual influence is a problem that each composer solves according to his preferences or interests. Among the works presented here there are examples of all kinds. Especially in the works written in 1935, which will be studied musically and literarily, as well as the relationship between both aspects, we will be able to see how the composers treat the texts of Lope de Vega.

The presence of musical manifestations in all human societies, and the use of the voice as a basic and fundamental musical instrument in the history of music, are facts that do not need to be established. The social and cultural success of the song is based on the fact that poetry functions, as a language, in an easier and more accessible way than music[31] , which, on the contrary, has structures that require specific learning, hence its rapid extension in various forms since the origins of mankind. It is not necessary to dwell too much on the consideration of the song as an almost unique genre in the field of pop music since the middle of the 20th century. Popular urban music, as it is nowadays called the very varied set of styles, from waltz, tango, salsa or copla, to pop and rock, is evolving more and more towards the vocal, and formally it can be assimilated to what we understand as a song. Apart from other resources, its enormous social success lies in the brevity of the text, repetitions in the form of refrains, simple structures and the use of a language close to the colloquial[32] .

But this tendency towards song as a genre is not a phenomenon exclusive to music today.

---

[28] The dictionary of the RAE, joining the two components, the musical and the poetic, defines the term from both perspectives: "Composition in verse that is sung, and music with which this composition is sung". *Diccionario de la Real Academia,* 22ª edition [online], <http://buscon.rae.cs/draeI> [accessed: 17-7-2011].

[29] RIEMANN, Hugo, "Lied", *Musik-Lexikon*, Leipzig, 1882. Cited in: PEAKE, Luise Eitel, "Song", *The New Grove Dictionary of Music and Musicians*, vol. 17, Stanley Sadie (ed.), Macmillan Publishers, London, 1980, p. 511.

[30] STEINER, G., *After Babel,* London, 1975. Quoted in *The New Grove..., op. cit.,* "Song", vol. 17, p. 510.

[31] BROWN, Jane K., "In the begining was poetry", *The Cambridge Companion to the Lied*, James Parson (ed.), Cambridge University Press, Cambridge, 2004, p. 12.

[32] See TORREGO EGIDO, Luis Mariano, *Cancion de autor y education popular (1960-1980),* Ediciones de la Torre, 1999, p. 85-87. Torrego takes some of the ideas set out in VAZQUEZ MONTALBAN, Manuel, *Antologa de la "noaa cango "catalana,* Ediciones de Cultura Popular, Barcelona, 1968, p. 18.

Medieval literature already appears in many cases linked to music, thus accentuating its difference with the current language. The text is supported by the melody and becomes a song[33] . Francisco Lopez Estrada, speaking about medieval popular lyric and its relationship with music, points out that:

"The song has served for the verse to manifest itself from its origin in modules of a marked rhythmic sense, and the structure of the melodies has favoured the strophic disposition in a rigorous way. The primitive lyric, whether popular or cultured, appears with this conditioning, which was maintained for a long time and went beyond the medieval period; the musical condition of the cancioneril lyric made possible the great development of the mëtrica in terms of the rigour of the measure and the richness of the combination of stanzas and the complexity of rhymes"[34] .

Lopez Estrada himself warns of the difficulty of studying this relationship in its origins due to the lack of knowledge of "the musical melodies that would maintain the integrity of the text". However, these words reflect the interdependence of both elements in the genesis of the song, although the balance between them depends, as we have seen, on the style or preferences of the author in the creative process. The history of the genre that concerns us here, that of the song with piano, as will be seen below, is the history of the search for the proportion between music and poetry, with minimal instrumental means, and in a context, the concert, which helps to focus on its essence.

THE SONG FOR VOICE AND PIANO

Music written for voice and piano or another polyphonic instrument, because factors such as instrumentation, vocal polyphony, timbre, or scenic issues disappear or remain in the background, has in the text a fundamental and generative element. The musical recitation of the text, the transmission of its semantic content, the sonority of the verses, their lyricism or drama, the necessary collaboration of the piano, with greater or lesser conjunction with the text, are the essence of a poetic-musical genre, which seeks to endow poetry with a new dimension through music.

The musical compositions originally written to be sung by a solo voice and accompanied by a piano constitute a very particular genre that has known throughout history different denominations, applications and conceptions. The need to give the recitation of a poetic text a new sound dimension by incorporating a melodic line and providing it with an instrumental accompaniment that sustains tonally and harmonically, or even provides musical commentaries that represent the character of the text, is at the origin of the genre. This type of work is the logical evolution of the compositions for one voice with the accompaniment of a polyphonic instrument that have been present throughout the history of music. The origin of these compositions can be traced back to the songs of all kinds that singers, even in ancient times, sang accompanied or accompanied by citaras, bagpipes, fidulas, lyres, harps or other instruments .[35]

In the Middle Ages and the Renaissance it was customary to sing one of the voices in polyphonic works for which the musicians improvised the instrumental accompaniment from the rest of the voices. This could be done with several instruments, with a keyboard instrument with or without bass reinforcement by another instrument, or it could be a single instrument, such as the lute, but even with this procedure the composer conceived the work as a polyphonic construction. Dietrich Fischer-Dieskau is of the opinion that the origins of the cancion culta are to be found in the writing of works for a single voice and a harmonic or polyphonic instrument:

It does not seem appropriate to use performance as the sole criterion, since the information we have about it rarely offers absolute historical certainty. On the contrary, I believe that what is decisive is the notation, in our case the

[33] LOPEZ ESTRADA, Francisco, "Caracteristicas generates de la Edad Media literaria", *Historia de la literatura espanola,* tomo I: *La Edad Media,* Jose Maria Diez Borque (coord.), Taurus, Madrid, 1980, pp. 70.
[34] Ibid.
[35] For a more detailed study of the history and evolution of monodic art see the first chapter of FISCHER-DIESKAU, *Dietrich, Hablan los sonidos, suenan las palabras. Historia e interpretacion del canto,* Turner, Madrid, 1990, pp. 15-28.

accompaniment written for a harmonic instrument. Seen in this light, the history of the song for one voice with accompaniment has its beginnings in the first decades of the 16th century[36] .

With the Renaissance, not only did this format of composition appear, but also, taking from the resources of the Renaissance madrigal, various formulas of musical interpretation were introduced, the so-called madrigalisms, as forms of description of the feelings expressed by the text. *Tempi*, binary or ternary accentuation, major or minor mode, short or wide intervals, are used to express the meaning of the words conveyed by the melody. The struggle against counterpoint, the so-called *stle rappresentatvo* and *stle narratvo,* the triumph of monody and the basso continuo, granted the sung voice an independence that allowed it a more subtle interpretation of the text, without being subordinated to the other voices[37] .

However, in Philip Radcliffe's opinion the omnipresence of the basso continuo was an impediment to the true development of independent accompaniment and, "until it emerged, the solo solo self-contained song was a pale reflection of the things that were said most vividly in the larger pieces"[38] .

From the 16th century, the interest of composers in "imitating" the text in their compositions led some to employ stereotypes of musical figures associated with certain words and expressions[39] , influenced by the principles of rhetoric, a discipline in which some composers had a solid formation[40] , which gave rise to the first musical resources or mechanisms linking sound discourse to the word. These procedures, which emerged in polyphonic vocal music, were used as technical routines in the compositional process, both in the formal organisation of the work and in the use of certain musical figures that constituted the equivalent of decorato-rhetoric[41] . The importance of the music-word relationship is such that from the Renaissance onwards the song can be judged in relation to its fidelity in the declamation of the text and according to its expressiveness. For this reason, those which presented a deficient interpretation of the text were often criticised[42] .

The expansion of the piano from the middle of the 18th century made it the main domestic and professional instrument in the 19th century[43] , present in homes of a certain economic and cultural level, as well as in institutions of all kinds. This placed it in the role of accompaniment to the voice in the repertoire of songs with accompaniment. Its sonority, its dynamic and expressive possibilities, its capacity for *legato* and *cantabile* sound, together with its generalisation in all musical environments, won the composers' favour for this instrument as a collaborator of the voice in the genre of songs with accompaniment. From the beginning of the century, the voice and the piano became the best combination for the song, for economy of means and expressive potential[44] .

Since the beginning of the 19th century, there has been a wide-ranging division in the genre of song between the popular and the cultivated. The repertoire, comprising solo songs with piano, is enriched by occasional additions of other voices or *obbligato* instruments, as well as by arrangements of theatre parts, hymns, etc. In many cases, the type of piano accompaniment is the key to distinguishing serious repertoire from popular repertoire[45] . In the serious repertoire, the piano is taken as equal to the voice, with which it collaborates in the expression of feelings. The

---

[36] *Ibid.,* pp. 29-30.
[37] *Ibid.,* p. 35.
[38] RADCLIFFE, Philip, "Germany and Austria", *History of Song, op. cit,* pp. 135.
[39] GHEW, Geoffrey, "Song", *The New Grove..., op. cit,* vol. 17, p. 511.
[40] Music, belonging to the *quadrivium*, and rhetoric, part of the *trivium*, were related as two of the Seven Liberal Arts on which higher education was based from the Middle Ages onwards. See: BARTOLOME MARTINEZ, Bernabe, *Historia de la educación en Espana y America,* vol. 1, SM, Madrid, 1992, p. 192.
[41] See BUELOW, George J., "Rethoric and music", *The New Grove..., op. cit,* vol. 15, pp. 793-803. A reference bibliography on this subject is included in this article.
[42] GHEW, Geoffrey, "Song", *The New Grove, op. cit.*, vol. 17, p. 510.
[43] For a history of the technical evolution, expansion and instrumental practice of the piano see: RIPIN, Edwin M.; BELT, Philiph R.; MEISEL, Maribel *et al.*, "Pianoforte", *The New Grove, op. cit.*, vol. 14, p.682-714; RATTALINO, Piero, *Historia del piano,* Idea Books, Barcelona, 2005.
[44] GHEW, Geoffrey, "Song", *The New Grove..., op. cit,* vol. 17, p. 518.
[45] Idem.

interest of the great composers in songs with piano raised the technical and expressive demands. Just as the popular song was generally based on stereotyped melodies which were repeated for the stanzas of the text, the serious song opened the way to modified strophic songs and compositions with a freer formal structure adapted to each stanza of the text, the so-called *durchkomponiert* style[46] , in order to reflect a correct declamation of the text in all its details. Ideas like those of Richard Wagner in *Oper und Drama,* where the accompaniment, in its broadest sense, is seen as a means to reinforce the emotional force of the verse, had a great influence, not only on German *Lied* but also on the whole repertoire[47] .

Paradoxically, in popular song, made with simpler and more predictable musical structures, and with generally lower vocal demands, the listeners' understanding of the text is facilitated. In the cultured song, the technical difficulty of the voice part and, in general, the greater musical complexity that multiplies the sonorous and intellectual stimuli, can make it difficult for the audience to understand the text. For Edward F. Kravitt, Wagner was the one who fought most forcefully against the problems of diction and understanding of the text arising from the predominance of Italian vocalism in Western music until well into the 19th century, calling for the need for a genuinely Germanic school of singing[48] . Such problems are not only attributable to the singers, who with proper articulation of sound can more effectively convey the sonorous aspect of the text. The composers are responsible for ensuring that the organisation of the sounds facilitates their correct transmission and enhances their deeper meaning, as Wagner advocated in his aesthetic credo.

In the 20th century, after the First World War, the genre was subjected to experimentation, as was the case with other genres. The abandonment of tonality, the search for new timbral sonorities, extreme vocal virtuosity, new ideas in the declamation of the text and the incorporation of the spoken word, often turned the song into "absolute" music, an unprecedented development, perhaps contrary to its origins[49] .

However, the union of the two instruments is not enough to delimit a type of composition that requires a third fundamental element: the text. Composers have generally chosen poetic texts for their songs because they have an implicit rhythm and prosody comparable to musical prosody, and, no doubt, because they rise above prose in the attempt to express feelings, ideas, concepts and dramatic situations with an aesthetic component. Music in these cases comes to enhance the poet's aesthetic intentionality.

Perhaps the purpose of the composition is missing in this exposition of its components. Although this factor is more imprecise and not infrequently unknown, the genre we are trying to define was born with the purpose of being heard in the nineteenth-century salon, concert halls or audiovisual media of any kind, without the intervention of external visual scenic elements, although the dramatic components that the text may incorporate and that the interpreters try to transmit. The evolution of the technical possibilities, the tastes and current social customs, has allowed us to

[46] German expression referring, as opposed to strophic form, to musical compositions written in a continuous flow of different musical ideas for each stanza or poetic section. The English term is also used: *through-composed.* The term is applied to songwriting in which the music for each stanza is different, not repeating from stanza to stanza. The resulting musical form is not necessarily determined by the poetic form, continuity being achieved because the music responds momentarily to the flow of ideas, images and situations in the verse, not excluding the recurrence of thematic motifs. TILMOUTH, Michael, "Through-composed", *The New Grove..., op. cit.*, vol. 18, p. 794. This compositional approach in vocal music based on a poetic text is not new; this type of composition has its origins in the motet of the second half of the 15th century. In it, each phrase of the text has a different music according to its meaning.

[47] GHEW, Geoffrey, "Song", *The New Grove..., op. cit,* vol. 17, p. 519.

[48] Quoted in KRAVITT, Edward F., *The lied: mirror of late romanticism*, Yale University Press, Michigan, 1998, p. 52.

[49] Three different ways are those of Schoenberg in *Pierrot hrnaire,* Stravinski in his *Three Japanese Lyrics,* or Ravel in *Trois poemes de Stephane Maharme.* Bela Bartok, for his part, brings new conventions of declamation suggested by popular music, and Charles Ives experiments with spoken text. GHEW, Geoffrey, "Song", *The New Grove..., op. cit.,* vol. 17, p. 520.

have some punctual experiences in which a scenic and/or cinematographic component, not foreseen by the composers, is added to reference works of the liederistic repertoire.

THE *LIED* MODEL

Compositions for voice and piano are given different names depending on the geographical area from which they originate and the language in which they are written. Even composers of the same pals use different designations in the headings of the scores or when referring to them. These works, or the composer's own adaptations for these two instruments from works for voice and orchestra or any other instrumental combination, serve different purposes and motivations on the part of their creators and performers. The palses of the Germanic area created in the 18th and 19th centuries a great compositional and interpretative school of this genre that was imposed as a model, and that with greater or lesser speed and intensity spread throughout Europe and America, adopting the term *Lied* to denominate this type of compositions, of which those of Franz Schubert, Robert Schumann, Johannes Brahms, Hugo Wolf and Gustav Mahler stand out for their quantity, quality and diffusion[50] .

By extension, this term is applied to analogous works written in languages other than German, although other terms such as *song, art song, chanson, melodie,* cancion, cancion dc concierto or cancion de arte are used, depending on the pals and the language of the text. It is necessary to point out the difficulty of establishing the boundary between what is understood by *Lied* and the mere song with piano accompaniment, as well as the differences between the different terms listed here, regardless of the title chosen by the composer for the work. Being aware of this difficulty, and being far from our intention to judge and qualify the songs that we present by giving them one appellative or another, in the present work, we have chosen the term "Lied" as the one that best suits the composer's taste and the composer's choice of title.

We have opted for the term "song for voice and piano", which, although descriptive and aseptic, is clear and unambiguous. The evident influence that the masterpieces of the German *Lied* exerted, and possibly still exert, on the development of the song with piano and the perception that we currently have of these works, throughout the world and particularly in our country, obliges us to take a closer look at their historical evolution.

According to *The New Grove*, in the entry "Lied"[51] , in 1752 Christian Gottfried Krause defines the term as a composition singable by amateurs which expresses the character and meaning of the text, and has a simple and independent accompaniment so that the song can be sung without it. This simplicity to which Krause alludes is what E. T. A. Hoffmann defends when he warns of the true essence of the *Lied*:

[...] to stir the innermost soul by means of the simplest melody and the simplest modulation, without affectation or straining for effect and originality: therein lies the mysterious power of true genius[52] .

Evidently, as *The New Grove* explains, this concept was enriched as more complex works were written melodically, n'tinica and harmonically, giving greater importance to the piano part, until the model was established in the 19th century as a form in which the ideas suggested by the text took shape in the organisation of those words in the voice and piano, both to provide formal unity

[50] To get an idea of the popularity of this genre, James Parsons notes that in Berlin, between 1900 and 1914, more than twenty *Liederabende* (*Leder* recitals) were given each week, apart from the private sessions. PARSONS, James, "Introduction: Why the Lied?", *The Cambridge Companion..., op. cit.*, p. 4.

[51] BOKER-HEIL, Norbert, "Lied", *The New Grove..., op. cit,* vol. 10, p. 830.

[52] "[...] to touch the innermost recesses of the soul by means of the simplest melody and the simplest modulation, without affectation and without forcing a search for effect or originality: therein lies the mysterious power of true genius." [author's translation]. Quoted in PARSON, James, "The eighteenth-century Lied", *The Cambridge Companion to the Lied*, James Parson (ed.), Cambridge University Press, Cambridge, 2004, pp. 36. In the same vein, Johann Christoph Gottsched, professor of rhetoric at Leipzig, in his essay *Versuch einer aitschen Dichkunst* (Critical Essay on the Art of Poetry) of 1730, relates poetry to songs, arguing that these should be short and relatively simple, pi'caras bachic or love songs. *Idem.* p. 16.

and to enhance certain details inherent in the poetry of the musical composition[53] . This concept that Boker-Heil applies to the term *Lied* is extensible to the different denominations of the genre in different countries.

One of the definitions of the term *Lied* that we have found most interesting for its concision and accuracy is that of Carlos Gomez Amat, for whom the universalisation of the German word gives name "to a genre of particular characteristics, whose best virtues are dramatic condensation and the intimate union of text and music in an indissoluble whole"[54] . For his part, Eduard Toldra, considered by many historians and interpreters to be one of the greatest exponents of Spanish song, left us these words, which Antonio Fernandez-Cid includes in his book on Spanish song:

Dina that the song is music itself, substantively, without adjectives; music in its most intimate and naked state. Dina that the song must be written in a state of grace. And that it is a real touchstone for composers and performers[55] .

The primary idea of the word *Lied*[56] refers to a song in the German language, from which it has come to denote different types of compositions in the course of history. The polyphonic *Lied,* which experienced its heyday around 1500, is based on a not necessarily vocal construction which uses a pre-existing song melody for its elaboration. The influences of the Italian madrigal, with the *seconda prattica*, the accompanied monody and the expression of the *affetti*, introduce concertante elements with *obbligato* instruments, interludes and *ritorneli* which expand the possibilities of musical construction, based on the principle of the strophic song and the cantabile melody[57] , as well as certain rhythmic-melodic effects, ornaments, echoes, the so-called madrigalisms, as well as poetic metres. In the late Baroque period it gave way to the *Lied* with soloist and basso continuo, the *Generalbass Lied* or *Lied* con continuo, a generally secular composition following the principles of the strophic model with instrumental participation in the *ritornellos, with* vocal parts with more or less ornamentation[58] .

Perhaps most remarkable about the practice of *Lied* in the Germanic area is its dependence on poetry from very early times, which may have influenced the later evolution of the genre. Jane K. Brown points out that the development of German *Lied* is a direct consequence of the flowering of Romantic poetry and Goethe in particular, and spread in the form of numerous publications of song collections with piano accompaniment for domestic use, written by good composers familiar with the poetic literature of the time[59] . Many song collections were compiled by the poets themselves, who could commission music for their poems from minor composers. When composers were in charge of publishing the song collections, they were generally more ornate and elaborate, until the criteria of simplicity in the compositions, in favour of clarity and comprehensibility of the text, were imposed towards the middle of the 17th century .[60]

Another important peculiarity is the use to which the songs were put. While in France, Italy or Spain the collections published were mainly intended for the aristocratic sectors, in Northern

---

[53] BOKER-HEIL, Norbert, "Lied", *The New Grove, op. cit.,* vol. 10, p. 838. Jane K. Brown ventures to give a date for the beginning of the German *Lied* as an adult genre, 19 October 1814, when Schubert composed his *Gretchen am Spinnrade*. BROWN, Jane K., "In the begining was., *op. cit*., p. 12. Similarly, Marie-Agnes Dittrich, discusses the idea of *Gretchen* as the beginning of modern lied. DITTRICH, Marie-Agnes, "The Lieder of Schubert", *The Cambridge Companion, op. cit.*, p. 85.

[54] GOMEZ AMAT, Carlos, *Historia de la musica espanola, s. XIX,* Alianza, Madrid, 1988, p. 93.

[55] FERNANDEZ-CID, Antonio, *Liederycanciones..., op. cit,* p. 2.

[56] For a more detailed history of *Lied,* especially German Lied, see the collected studies: BOKER- HEIL, Norbert; BARON, John H.; BARR, Raymond A. and others, "Lied", *The New Grove..., vol. 10, p. 830-847, op. cit.,* vol. 10, p. 830-847; FISCHER-DIESKAU, Dietrich, *The sounds speak, op. cit.*; PARSON, James (ed.), *The Cambridge companion, op. cit.*; KRAVITT, Edward F., *The lied: mirror, op. cit.* For a broader view of the song genre: STEVENS, Denis (ed.), *Historia de la cancion,* Taurus, Madrid, 1990 *[A History of Song*, Hutchinson, London, 1960].

[57] BOKER-HEIL, Norbert, "Lied", *The New Grove, op. cit.,* vol. 10, p. 830.

[58] BARON, John H., "Lied", *The New Grove..., op. cit,* vol. 10, p. 834.

[59] BROWN, Jane K., "In the begining was poetry", *The Cambridge Companion to the Lied*, James Parson (ed.), Cambridge University Press, Cambridge, 2004, p. 12.

[60] Idem.

Europe the recipients were generally the literati, students and cultivated middle classes, an entertainment for the prosperous bourgeoisie who wanted to imitate the upper classes[61] , which greatly facilitated their dissemination while making the genre an increasingly integrated element in the common culture.

Towards the middle of the 18th century Berlin became the main centre of *Lied* composition, reflecting the cultural and artistic environment promoted by Frederick the Great. Christian Gottfried Krause established the terms on which the first Berlin school developed in the above sense, resulting in numerous songs composed in a diatonic style, with simple rhythm and harmony. The simplicity of these early cases was tempered by the contributions of composers such as August Bernhard Valentin Herbing, precursor of the ballads, who introduced stories and fables with a more elaborate harmonic treatment, or the case of Christian Gottlob Neefe, Beethoven's first teacher, who introduced modifications in the form of the strophic *Lied*, freeing the *Lied* form from the restrictions imposed by the Berlin School. His technique allowed the repetitive structure to be altered when it did not suit the text of the stanzas that demanded it[62] , thus opening the way to the idea of the *durchkomponiertes Lied.* However, the above-mentioned principle of simplicity will not disappear in the history of the song despite the later evolution towards more elaborate forms. Some of the future great masters of the *Lied* will not resist the composition of pieces which, although imbued with genius, are still in keeping with the idea of simplicity in their construction. In some of the works presented in this work, already in the 20th century, this is a substantial characteristic, especially in those in which the poetic text written by Lope is nourished by the simplicity of the popular style, so characteristic of his work.

In the last third of the 18th century the composers of the so-called second Berlin *Lied* school, following the evolution of those mentioned above, wrote songs with a greater melodic, rhythmic and harmonic complexity, with more elaborate keyboard accompaniments and with a different musical treatment for the different stanzas. "These developments, together with the personal demand to work with good poetic texts, led the most prominent composers of the genre, Carl Friedrich Zelter, Johann Abraham Peter Schultz and Johann Friedrich Reichardt, to the compositional technique of the *durchkomponiertes Lied.* Schultz, for example, insisted on avoiding tasteless texts and resorted to the works of the best poets"[63] . The influence of these composers spread throughout the Germanic area, influencing others who devoted themselves especially to *Lied*, such as Christian Friedrich Schubart or Johann Rudolf Zumsteeg, until it became established as a genre that was cultivated by all composers of the time. The discreet contributions of Christoph Willibald Gluck, Carl Philipp Emanuel Bach or Haydn were expanded by Mozart, who wrote some 40 songs. His rich, widely recognised lyrical talent is combined with a subtle accompaniment, with a special sense of emphasising the relationship between verse and music, with the latter sometimes leading the latter, as in *Das Veichen and Abendempfndung,* expressing the character and meaning of the texts he used in the style of the *durchkomponiertes Led,* even though he regarded the song as a minor genre[64] .

In the 19th century the *Lied* became a well-defined type of composition, referred to as a romantic *Lied*, where the ideas suggested by the poetic text take shape in the musical construction and in the relationship between voice and piano. The expansion of the *Lied* presupposes a renaissance of German lyric poetry, whose popularity among composers and audiences stems from the consideration that music can be derived from the poetic text, as well as a wealth of musical devices and techniques for expressing this interrelation. Johann W. Goethe, Ludwig H. C. Holty, Johann Mayrhofer, Wihelm Muller, Friedrich G. Klopstock, Matthias Claudius, Johann G. Herder and

---

61 BROWN, Jane K., "In the beginning,..., *op. cit,* p. 17.

62 BARR, Raymond A., "Lied", *The New Grove..., op. cit.,* vol. 10, p. 836.

63 Reichart, and especially Zelter, were composers who collaborated directly with Goethe. See in BROWN, Jane K., "In the beginning,^, *op. cit.,* p. 14.

64 RADCLIFFE, Philip, "Germany and Austria", *op. cit.*, pp. 138-139.

Friedrich Schiller were the main German-language poets who served the Romantic *Lied.* Franz Schubert, more than the creator, was the composer who gave it its full poetic-musical dimension by being able like no other to fuse the meanings of music and words. In Schubert, the infinite variety of styles and forms, melodic lines, modulations, accompaniment figures, are essentially the result of his ability to respond musically to the stimulus of poetry[65] . His aim was to find expressive mechanisms that could be used as structural elements in music. These mechanisms already appear in his predecessors, but Schubert develops them by applying them to his own music.

[...] musical metaphors for human movement and emotions: rhythms of walking or running; tonic or dominant inflections for questions and answers; stormy or calm character; major-minor contrasts for smiling or crying, joy or sorrow; pleasant or melancholy melodies modulated by the form and tension of the verse. These elements were already to be found in Schubert's precursors, especially in Zumsteeg, in whose works they are closely and deliberately modelled[66] .

From Schubert onwards, the *Lied* continues to expand in a golden age in which the greatest composers of the time devote their attention to the genre. Robert Schumann, called the poet of the piano, unites music and poetry like no other. He considered poetry as a unity of form and content, and composed on the basis of the central idea of the poem, interpreting it through music[67] . Carl Loewe and Robert Franz have an abundant production of ballads in a narrative style closely linked to the dramatic scene, composers who, together with Peter Cornelius, Adolf Jensen, Fanny Hensel and Clara Schumann, are among the least known but no less important composers. Felix Mendelssohn shows in the *Lieder* his tendency towards a simple style and the character of popular song. Brahms seeks the sonorous expression of experiences and feelings, avoiding excessive passion as a reflection of the bourgeois attitude with which he moved as a man and composer[68] . Hugo Wolf, devoted almost exclusively to *Lied,* makes the melody flow according to the rhythm of the language, achieving unity with the motifs that the piano varies or repeats, confronts or connects, making the musical cohesion emanate from the text[69] . Gustav Mahler, Hans Pfizner, Richard Strauss, and Max Reger are the most outstanding in their dedication to the *Lied* at the turn of the century, joined by many other composers, since there are few at this time who resist this genre. The same is true of other composers from neighbouring countries, among whom, due to the importance of their output, Franz Liszt, fully integrated into Germanic tradition and culture, Frederic Chopin, Edvard Grieg, Antonin Dvorak and Modest Moussorgsky should be mentioned. The nationalist currents of the 19th century, with the artistic impulse of the autochthonous languages, saw in the *Lied,* as in opera, an ideal medium for the musical treatment of national poetry with the help of influences from folk music. From Grieg to Leos Janacek or Bela Bartok, the composition of *Lieder* was an important part of musical production and played an important role in the musical evolution of nationalism[70] .

The school created in France deserves special mention. In Fischer-Dieskau's opinion, the

---

[65] SAMS, Eric, "Lied", *The New Grove..., op. cit,* vol. 10, p. 839.

[66] *Idem.* "[...] the musical metaphors of human motion and gesture: walking or running rhythms; tonic or dominant inflections for question and answer; the moods of storm or calm; the major-minor contrasts for laughter and tears, sunshine and shade; the convivial or melancholy melodies moduled to the shape and stress of the verse. All these abound in Schubert's precursors, notably Zumsteeg, on whose work his own is often closely and deliberately modelled." [Author's translation].

[67] FISCHER-DIESKAU, Dietrich, *The sounds speak..., op. cit.,* p. 82. In the same way Jurgen Thym describes Schumann's *Lieder*, a union of poetry and music, making the poem his own with the addition of piano commentary. THYM, Jurgen, "Schumann: reconfiguring the Lied", *The Cambridge Companion..., op. cit.*, p. 135.

[68] *Ibid.,* p. 93.

[69] Federico Sopena points out that "for Wolf the verse is the source of inspiration, for the previous ones it is the melody that turns the text almost into a pretext". The search for the essence, for the instant created by the concrete poem, creates a maximum tension of an expressionist mood that already brings him close to the *Sprechgesang* of the second Viennese school. SOPENA, Federico, *Enacionalsmoy el "He"".* Real Musical, Madrid, 1979, p. 69.

[70] "...] thefact that nationalism is inseparable from the passionate cult of one's own language is decisive for the structure of the lied". *Ibid.,* p. 6.

particularity, popularity and continuity of the *melodie* was due to the profusion of French translations of Schubert's *Lieder*, performed by singers of prestige[71] . The fact is that the interest in vocal music in France goes back a long way. In the 17th century song was a very popular genre, even King Louis XIII himself composed and sang them, and composers such as Pierre Guedron, Antoine Boesset and Gabriel Bataille became famous for the anthologies of songs they published[72] . The troubadour romance gave way to the elaborate song, until the time of Berlioz, when the word *melodie* came to denote the *Lied* genre in France. David Cox characterises this type of music as a "combination of rhythmic flexibility, melodic subtlety and harmonic richness", characteristics that would achieve a high degree of perfection with Gabriel Faure, Henri Duparc and Claude Debussy[73] . The songs of Charles Gounod and Jules Massenet have a special interest in the prosody of verse, albeit with piano accompaniments in the background. These two composers gave way to the golden age of the *melodie*, in the last third of the 19th century, with Dupark, Faure, Cesar Frank, Ernest Chausson, Joseph Guy Ropartz, Emmanuel Chabrier and a whole pleyade of minor composers, some of whom had in the *melodie* their main field of action, such as Pierre de Breville, Alexis de Castillon, Louis Vierne or Guillaume Lekeu, up to the now modern creations of Maurice Ravel, Francis Poulenc and, especially, Debussy.
The *Lied* model spread throughout Europe, forming various national styles from the end of the 19th century. Its adaptation to the different cultural realities was varied, generally defined by linguistic peculiarities, and influenced by autochthonous music. In some cases, a lieder style of its own did not materialise, as the musical indefinition of this style was joined by the enormous weight of the *Lied* and the *melodie* on the one hand, and on the other by the omnipresent influence of Italian music, closely linked to the stage repertoire. This is the case of our par's, as we shall see below.

THE CONCERT SONG IN SPAIN

The development of song in Spain, perhaps also in other countries, has inevitably had the German *Lied* as a point of reference. In some cases, in order to have a model to follow, in others, as a revulsive to find a more personal and linguistically national manifestation. In any case, in the words of Celsa Alonso, Spanish song has suffered, on the part of critics and historiography, the "comparative insult of the German *Lied* [...] since the writings of Felipe Pedrell"[74] . The musical quality, the concreteness of the fundamentals of the genre, and the enormous dissemination of the works of the great Germanic *Lieder* composers of the nineteenth and early twentieth centuries, marked the evolution of the piano song throughout Europe. Federico Sopena laments the fact that the great European *Lied* repertoire did not penetrate into Spain, with only a few examples of Schubert translated into Spanish, no reference by writers and musical scholars, and a total absence in the conservatory environment[75] . Perhaps this judgement by Federico Sopena is not entirely accurate, since the first attempts to establish a quality Spanish *Lied* with its own characteristics come from Pedrell, for whom the Hispanic *Lied* was to be a transformed popular song, based on the internalisation of the natural music of a nation, following the model of the Germans[76] . The recognition of a particular Spanish style, based on picturesqueness, casticismo and the importance of the popular element, together with the consideration of superficiality and lack of musical quality

---

[71] FISCHER-DIESKAU, Dietrich, *The sounds speak..., op. cit,* p. 110.
[72] COX, David, "France", *Histoiia de la cancion,* Denis Stevens (ed.), *op. cit.* p. 270.
[73] *Idem.* p. 276.
[74] ALONSO, Celsa, "La cancion espanola desde la monarquia fernandina a la restauracion alfonsina", *La musica espanola en el siglo XIX,* Universidad de Oviedo, Oviedo, 1995, p. 245.
[75] SOPENA, Federico, *E "Hed "romantco,* Moneda y Credito, Madrid, 1973, p. 133.
[76] PEDRELL, Felipe, *Por nuestra musica,* Henrich and C[a] . Barcelona, 1891, pp. 40-41. Pedrell acknowledges that this consideration belongs to the critic P. Uriarte, a contemporary and friend of his, and then goes on to state that the drama lmco national would be the same *Lied* magnified. There is a reprint of this book by Pedrell by Francesc Bonastre, Universidad Autonoma de Barcelona, Bellaterra, 1991.

in many cases, can be found in Spanish musical historiography when referring to the cancion[77] . It was not until the end of the 19th and beginning of the 20th century that this tendency was reversed, although this change is only seen in the cases of Enrique Granados, Manuel de Falla, Joaquin Turina, Eduard Toldra, or Joaquin Rodrigo, when some of their songs became part of the international repertoire.

On the other hand, the delay in the knowledge of German *Lied* in our country was responsible, in the opinion of Pedrell, followed by Federico Sopena, for the delay in the development of romantic song. The pretension of taking German *Lied* as a model led to the discrediting of the abundant national production, due to the accusation of being populist and chauvinistic, until the arrival of some composers who, at the end of the 19th century, following the approaches of the genre in Germany and France, composed songs of a musical elaboration and expressive depth hitherto unattained in Spain.

The social and political framework in which the song develops cannot be forgotten when it comes to understanding its evolution. Alonso points to the "plebeianism" of the Spanish aristocracy and the "majismo" of the bourgeoisie[78] , as cultural conditioning factors that prevent the development of a song of true musical and poetic quality. On the other hand, Gomez Amat warns of the differences in the salon repertoire between the Anglo-Saxon world and Spanish culture, where the relations between this repertoire and theatrical music are closer[79] , hence the models of stage music were transferred to the salon repertoire.

The composition of works for voice and piano has developed as a genre since the 18th century in the form of salon pieces. Celsa Alonso, like Jose Subira and Rafael Mitjana, whom she quotes, states that the origins are to be found in the tonadilla escenica, from which some of the most popular numbers were extracted, based on the rhythms and formats of seguidillas, polos and tiranas, and passed to the aristocratic salon where the voice was accompanied by piano or guitar[80] . The popular substratum, and therefore its popularity, was fundamental for its development, and the poetic and musical structure was established by tradition. The ternary rhythm, the syllabic vocal line with slight melismas at the end of the verse, upper flourishes, broken syncopations, chained triplets, presence of the augmented second, descending phrygian tetrachords, modal turns, or the rhythmic accompaniments subordinated to the voice, made up a musical style anchored in folklore[81] . Over time this style was enriched by the contributions of Italian vocal music, with a great influence of operatic bel canto. Fernando Sor and Manuel Garcia are the Spanish composers of the late 18th century who contributed most to the expansion of the genre, making their songs and the style of Spanish song known, due to their international artistic trajectory, in England, France and Italy. "Versatility and the capacity to assimilate the languages of his environment" are, in the opinion of Andres Moreno Menjibar, the defining features of Garcia's music, always endowed with originality[82] , but always marked by the breath of stage music, first of the tonadilla, later of Italian opera[83] . The phrase with which Celsa Alonso summarises the stylistic elements of

[77] The opinions of Subira, Salazar, Mitjana or Sopena, are in the same sense, the recognition of a very large repertoire, of its national particularity, but of a certain musical and poetic superficiality which has prevented it from transcending to the international repertoire. See ALONSO, Celsa, "La cancion espanola desde la monarquia fernandina", *op. cit*, p. 246.

[78] ALONSO, Celsa, "Cancion", Diccionario de la Musica Espanola, op. cit., vol. 3, p. 1.

[79] GOMEZ AMAT, Carlos, Historia de la musica, op. cit. p. 18.

[80] ALONSO, Celsa, "Cancion", *Diccionario de la Musica Espanola..., op. cit,* vol. 3, pp. 1-19. For a more detailed study, by the same author we have previously noted *Cancion lrca espanola en el siglo XIX,* Instituto Complutense de Ciencias Musicales, Madrid, 1998, as well as "La cancion espanola desde la monarquia fernandina a la restauracion alfonsina", *La musica espanola en el siglo XIX,* Universidad de Oviedo, 1995.

[81] ALONSO, Celsa, Diccionario de la Musica Espanola, op. cit., vol. 3, p. 1.

[82] MORENO MENJIBAR, Andres, "Manuel Garcia en la perspectiva", *Manuel Garaa, de la tonadila escenica a la opera (1775-1832),* Alberto Romero Ferrer, Andres Moreno Menjibar (eds.), Universidad de Cadiz, Cadiz, 2006, p. 107.

[83] Of a style close to that of the tonadilla is the song *La barca de Amor*, with lyrics by Lope de Vega, which we include in our catalogue.

the songs of Manuel Garcia, whom she describes as the precursor of the genre, may well serve as a summary of what would be experienced in Spain for a good part of the century, and which would survive well into the twentieth:

[...] Italian *bel canto*, French operetta, romantic virtuosity and picturesqueness, without forgetting the importance of populist myth, the mystification of popular song and colonial exoticism[84] .

The 19th century began by consolidating the trajectory initiated in the previous century. After a first period in which patriotic songs and hymns became fashionable, motivated by the political events between 1808 and 1814, during the reign of Fernando VII the populist aesthetic was consolidated with a profusion of seguidillas-boleras and tiranas, mostly with guitar accompaniment[85] . The style and effects of the guitar as an accompanying instrument would be transmitted to piano writing as an important element of the Spanish nationalist spirit[86 87] valid well into the 20th century. The compositions of Federico Moretti, Jose Melchor Gomis, Manuel Ruckert, Ramon Carnicer appeared in different song collections, between 1812 and the 1930s, with a tendency to abandon the bolera for the Spanish song or the Andalusian tirana. Mariano Rodriguez de Ledesma, then in London, was highly valued as a composer of *canzonettas* and romanzas, in a style strongly influenced by Italian opera, a tendency which became stronger from the 1920s onwards. The predilection for neoclassical poetry, together with a Rossinian musical style, coexisted with the incipient pre-romantic poetry, with more bel canto-like melodic lines, rich in appoggiaturas and ornaments.

The two trends in Spanish cancion de salon, Italianism and populism, marked a double direction in this period. On the one hand, the Italianate taste of opera was imported and influenced the repertoire of the cancioneril, and on the other hand, in Europe a taste for genuinely Spanish songs was forged, which composers such as Narciso Paz, Fernando Sor, Mariano Rodriguez de Ledesma, Manuel Garcia, Manuel Ruckert, Ramon Carnicer, Jose Melchor Gomis, Federico Moretti and Salvador Castro de Gistau published and disseminated abroad. Thus, "Europe came into contact with Spanish music through those national airs, in which there was a strong presence of the Andalusian element, reinterpreted as a vestige of Arab culture. This fact is fundamental to understand what, in later years, ended up becoming the so-called French musical Hispanism [...]"[87].

Gilbert Chase sums up the populist style of nineteenth-century Spanish song in this way:

Many canciones lmcas of nineteenth-century Spain can be characterized as popular and artistic in style, employing picturesque texts and exposing the fabric of Spanish culture-majas (attractive Castilian women), mozos (young men), Andalucian cities, forbidden love, lost love, bullfighters, the strength of the Catholic faith, and an intense devotion of all that is Spanish. The mood is charming, with accompaniments providing an unobtrusive background built on simple rhythmical dances. Spoken interjections, syncopations, ornaments, triplets, appoggiaturas, and turns-- all of which can be traced to the cante flamenco-- abound. Rhythms, harmonic movement, and melodic design were based on the popular dances of Spain. The life of the typical working-class Spaniard was idealized and immortalized .[88]

These considerations may respond to the model of cancion, and in general of Spanish music, which spread to the rest of the world. Although this style was widely promoted at this time, it is no less true that Italianism was another important factor, as in so many other countries, and that the

---

[84] ALONSO, Celsa, "Manuel Garcia, compositor de canciones", *ibid.* p. 177.

[85] ALONSO, Celsa, *La cancionlirica espanola en elsiglo XIX,* ICCMU, Madrid, 1998, p. 39.

[86] CHASE, Gilbert, *The music of Span,* Dover, New York, 1959, p. 62.

[87] ALONSO, Celsa, Diccionario de la Musica Espanola, op. cit., vol. 3, p. 4.

[88] Many lyrical songs from 19th century Spain are characterised by their popular and artistic style, employing picturesque texts and exposing the social structure of Spanish culture: majas (attractive Castilian women), mozos (young men), Andalusian towns, forbidden loves, lost loves, bullfighters, the strength of the Catholic faith, and an intense devotion to all things Spanish. The atmosphere is enchanting, with accompaniments providing a discreet background built by simple rhythmic dances. There is an abundance of spoken interjections, syncopations, ornaments, triplets, appoggiaturas and turns, elements that can be attributed to flamenco singing. The rhythms, harmonic movement and melodic design were based on the folk dances of Spain. The life of the typical working-class Spaniard was idealised and immortalised [author's translation]. CHASE, Gilbert, *The music of Spain,* op. cit., p. 130. Quoted by DRAAYER, Suzanne R., *Art Song Composers of Spain. An Encyclopeda,* Scarecrow Press, Maryland, 2009, p. 1. Draayer offers in the following pages an interesting typology of 19th century Spanish songs.

works of some composers dignified with their quality both the purely Spanish style and other attempts to transcend these two deep-rooted tendencies.
The period of Isabella II allowed the liberal development and the penetration of French-style romanticism, with the result that French customs such as the *soirees*[89] were introduced into musical circles. Italian music continued to be the international point of reference, with a style derived from the successes of Gaetano Donizetti and Vincenzo Bellini, which had a notable influence on the song. The vocal melody uses diminished intervalic leaps for expressive purposes, chromaticisms, and the typical appoggiaturas and ornamental groupings, while the piano, sometimes also indicated for guitar and even harp, is subordinated to the voice, although more or less extensive preludes and interludes are included, with duplications of thirds or sixths, typical of opera. Populism becomes more and more Andalusian, in many occasions, due to the great demand, songs of very elementary construction and demands, destined to amateurs, largely based on dance rhythms[90] . The most elaborate songs, with the most prominent treatment of the piano, are those of Sebastian Iradier, the most outstanding composer of songs which draw on Andalusianism, criollismo and Italianism[91] , those of Jose Espi y Guillen, Cristobal Oudrid, Mariano Garcia and Mariano Soriano Fuertes. Hipolito Goldois, moving away from picturesqueness, tries a more serious style of romantic style.
Jose Inzenga marks a line of great quality and refinement, following the precedent of some songs by Santiago Masarnau and Jose Espi y Guillen. His songs are nourished by a certain eclecticism that ranges from Italian operatic music, French refinement and some folkloristic twists[92] , but fleeing from the Andalusian and criollismo that was so fashionable, such as the rhythms of habanera, guajira or guaracha, and banal themes. Inzenga endows the melody with a declamation originated by the verse and the piano with a strong expressive component generated by the text of the song.
The last third of the 19th century, while maintaining the tastes of the bourgeois salon, with the growth of Moorish songs, the fruit of an Arabist aesthetic that permeated the plastic and decorative arts, saw a progressive interest in French and German lyric poetry, as well as in the pre-Bekquerian and Bequerian Spanish poets. These works show a more Europeanist tendency, with neo-romantic melodies in a more refined style. Along the lines of what Jane K. Brown points out[93] , just as the development of German *Lied* is a direct consequence of the flowering of Romantic poetry and of Goethe in particular, in Spain the development of the cancion only reached a certain level of quality after the development of Romantic poetry, in our country with many years of delay with respect to Central Europe. An intellectual elite, "driven by a new Germanism and a growing nationalism, developed the production of a group of composers who were the architects of the first Hispanic *Lied*"[94] . The most renowned composers of this period are Fermin Maria Alvarez, Jose Espi Ulrich, Felipe Pedrell and Gabriel Rodriguez. In addition to the use of romantic poems including foreign poets, these composers gave the piano an increasingly expressive task, with the use of modulations linked to the expressive content of the text and particular figurations, greater harmonic richness, while the vocal line is very elaborate and linked to the poetic text, with periods in the form of *ariosos* and recitals, within structures influenced by the *Lied durchkomponiert* which flee from strophic forms.

[89] *Ibid.*, p. 5.
[90] The most outstanding features of the Andalusian style of this period are defined by Celsa Alonso in *La cancion Hrica espanola..., op. cit.*, pp. 244-245: modal or pre-tonal structures, ternary rhythms, the bipartite structure of copla and refran, the displacement of the guitar by the piano, and costumbrista themes and even the use of Andalusian slang on occasions.
[91] ALONSO, Celsa, Diccionario de la Musica Espanola..., op. cit., vol. 3, p. 6.
[92] The eclecticism of which Alonso speaks when referring to Inzenga's work takes the form of: "French elegance and refinement, Italian vocalism, stanzas of Hispanic roots, good poetry and popular rhythms if it was convenient". ALONSO, Celsa, *La cancion Hrica espanola..., op. cit.*, p. 294.
[93] BROWN, Jane K., "In the begining was.", *op. cit.*, p. 12.
[94] ALONSO, Celsa, Diccionario de la Musica Espanola, op. cit., vol. 3, p. 8.

Pedrell was the first in Spain to use the word *Lied* to name some of his songs published on various albums, as well as being the first to theorise about the term, promoting the creation of a school of Hispanic *Lied*[95] . Pedrell's proposals do not exclude the popular in his writings or in his compositions; on the contrary, both he and the group of composers responsible for this new romantic impulse use the purification of folklore as a starting point to develop an essentially Spanish *Lied*, in a "symbiosis between the popular and the cultured"[96] . The influences of both are varied, proposing solutions ranging from imitation of the models of German *Lied* and French song, to songs of popular origin with a refined and elaborate treatment. Among the poets to whom music is set, Becquer stands out, to whose texts almost all the composers of the time, the Becquerian poets such as Jose Selgas, Antonio de Trueba, Antonio Arnao, or Ventura Ruiz Aguilera[97] , and in some cases foreign poets from the Germanic (Ludwig Uhland) and French (Victor Hugo, Alphonse de Lamartine, Armand Silvestre) areas.
Gabriel Rodriguez and Jose Espi Ulrich show more Germanic influence, having Schumann's *Lieder as* the model for their songs, especially the role of the piano in the construction and expressiveness of the song. Marcial del Adalid composed in a distinctly French style, almost always with poems by French writers. Fermin Maria Alvarez, the most prolific in song composition, worked on both the refined populist song and the lyricism of Spanish, French and Catalan songs, always in a markedly French style. All these efforts in the search for a Spanish liederlstic genre were accompanied, evidently, by a large production of commercial works destined for the bourgeois salon, along the lines of the French romantic consumer melody, as well as the omnipresent Italianism. At the end of the century, compositions linked to nationalist currents also flourished, based on a regionalist folklorism which in some cases reached a certain stylisation, with examples close to the *Lied.* This type of compositions were found in areas where a more or less enlightened and regionalist bourgeoisie demanded works for the pequenobourgeois salons, as well as folkloristic manifestations of the choral societies, as in the case of the circle of composers linked to the poets of the Catalan *Renaixenca* and the Orfeo Catala, or the compositions in Basque by Jose Marla Iparraguirre, and the cancioneriles manifestations of the Galician *Rexurdimento* or the Valencian *Renaixenca.*
The song production of the first decades of the 20th century is closely related to the ideas of musical nationalism,

[...] at the same time diversifying into several apparently distant worlds: the сиplё, the Lied of neo-Romantic flavour, the continuity of nineteenth-century Andalusianism, the attempts to assert an Iberian Lied and the refined Casticism of Granados and Fernando Obradors, paving the way for the so-called transubstantiation of folklore[98] .

The interest in songs with piano declined in favour of symphonic or chamber music, although we find fundamental works by Albeniz, Granados, Falla and the Catalan composers of the Orpheus circle. The *Siete canciones populares* by Falla and the *Tonadillas en estilo antiguo* by Granados

---

[95] For a study of the relationship between Pedrell and the *Lied* see ALONSO, Celsa, "Felip Pedrell y la cancion culta con acompanamiento en la Espana decimononica: la dificil convivencia de lo popular y lo culto", *Recerca Musicologica,* XI-XII, 1991-1992, pp. 305-328. 305-328; SANCHEZ DE ANDRES, Leticia, "Gabriel Rodriguez y su relación con Felipe Pedrell: hacia la creación de un lied hispano", *Cuadernos de musica iberoamericana,* vol. 10, 2005, pp. 97-136; ZABALA, Alejandro, "La production liedenstica de Felip Pedrell", *Recerca Musicologica, XI-XII, 1991-1992, pp.* 97-136; ZABALA, Alejandro, "La production liedenstica de Felip Pedrell", *Recerca Musicologica, XI-XII, 1991-1992, pp.* 97-136.
Musicologica, XIV-XV, 2004-2005, pp. 325-334.
[96] ALONSO, Celsa, *Diccionaiio de la Musica Espanola..., op. cit.,* vol. 3, p. 9. In the same way Gilbert Chase expresses himself in recognising Pedrell and Barbieri as responsible for the revitalisation of Spanish music, and of cancion in particular, in the early years of the 20th century, "who discovered the musical treasures of the country's past, while at the same time drawing on the wealth of living folklore preserved in the popular and oral tradition". CHASE, Gilbert, "Espana", *Historia de la cancion, op. cit.*, p. 201.
[97] See ALONSO, Celsa, "La poesi'a prebecqueriana y becqueriana: un fermento del lied espanol", *Homenaje a Jose Maria Martinez Cachero,* Universidad de Oviedo, 2000, pp. 41-61.
[98] ALONSO, Celsa, Diccionario de la Musica Espanola, op. cit., vol. 3, p. 11.

are two collections of reference for the future creations of the genre[99] . Falla's influence on the composers of the time is enormous, coexisting his impressionist and neoclassical style, of French orientation, with other clearly neo-romantic aesthetics, as is the case of Conrado del Campo, Julio Gomez, Andres Isasi or Jose Marla Guervos. Although in some compositions the influence of Germanic *Lied* aesthetics is very marked, the general tendency is the "invocation of popular song [...] which guarantees the national character to create the Liediberico"[100] . The contributions to the song are very varied, ranging from the mere harmonisation of popular melody by Benito Garcia de la Parra, Angel Mingote or Jose Maria Franco, the populist nationalism of Fernando Obradors and Joaquin Nin Castellanos, to the romantic Andalusian style of Joaquim Turina. Turina's songs are one of the references of the genre, works of great sonorous amplitude, lyrical, with reminiscences of the cante jondo and great romantic breath. From his abundant production we can highlight the *Poema en forma de canciones*, the *Rimas* de Becquer, the *Saeta* or the *Homenaje a Lope de Vega* that we will deal with here.

The musicians of the Generation of the Republic, immersed in a crossroads of impressionist aesthetics, neoclassicism, the artistic avant-garde and the ideas of musical nationalism, sought in song, as in other repertoires, to reconcile folklore and new aesthetic positions. The personal relationship and artistic collaboration between artists from different disciplines, especially poets and musicians, makes the song a product opposed to the spirit of the romantic salon, aimed at the concert hall and in which the composers turn to the musical aesthetic to which they are most akin. The works of Julian Bautista, Oscar Espla, Salvador Bacarisse, Rodolfo Halffter, Ernesto Halffter, and to a lesser extent those of Adolfo Salazar, Enrique Casal Cliapi, Gustavo Pittaluga, Fernando Remacha, Gustavo Duran or Jesus Bal y Gay stand out. Eduard Toldra, Roberto Gerhard, Joaquin Rodrigo, Frederic Mompou, Rafael Rodriguez Albert and Arturo Menendez Aleyxandre also began their compositions for voice and piano at this time, although their vocal production extended and evolved until the sixties or seventies.

Despite the survival of the genre in these composers, in the post-war period the great renovating impulse of the Republic generation was lost, and the official authorities promoted a return to a type of compositions based on the harmonisation of popular songs, a regionalism which, without going as far as that, sought to take influences from the work of Turina and the *Siete canciones populares* by Falla. The general tendency is nuanced by the preferences and possibilities of each composer: Jesus Garcia Leoz follows Turina in his aesthetics, Jesus Guridi elaborates in more detail the piano part, Joaquin Nin-Culmell a neoclassical li'iiea, Manuel Palau achieves true *Lieder* with a vocal line of folkloric essence and an almost orchestral treatment of the piano, Xavier Montsalvatge successfully attempts the path of South American exoticism, and Vicente Asencio and Matilde Salvador write in a line that combines French impressionism and the works of Falla. Alongside these more prominent cases, there are numerous songs written in a populist vein that often do not transcend mere localism. The authors with a more avant-garde aesthetic, in which the piano is sometimes replaced by a small instrumental group in the search for new sonorities for the poetic text, all of them from the Catalan area, are Joaquim Homs, Josep Casanovas, Joan Comellas, Manuel Valls and Manuel Blancafort.

The song went into decline in the middle of the 20th century, although it continued to produce interesting results. The composers who took over, the so-called generation of '51, were Ramon Barce, Cristobal Halffter, Carmelo Bernaola, Luis de Pablo, Blancafort himself, Manuel Moreno Buendia and Anton Garcia Abril. Their contributions are irregular and sporadic. They include avant-garde compositional techniques, atonal, serial and aleatoric elements. Different instrumental combinations are the basis for the most avant-garde works, while when the piano is used, the

---

[99] FERNANDEZ-CID, Antonio, *Canciones de Espana..., op. cit.*, p. 18.
ALONSO, Celsa, Diccionario de la Musica Espanola, op. cit., vol. 3, p. 12.

composers tend to move away from these tendencies[101] . Alongside this group are works by Josep Maria Mestres-Quadreny, Gerardo Gombau, Josep Cercos and Agustin Gonzalez Acilu, who use both the piano and instrumental groups in serialist compositions. Josep Soler, in comparison with the trend of the time, has a large number of works for voice and piano with texts by Catalan, Italian, German and French poets, based on dodecaphonism with expressionist undertones[102] .

In the last quarter of the century, two opposing tendencies coexist. On the one hand, a return to nationalism and tradition as a counterbalance to the communication problems of the avant-garde, sometimes giving rise to the paradox that the songs of some composers are more conservative than their instrumental compositions. This is the case of Amando Blanquer, Rogelio Groba and Anton Garcia Abril. Miguel Asins Arbo, Pascual Aldave, Manuel Castillo, Juan Jose Falcon Sanabria, Angel Barja, Felix Lavilla and Leonardo Balada are examples of this conservative tendency in which a clear and comprehensive melody is the basis of the composition. Alongside them, the avant-garde exploits the possibilities of the voice united or manipulated by electronic means. The compositional work of songs by Miguel Angel Coria, Tomas Marco, Francisco Cano or Gerardo Gombau is insignificant since for these authors the voice and piano genre "is synonymous with conservatism"[103] , moving away from the essence of the *Lied* by using the voice as just another instrumental element and abandoning the communication of the text as a priority objective.

After a first approach, using as references the aforementioned *Catalogo anotado de la musica espanola contemporanea basada en la literaUra espanola* by Roger Tinnell and the study by Celsa Alonso *Cancion lrica espanola en el siglo XIX,* we can affirm that it was not until the beginning of the 20th century that Spanish composers turned their attention to the classical poets of the Golden Age[104] . The interest shown by poets in the first decades of that century, especially those of the generation of 27[105] , and the impulse of the celebrations of the centenaries of Cervantes, Gongora and Lope de Vega are at the origin of this new source of inspiration that led to the scores for voice and piano the poems of the main writers of the Golden Age as well as anonymous texts or others less known.

In the case in point, we will continue to focus on the relationship between music and the Lopesque theatre, given that most of the lyrics of the songs we will catalogue and study have their origin in the enormous stage work of El Fenix.

---

[101] *Ibid.,* p. 17

[102] *Ibid.,* p. 18.

[103] *Ibid.,* p. 19.

[104] The lyrics of the Spanish poets of the Golden Age have been practically absent in the song repertoire during the 19th century. Vtfanse the few references to songs with lyrics by Golden Age poets that Celsa Alonso includes in *La Cancion Lmca Espanola...,* those of Manuel Garcia (p. 179, 180, 183) and Bernardino Valle (p. 479). Alonso includes a quotation from Mesonero Romanos (p. 90), taken from his *Memorias de un sesenton,* published in 1881, in which he quotes such a lofty title as "Madre unos ojuelos vi" without indicating its author. We do not know who the author may be. In our catalogue there is only one song with this title composed in the 19th century, by Jose Maria Espinosa y Casares de los Monteros, probably written in the last decade.

[105] On the reception of the golden tradition in twentieth-century poets, see DIEZ DE REVENGA, Francisco Javier, *La tradicion aurea: sobre la recepcion del Siglo de Oro en poetas contemporaneos*, Biblioteca Nueva, Madrid, 2003. The author indicates in the introduction to this study (p. 13) that Spanish poetry between 1920 and 1936, nourished by tradition and avant-garde, recovered and assimilated the legacy of the poets of the 16th and 17th centuries, the golden tradition, such as Garcilaso, Fray Luis de Leon, San Juan de la Cruz, Cervantes, Gongora, Quevedo or Lope de Vega. This is the origin of the composers' interest in these poets.

Part II

MUSIC IN THE GOLDEN AGE AND IN THE WORK OF LOPE DE VEGA

WORKS OF LOPE DE VEGA

MUSIC IN THE GOLDEN AGE THEATRE

The use of music in the Spanish theatre of the Golden Age is an evolutionary consequence of its presence in scenic manifestations since ancient times. It is with the authors of the Spanish pre-Renaissance, Inigo de Mendoza, Gomez Manrique, Juan del Encina, Suarez Robles, Torres Naharro, Lucas Fernandez and Fernan Lopez de Yanguas, that carols and songs began to enter the Spanish stage, with Gil Vicente (1465-1536) being the one who used music most prominently[106] . The first example of a popular carol inserted into a literary text is the verse from *E libro de buen amor:* "Senora Rama, yo que por mi mal os vi / que las mis hadas negras non se parten de mi'"[107] . A similar case is Melibea's dawn song in *La Celestna* ("Papagayos, ruisenores / que cantais al al alborada"). Among the pre-Renaissance authors, Juan del Encina, given his condition as a musician and playwright, is supposed to have worked in a relationship between the two disciplines. Diez de Revenga is of the opinion that "he knew how to combine the musical and the dramatic like no one else, and if in his work there is an important musical songbook, it is not unusual for his theatre to be nourished by splendid musical representations"[108] . Lucas Fernandez is notable for the religious carols that appear in his performances of Christmas-themed cars. But, as mentioned above, it is Gil Vicente, for his great ability to combinc the lyrical and the dramatic, who can be considered practically the inventor of the procedure that Lope de Vega and some of his school would later raise to the highest level. He is the one who

He invented the ideal magic formula to be developed by those who came after him. In order to make a song in a car, to which he himself sets the music, he has made use of traditional schemes belonging to the popular genre[109] .

Cervantes also includes songs in his dramatic works, sometimes taken directly from the popular tradition, connecting them with the development of comedy[110] . He himself says that the first to include music, in the form of ancient romance, is a certain Nabarro de Toledo, of Lope de Rueda's time. In the latter's time, the music was usually off-stage accompanied by a guitar, which leads us to suppose that it was vocal music, heard especially in the intermissions as entertainment. Agustin de Rojas mentions the lute and the vihuela as common instruments in the companies, Juan Rufo that in Lope de Rueda's plays only two flutes and a tambourine were used. Likewise, Rojas says that "romances and lyrics" were sung in the theatre at the end of the 16th century and "a little dance at the end of the piece to make the audience happy"[111] .

The popular romances of the ancient lyric, many of them included in the so-called cancioneros or romanceros[112] , were the source of inspiration for most of the lyrics to be sung in the comedies of the 17th century[113] . These texts, together with melodies well known to the public, contributed enormously to endowing the plays with the verisimilitude typical of the scene of the time, explained with the metaphor of "comedy as a mirror of life". Agustin Duran explains in this way the survival of popular poetry throughout the centuries and its inclusion in the theatre of the 17th century:

---

[106] UMPIERRE, Gustavo, Songs in the Plays of Lope de Vega..., op. cit., p. 1.

[107] ESTEPA, Luis, "Voz femenina: los comienzos de la lirica popular hispanica y su relación con otros gëneros literarios", in *Cuadernos de Teatro Clasico,* 3, 1989, p. 13. See also FRENK ALATORRE, Margit, *Nuevo corpus de la antgua lricapopular hispanica, siglosXVa XVII,* UNAM, Mexico, 2003, p. 583.

[108] DIEZ DE REVENGA, Francisco Javier, "Teatro clasico y cancion traditional", *Cuadernos de Teatro Clasico,* 3, 1989, p. 31.

[109] *Ibid.*, p. 33

[110] *Ibid.*, p. 34-35

[111] STEIN, Louise K., Songs of Mortals, Dialogues of the Gods. Music and Theater in Seventh Century Spain, Oxford, 1993, pp. 15-16.

[112] On the romanceros published during Lope's time, see RODRIGUEZ-MONINO, Antonio, *Manual biblografco de cancioneros y romanceros impresos durante el siglo XVII,* Castalia, Madrid, 1977-1978. For Lope's romances in particular, see PEDRAZA JIMENEZ, Felipe B., *Euniversoportico de Lope de Vega,* Laberinto, Madrid, 2003, pp. 18-50.

[113] STEIN, Louise K., *Songs of Mortals..., op. cit,* p. 18. In this respect, the author is of the opinion that in one sense Lope and his contemporaries destroyed the tradition of ancient lyric by modifying it, but on the other hand they contributed greatly to preserving it by including it in their comedies.

The same origin had and the same course followed among us as everywhere else the poetry of the people, which from its first steps until the end of the sixteenth century was preserved in the pithy and narrative form of the octosyllabic romance, and of certain rich and simple lyrics sung by the people. But as the progress of civilisation had spread and the Nation had advanced in intelligence and a great deal of knowledge, in the seventeenth century the national poetry was merged into the drama of the novel, which, adapting it for the basis of its creation, converted its narrative essence into action and dialogue, but kept it within the reach of the people, but keeping it within the reach of the people as their child and as a repository of their historical, civil and religious notions, where the original and indelible type of their character, their habits, customs, faith, tastes, pleasures, sentiments and progress would be recorded[114] .

The use of music in the performances of the comedies responded to various functions. The most elementary was the use of music as a structural or decorative device, but vocal music, in particular, went further, being used as a vehicle for the expression of social affectivity, thus responding to the principle of the "mirror of life". Songs, many of them familiar to the public, were essential to give dramatic verisimilitude to the scenes in which they occurred[115] . A not inconsiderable function was that of seeking a certain familiarity with the spectator with respect to songs and lyrics that he or she had assumed by tradition[116] .

From the middle of the century the Madrid stage underwent a process of change due to the strong demand for new works for the court in the period of consolidation of artistic patronage as a form of legitimisation of the monarchy of Philip IV[117] . The consequent increase in the professional and economic profits of the theatre companies meant that they withdrew their activity in the public theatres in the face of the constant demand from the court theatres. The authors of Calderon's generation living in Madrid aspired to write for the court stage. The increase of means in these productions facilitated the development of musical theatre and paved the way for Calderonian semi-operas and operas and zarzuelas. Even so, comedy continued to be cultivated in public theatres and the use of the romancero as a source of lyrics to be sung in performances.

LOPE DE VEGA AND MUSIC

It was Lope de Vega with his *Arte nuevo de hacer comedias* who contributed decisively not only to the inclusion of music on the stage as a decorative element, but also to its standardisation as an important component that would play various dramatic functions in theatrical works. Lope's relationship with music seems to have been close, not only because of his friendship with some of the most important composers of the time, the most notable case being Juan Blas de Castro, but also because of his knowledge of the musical art beyond that of a mere amateur. Indeed, Barbieri refers to some passages in *La Dorotea* in which the comments of the characters indicate that:

[...] whoever wrote this not only knew music theoretically, but was initiated in the smallest accidents, usually reserved only for those who frequently practice the art[118] .

Umpierre reminds us of what seems unnecessary, that "Lope lived in the period of greatest splendour of Spanish music, that of Victoria, Morales, Salinas and Cabezon, whose *Diferencias sobre el canto del caballero* uses the same theme as the popular song that is believed to have given Lope the idea for *El caballero de* Olmedo"[119] . This fact, of enormous transcendence, is interesting to link to some biographical information about our poet in order to understand Lope's relationship with musical art and the influence of this relationship on his dramatic work.

Lope learnt the first rudiments of music and poetry with the poet and musician Vicente Espinel, at

---

114 DURAN, Agustin, "Poesia popular, drama novelesco", *Obras de Lope de Vega,* RAE, Vol. 1, Rivadeneyra, Madrid, 1890, p. 7.

115 STEIN, Louise K., *Songs of Mortals..., op. cit,* p. 19.

116 DIEZ DE REVENGA, Francisco Javier, "Teatro clasico y cancion...", *op. cit.,* p. 36.

117 STEIN, Louise K., *Songs of Mortals..., op. cit,* p. 49.

118 BARBIERI, Francisco Asenjo, *Lope de Vega musico y algunos musicos espanoles de su tempo,* 1864; quoted by BAL y GAY, Jesus, *Treinta condones de Lope de Vega,* Residencia de Estudiantes, Madrid, 1935, p. 97. The same reasoning, with the addition of some examples, is given by QUEROL, Miquel, *Cancionero musical de Lope de Vega, III. Poesi'as cantadas en las comedias,* Barcelona, CSIC, 1991, p. 11-13.

119 UMPIERRE, Gustavo, *Songs in the Plays..., op. cit,* p. 1.

a time when the learning of both arts was almost inseparable. He studied at the University of Alcala, where he had to study music in order to obtain the title of Bachiller, as well as in Salamanca, where he attended the lessons of the composer Francisco de Salinas[120] . Throughout his life he was in contact with renowned Spanish musicians. With Espinel, in addition to his childhood lessons, he maintained later contact, and as a token of his admiration he dedicated to him *El caballero de Illescas,* and mentioned him on other occasions in some of his works[121] . Gabriel Diaz, Juan Palomares, and especially Juan Blas de Castro, were the musicians he dealt with most. Lope mentions Castro in *El acero de Madrid,* in La *Jerusalen conquistada,* in *La Filomena* and, especially, in *Elogio en la muerte de Blas de Castro*, included in *La vega del parnaso*[122] . The two spent part of their youth together, and Castro set to music the poems that Lope supplied him with as a confidant of his youthful loves. In the *Elogio* Lope recalls Castro's involvement in singing of his first great love, Filis. Considered to be by an anonymous author, Miquel Querol attributes to Castro the music preserved in the Turin Songbook of one of the fifteen romances to Filis from the *Romancero General, "Ay* amargas soledades / de mi bellisima Filis"[123] . Alfredo Rodriguez and Ruiz-Fabrega provide us with conclusive data on the importance Lope gave to music on stage: of Lope's 343 comedies, 175 contain songs or singable fragments, in a total of 341 songs and lyrics, directly or indirectly related to the Castilian popular tradition[124] . Added to this is the fact that at least two comedies, Peribanezy *El Caballero de Olmedo,* arise from a pre-existing song, which constitutes the structural and argumental basis on which the work is based[125] .

MUSIC IN LOPE'S THEATRE

The references to musical elements that can be found in the stage notes of Lope's comedies[126] show how songs, dances and the use of different instruments were used for the structural division of the text. The functional use of music to mark action, transitions or thematically unify a scene was developed by Lope in countless plays and remains a basic resource in 17th century comedy[127] . In the didascalias there are shawms, flutes, caramillos, bagpipes, guitars, harps, drums, tambourines, rattles or bells, which sound independently or accompany the voices in a song or dance. Among these we find the chacona, the seguidilla, the gallarda, the pavana, the zambra, the canario, "saraos", or generic dances of Indians, blacks, Portuguese or shepherds[128] .

Among the instruments mentioned, there are many percussion instruments: atabales, tambourines and all kinds of drums, rattles and castanets. Stringed instruments include the guitar, vihuela and harp. Among the wind instruments, trumpets, clarinets, flutes, shawms, and sometimes the organ[129] . Trumpets and drums were associated with military scenes, marked the division of scenes at the entrances of higher-ranking characters, announced battles offstage, or served to interrupt the

[120] QUEROL, Miquel, Cancionero musical de Lope de Vega, vol. I: Poesi'as cantadas en las novelas, CSIC, Barcelona, 1991. p. 11.

[121] In the "Romance para la conclusión de la Justa Poelica celebrada con motivo de la beatification de San Isidro", in the *La Arcadia, La Fiomena* and in a sonnet, "Aquella pluma, cëlebre maestro". QUEROL, Miquel, *Cancionero musical de Lope de Vega,* vol. II: *Poesias sueltas puestas en musica,* CSIC, Barcelona, 1991, p. 89.

[122] *Ibid.,* pp. 10-11.

[123] *Ibid.,* p. 12. On this melody Felix Lavilla composed a song with piano, see our catalogue.

[124] RODRIGUEZ, Alfredo and RUIZ-FABREGA, Tomas, "En torno al cancionero teatral de Lope", *Lope de Vega y los origenes del teatro espanol. Actas del Congreso Internacional sobre Lope de Vega,* Edi-6, Madrid, 1981, p. 524. The authors relate the origin and popular setting of the songs to the predominant use of octosflabos in romances, redondillas and seguidillas (*Ibid.,* pp. 526-527).

[125] DIEZ DE REVENGA, Francisco Javier, "Teatro clasico y canci6n...", *op. cit.,* p. 39.

[126] Stein offers a list of the musical notes of more than a hundred of Lope's plays (STEIN, Louise K., *Songs of mortals..., op. cit.,* pp. 337-347), which in turn is taken from Morley and Bruerton: MORLEY, Griswold; BRUERTON, Courtney, *Cronologa de las comedias de Lope de Vega,* Gredos, Madrid, 1968.

[127] STEIN, Louise K., *Songs of mortals..., op. cit.,* p. 20.

[128] Querol offers an extensive list in the introduction to vol. I, QUEROL, Miquel, *op. cit.*, p. 13.

[129] See the list given by Querol, p. 13, and the list of Stein's notes, taken from Morley-Bruerton.

action at scene section changes[130] . Shawms or sackbuts were associated with religious plays, and there is even an annotation referring to groups of instruments playing in different locations, in the style of the *cori spezzati*[131] . Rustic folk instruments were used in peasant scenes, with the guitar, harp and vihuela serving as accompaniment. There are cases in which instruments are used with a realistic function when a character sings and is accompanied by an instrument. Sometimes the sound of the instruments or the voices were also used to cover the noise of the stage machinery, or the machinery was activated by the sound of the music on the stage.

In Lope, the song, on or off stage, in addition to defining a scene or subsection, is linked to the content of the scene in which it is used and thus contributes to the development of the play's plot. Songs are sometimes used to provoke changes in the prevailing mood. Vocal music was generally used as a vehicle for dramatic continuity, maintaining or reinforcing the mood or atmosphere of the scene, as an element of verisimilitude. Wedding scenes are reinforced by song, rustic and pastoral scenes include groups of peasants singing, whose songs tend to be based on popular lyrics, servants or confidants sing to noble characters, and religious scenes require songs sung off-stage by angelic voices[132] . Most songs in Lope have more than one function. The same song can serve to formally mark the scene, to set it in context and to introduce a message related to the plot[133] .

Some songs he wrote ex profeso for each play, although based on borrowed material, others already existed before he included them in some of his comedies[134] . This is the case of *Mira Nero from Tarpeya* or the song from *El caballero de Olmedo.* Referring to the melodies, or the polyphonic compositions based on them, which circulated prior to the writing of the stage work, Stein believes that "it is very possible that these are the melodies that Lope associated with the pre-existing lyrics when he wrote them for his comedies"[135] . The fact that the texts of the musical works with theatrical texts that have survived[136] differ from those that appear in Lope's plays, and the style and polyphonic complexity of some examples, leads us to doubt that many of the works that have survived today were performed in the theatre as they are in the scores[137] , but rather they could be arrangements of melodies and lyrics that had achieved a certain fame, independently or not of their inclusion in one or another comedy.

The textual variants, so frequent in the songs that Lope intercalated in his comedies, are the consequence of the adaptation of pre-existing material, which was a practice that was not limited to poetry. Like poets, composers borrowed melodies and musical ideas to compose their polyphonic works. "Composers and poets had the same technique: using known melodies and

---

[130] STEIN, Louise K., *Songs of mortals..., op. cit.,* p. 21.
[131] In Act II of *La ninez del padre Rojas. Ibid.,* p. 22.
[132] *Ibid.,* pp. 23-24.
[133] *Ibid.,* p. 24.
[134] In FRENK ALATORRE, Margit, *Nuevo corpus..., op. cit,* we find numerous references to letrillas used by Lope in some of his comedies of which the author gives the sources and survivals, on many occasions prior to the writing of the plays.
[135] STEIN, Louise K., *Songs of mortals..., op. cit,* p. 30.
[136] Stein collects 17 compositions, included in different songbooks, with lyrics by Lope or attributed to him. These works are also included in the works by Jesus Bal y Gay, *Treinta canciones..., op. cit,* and Miquel Querol, *Cancionero musical..., op. cit* Querol includes in his songbook both works that he himself attributes to Lope and others with lyrics by other poets that Lope uses in some of his comedies, such as the *Coplas* by Jorge Manrique. He also notes that two of the thirty songs collected by Bal y Gay are not by Lope.
[137] STEIN, Louise K., *Songs of mortals..., op. cit,* p. 30. This opinion is shared by Carmelo Caballero Fernandez-Rufete, who adds, referring to the testimonies that have come down to us, that "all of them were certainly destined for areas of musical life outside the theatre: the palace chamber, the temple or the non-dramatic feast". CABALLERO FERNANDEZ-RUFETE, Carmelo, "La musica en el teatro clasico", *Historia del teatro espanol,* vol. 1, *De la Edad Media a los Siglos de Oro,* Javier Huerta Calvo (dir.), Gredos, Madrid, 2003, p. 680.

lyrics for their works. The test of mastery for both lay in the refinement and intelligence in adapting borrowed materials"[138] . The choice of lyrics and music was a function of the type of scene in which they were inserted, whether popular, peasant, courtly or exotic, of the dramatic function of the music, and of the principle of verisimilitude that governed the scene of the time, so that they often responded to conventionalisms and stage stereotypes.

The musical compositions that are preserved, collected in songbooks, are works closer to the courtly or chamber style than to popular music[139] . Tirso de Molina, in *Cigarrales de Toledo compuestos por el maestro Tirso de Molina*, describing a performance of *E vergonzoso en palacio* mentions the composers Juan Blas and Alvaro de los R'os as the "authors of the tones" that were played. Both were court musicians of Philip III and probably did not compose for public performances, in this case for an aristocratic and private performance[140] . It is clear, then, that the music played in the Lopesque comedies is unknown to us. Carmelo Caballero sums up the situation of studies on the subject by saying that:

Most of the pages published on the history of aurisecular theatre music, and especially those referring to the first half of the century, have been written in the total absence of direct testimonies, that is to say, of scores. It is absolutely impossible to write a history of musical texts for the theatre. In the absence of ëstos, the documentary basis for the elaboration of the account has been limited almost exclusively to the dramatic texts themselves; His method of work has consisted basically in the compilation of the sung fragments and the didascalias referring to the music inserted in them, and his final product, in the best of cases, an interpretative si'iitesis of these didascalias and lyric fragments, extrapolating from all this a series of conclusions about the role of music in certain plays, playwrights or periods[141] .

Likewise, the scores that are preserved are not usually dated, and in the few cases in which the date is known, it is usually very far from the date of the play's premiere[142] . The composers or musicians in charge of the theatre music are not usually mentioned in any document, and when they do appear they are related to performances at court[143] .

The principle of verisimilitude, already discussed above, dictates what kind of music should be introduced in what kind of scenes and how it should be introduced. It seems obvious that in allegorical scenes, those of mystical or supernatural content, with entrances of divine messengers, apparitions of images and altars, or ascensions or descents of saints from or to heaven, polyphonic composition was the most appropriate. However, in scenes of peasant settings, wedding songs, harvest songs, Moorish songs, Mayan songs, and all kinds of settings in which the popular is the referent, it is difficult to fit a polyphonic song, not so much because of its musical difficulty as because of the lack of scenic verisimilitude[144] .

---

[138] STEIN, Louise K., *Songs of mortals..., op. cit.,* p. 45.

[139] Stein gives as an example the case of the Cancionero de Olot, in which many songs belong to composers close to the court *(Ibid.,* p. 44).

[140] *Ibid.,* p. 35.

[141] CABALLERO FERNANDEZ-RUFETE, Carmelo, "La musica en...", *op. at.,* p. 677. Some of the most important studies on the theatrical praxis of the Golden Age include little or no reference to the music played in the performances, the performance of the musicians or the musical involvement of the actors. See RODRIGUEZ CUADROS, Evangelina, *La técnica del actor espanol en el Barroco: hipotesis y documents,* Castalia, Madrid, 1998; Quirante, Luis; RODRIGUEZ CUADROS, Evangelina; SIRERA Josep Lluis, *Practiques esceniques de l'edat mitjana als segles dor,* Universitat de Valencia, Valencia, 1999; RUANO DE LA HAZA, Jose Maria; ALLEN, John J., *Los teatros comerciales del siglo XVIIy la escenifcacion de la comedia*, Castalia, Madrid, 1994.

[142] CABALLERO FERNANDEZ-RUFETE, Carmelo, "La musica en.", *op. cit.*, p. 678.

[143] Remember the above mentioned in *Cigarrales de Toledo*.

[144] Bal y Gay expresses the same opinion in his commentaries on *Thirty Songs by Lope de Vega*: "the songs we present correspond partly to the theatre and partly to Lope's novelistic lyric. But the provenance of the musical manuscripts seems to indicate that these songs, even though some of them belonged to the stage, must have had their most repeated setting in the aristocratic salons of the time". BAL y GAY, Jesus, *Treinta canciones..., op. cit.,* p. 97. These thirty songs include both music written for original texts by Lope and songs that in some way are alluded to or used by him in his works.

But when in the stage notes or in some previous intervention of a character he refers to a certain rhythmic foot in dances or sung dances[145] .

[145] We refer once again to the list of names of dances and dances given by QUEROL, Miquel, *Cancionero musical de Lope de Vega...,* vol. 13, to which we could undoubtedly add, as they were very popular at the time, the canario, gambeta, el villano, la zarabanda, el paseme de ello, el Rey don Alonso, el escarraman, and all those mentioned by Cervantes in his work, collected by Querol in his study on music in Cervantes: QUEROL, Miquel, *La musica en la epoca de Cervantes,* Centro de Estudios Cervantinos, Madrid, 2005, pp. 109-168. Likewise, more information can be found in the entries "baile" and "danzas" in the *Gran Enciclopedia Cervantina*: MAESTRO, Jesus G., "baile", *Gran Enciclopedia Cervantina*, ALVAR, Carlos (dir.), Centro de Estudios Cervantinos, Castalia, Alcala de Henares, 2005-, vol. 2, p. 1058-1061; PROFETI, Maria Gracia, "danzas", *Gran Enciclopedia Cervantina*, ALVAR, Carlos (dir.), Centro de Estudios Cervantinos, Castalia, Alcala de Henares, 2005-, vol. 4, pp. 3163-3168.

Part III

THE WORK OF LOPE IN 20th CENTURY SPANISH MUSIC

Although our work focuses on the genre of the song with piano, we offer in this chapter a broader vision of the presence of Lope's work in the music composed in the 20th century, a century in which, as has already been mentioned, 93% of the songs included in the catalogue were produced. The interest of Spanish composers in Lope de Vega's work is obviously not limited to songs. Although his texts are present in vocal compositions, whether taken literally or by means of adaptations, the inspiration that the work of El Fenix represents for many composers is not exhausted here. Purely instrumental music is also abundant, whether as incidental music or soundtracks for film or television.
After a first section in which we will summarise the musical production based on Lope's work in musical genres other than the one we are concerned with here, we will now study the musical implications that the centenaries of the poet's death and birth, in 1935 and 1962 respectively, had for music in general and the liederistic production in particular. We find it interesting to compare the significance of these celebrations, as far as music is concerned, with those of the centenaries of Miguel de Cervantes and his *Don Quixote (*1905, 1915, 1916 and 1947), and of Luis de Gongora (1927). We will study the musical works generated as a consequence of these celebrations before going on to study the derivations of the tercentenary of the lopiano and two fundamental events for our work: the announcement of the National Music Prize of that year and the tribute concert offered by the Madrid Conservatory in the Teatro Espanol, events which generated most of the songs on which we will base our subsequent study.
With the intention of situating the production for voice and piano within the group of works inspired by Lope de Vega or based on his texts, and without wishing to be exhaustive in the description of Lope's influence on Spanish composers, we will study in this section the musical creations in musical genres other than the one that occupies us in this work. The vast oeuvre of the Fenix has served as a stimulus for a great number of compositions of all kinds of genres and vocal and instrumental combinations. It is important to distinguish between those that make use of an unabridged text by Lope and those that are an adaptation based on one of his works. Another level apart are those creations that make use of purely instrumental means in which the text is not presented explicitly, but as an expressive or argumental reference. In the first group we find works for solo voice accompanied by an instrument other than the piano, instrumental ensemble or orchestra. There are also numerous works for *a cappella* choir, with or without soloists, or with organ, harmonium, an instrumental ensemble or an orchestral formation. As we shall see below, there are also two cases of recitative over music.
Lope has also been used on occasion as a more or less extensive plot basis for stage works, whether in opera or zarzuela format. In all these cases the original text has been adapted by the corresponding librettists. Still in the field of the stage, the largest production is that of incidental music for theatrical performances of Lopean comedies, as well as scores for the soundtrack of films and television productions, as well as ballets.

VOCAL WORKS

The adaptation of many of Lope de Vega's texts to the field of sacred or specifically liturgical music has inspired some composers to write songs for one voice or choir in unison with organ or harmonium accompaniment, a fundamental instrument in church music. From the nineteenth-century Fermin Maria Alvarez (1833-1898) and Salvador Bartoli (18'75-(-?) "s, authors of numerous songs, to Angel Mingote (18911961) and Miguel Asins Arbo (1918-1996), who adapted for these instruments works written for piano or choir and vice versa, through a good group of ecclesiastical musicians such as Jose Manuel Adran, Rafael Lozano, Jose Font Roger, Francisco Laporta or Eduardo Torres, there are compositions with lyrics on Christmas motifs taken mostly from *Shepherds of Bethlehem*[14] .
Something similar occurs with the repertoire of choral music, where the list of works inspired by religious poetry, and especially by the aforementioned novel, is extensive. The earliest

[146] Composer of religious music, stage music and songs in Spanish and Catalan. His place of birth and date of death are unknown. See: DRAAYER, Suzanne R., *Art Song Composers..., op. cit.,* pp. 297298.
[147] Unless otherwise stated, the data on these works are taken from TINNELL, Roger, *Catalogo anotado.*

are those of Francesc Laporta (ca. 1890)[148] , Bernardino Valle Chinestra (1915), Jose Alfonso (1918) and Nemesio Otano (1935). From the post-war years are those of Joan M.ª Thomas (1944 and 1958), Angel Mingote (1944 and 1960) and Arturo Duo Vital (1952), increasing the production from the 1960s onwards with works by Padre Luis del Santisimo: (1959), Joaquin Hernandez (1964), M.ª Pilar Escudero (1966), Matilde Salvador (1970), Victorina Falco de Pablo (1972), Jesus M.ª Muneta (1976), Jose M.ª Sanmartin (1978), Jose Miguel Moreno (1983), Manuel Seco de Arpe (1983), P. Felix Remon (1985), Jose L. Zamanillo (1986), Angel Peinado (1987), Joaquin Broto (1989), Jose Luis Rubio Pulido (1989) and Antonio Celada (1994).

The flourishing of religious vocal music in these years can be explained, among other reasons, by the impulse of what is known as the *Motu proprio* Generation, the extensive group of composers, many of them ecclesiastical, driven by the papal declaration on sacred music of 1903, which took shape in Spain from the 1930s onwards. Federico Sopena defends the idea that some composers, he gives as an outstanding example Father Otano, wrote some songs with evident influence of some *Lieder* by Schubert, Schumann or Brahms, looking for a type of music that united simplicity and the style of popular song[149] . These musicians who, although they occasionally wrote other types of music, concentrated on the work of dignifying religious music[150] . The impulse that motivated and guided these composers can be found in the publication in 1903 of Pius X's *Motu proprio Tra le solecitudine*[151] , on sacred music. Three congresses of Sacred Music were held in Spain in response to this papal document: Valladolid in 1907, Barcelona in 1912, and Vitoria in 1928, the latter of special relevance[152] . The group of musicians who followed the new guidelines based their creations on the recovery of the Gregorian tradition and Renaissance and Baroque compositional techniques, as a reaction to the Italianism and general mannerism into which liturgical and religious music in general had fallen. This movement was weakened after the Civil War, although its later influence was notable due to the ideological conditions of the political regime. The work of this generation extended until the Second Vatican Council, when two other official documents, the *Sacrosantum Concilium*, the constitution on the sacred liturgy of the Second Vatican Council, of 1963, and the Instruction on music in the sacred liturgy *Musicam Sacram,* of 1967, which, according to Tomas Marco, "abruptly removed all liturgical music of a certain artistic height, not so concert music, which experienced a certain renaissance and continued to bear remarkable fruit"[153] . In the words of Jose Sierra Perez, "the great debate motivated by the *Motu Proprio* on how religious music should be, finally resolved, according to the most generalised opinion, by saying that the main quality of religious music is that it should be good music". In agreement with Marco, Sierra Perez is of the opinion that this generation was a generation frustrated in large part by the consequences of Vatican II[154] .

Among the most ambitious works with sacred text in terms of instrumental numbers, we find compositions by Jesus Guridi, *Pastores de Belen* (three sopranos and orchestra, from 1958), Jose

[148] *Fons Francesc Laporta i Mercader*, Biblioteca de Catalunya. Seccio de Musica. Inventaris, p. 11.
[149] SOPENA, Federico, *El "Leed" lornnntioo,* op. cit., p. 134-135.
[150] MARCO, Tomas, *Historia de la musica..., op. at.,* p. 107. Marco takes the denomination "Generation del Motu Proprio" from Josë Subira and Juan Alfonso Garcia.
[151] Tomas Marco confuses this papal declaration with an entidica entitled "Motu proprio". This term is given in the Catholic Church to a document issued by the Pope on his own initiative and authority. The title of this document, as a *Motu proprio,* taken as is traditional from the first words of the text is *Trale solecitudne* ("Among the cares"). *Ibid.,* p. 106.
[152] On the three congresses held in Spain, see: AVINOA, Xose, "Los congresos del "Motu Proprio" (1907-1928): repercusion e influencias", *Revista de Musicolog'a,* vol. 27, n° 1, 2004, pp. 381400. [This volume contains the proceedings of the International Symposium "The Motu Proprio of St. Pius X and Music (1903-2003)" (Barcelona, 26-28 November 2003)].
[153] MARCO, Tomas, Historia de la musica..., op. cit., 107.
[154] SIERRA PEREZ, Jose, "Presentation", *Revista de Musicologa..., op. cit.,* p. 17.

Ignacio Prieto, *Dos villancicos* (voice and orchestra, from 1976-79), Jose Font Roger, *Al sol de Belen* (soloists, choir and orchestra), Conrado del Campo, *Figuras de Belen* (soloists and orchestra, from 1946), Joaquin Rodrigo, *A la Clavelina* (choir and orchestra, from 1952). They also use sacred texts in the works *Alegraos pastores (*1952) by Arturo Duo Vital and *Dos poemas (Pastor que con tus silbos amorosos* and *Pues andais en las palmas,* from 1961) by Joaquim Homs, with a soprano and reduced instrumental ensemble.

The works with secular text are scarce in comparison with the previous ones. From the tercentenary year are two works for four-voice choir, *Cancion de velador* and *Villano,* by Manuel del Fresno[155] . Enrique Casal Chapi, a fundamental composer in our work, wrote in 1935 a *Cancion madrigalesca,* from the comedy *E acero de Madrid,* for three equal voices, flute and guitar[156] . The original songs for voice and piano later orchestrated by the composers themselves are the three by Bacarisse[157] and the *Elega al caballero de Olmedo* by Manuel Palau. Francesc Bonastre composed *Si os parterades al alba* for soprano and a small instrumental group, and Cesar Cano wrote *Quedito* in 1997, for four voices a cappella, with the same poem "Si os partierades al al alba, / quedito, pasito, amor, / no espanteis al ruisenor" from *E ruisenor de Sevilla.*

The cantata format[158] [159] is used by Julio Gomez in *Elegia heroica™, a* 1945 work for mixed choir and orchestra based on *La Arcadia,* while Jose Luis Turina de Santos resorts to a single poem included in the so-called *Codice del marques de Pidal* in one of the numbers of his *Musica ex lingua* (1989) for choir and chamber orchestra, and Juan Angel Quesada de la Vega writes *E caballero de Olmedo (*1983) for choir and piano soloists. Manuel Angulo uses a choir of two white voices and a reduced instrumental group for his *Dos canciones (*1962), a work intended for school-age performers[160] .

The use of the guitar as instrumental support for the solo voice has produced two interesting and timely collections of songs, Rafael Rodriguez Albert's *Cuatro canciones de Lope de Vega,* written in 1935, the year of the III centenary, and Gracia Tarrago's *Cinco canciones del siglo XVII,* published in 1963, a direct consequence of the celebration of the IV centenary in 1962. Tarrago would later write her version for voice and guitar of the popular *Tened los rat nos*" (1968). For this format Joaquin Rodrigo adapted his two songs for voice and piano *Pastorcito santo* and *Coplas del pastor enamorado.* The popularity of the poem *Zagalejo de perlas* also reached the world of singer-songwriters. Amancio Prada wrote the song *Hijo del alba,* which he himself sang accompanied by the guitar. A version of "A mis soledades voy" was also composed under the title *Soledades (*1975) by Jose Manuel Ipina and performed by the musical group Mocedades with an instrumental arrangement by Juan Carlos Calderon.

An unfrequented combination, at least as far as compositions created ex profeso for the recitation

---

155 First performed on 3-11-1935, in December of the same year they were performed in an act of homage to Lope de Vega in the Ateneo Popular in Oviedo. See: MARTINEZ DEL FRESNO, Beatriz, "La obra de Manuel del Fresno, un capitulo del regionalismo asturiano (1900-1936)", *Homenaje a Juan Una Ru,* vol. 2, Universidad de Oviedo, Oviedo, 1999, p. 1009.

156 BNE, signatures: M.CASAECHAPI / 3 and M.CASAECHAPI / 4. Probably for the staging of this comedy by the company Teatro Escuela de Arte directed by Rivas Cherif and Jose Franco. The performances were given at the Teatro Maria Guerrero in Madrid, the premiere being on 4-2-1935. See in GIL FOMBELLIDA, Mª del Carmen, *Rvas Cherif Margarita Xirgu y el teatro de la II Republica,* Fundamentos, Madrid, 2003, pp. 116 and 313.

157 Included in our catalogue.

158 Within this group, we have found no trace of Manuel Palau's *Poema lirico,* which Tinnell notes as having been composed in 1947, either in the SGAE's catalogue of Palau's works or in the doctoral thesis that Salvador Segui dedicated to his vocal work. SEGUI PEREZ, Salvador, *La praxis aimonico-contrapuntistica en la obra liederistica de Manuel Palau. Life and work of the Valencian musician.* Doctoral thesis. University of Valencia, Valencia, 1994. [Microfilm].

159 Work that received an accesit in the National Music Competition of 1945. MART'INEZ DEL FRESNO, Beatriz, *Catalogo obras de Julio Gomez,* Madrid, SGAE, 1997, p. 29.

160 These two songs were composed and premiered in the year of the celebration of the IV centenary of the birth of Lope de Vega. PLIEGO DE ANDRES, Victor, *Manuel Angulo,* Catalogos de compositores espanoles, SGAE, Madrid, 1992, p. 22.

of specific poems are concerned, is that employed by Juan Briz and Eduardo Rincon in writing works for reciter and keyboard instrument, the former with organ in *Engendra al hijo el padre (*1982), and the latter with his *Musica para tres sonetos de Lope de Vega (*1991) with piano.

STAGE MUSIC

Although the only work for orchestra inspired by a comedy by Lope, the *Fantasia en triptico sobre un drama de Lope (*Premio Nacional de Musica in 1961) by Rafael Rodriguez Albert, based on *El mejor alcalde, el Rey*, is not stage music as such but a symphonic composition for the concert hall, it serves to introduce an extensive group of compositions intended to serve as musical support for different stage manifestations, whether theatrical, filmic, television or ballet.

The most abundant are the incidental music written for the numerous theatrical performances of comedies[161] [162] and autos, many of which have not been preserved, as improvisation or the scarce transcendence of their music are at the origin of the lack of interest in preserving them. The composer who stands out above all others is Manuel Parada (1911-1973), author of an extensive catalogue of theatrical and cinematographic music, of whom up to ten scores of as many comedies by Lope have been preserved. The list of those known is extensive:

- *El acero de Madrid*: Paco Aguilera, 1995.
- *El amor enamorado (Love in Love)*, Tomas Bohorquez, 1991.
- *El caballero de Olmedo (The Knight of Olmedo)* Enrique Casal Chapi, 1935[163] [164] ; Manuel

Parada, 1946;

Salvador Ruiz de Luna, 1953; Luis Mendo, 1977; Gregorio Paniagua, 1990;

Luis Delgado, 2003.

- *El castgo sin venganza* Manuel Parada, 1943; Jose Garcia Roman, 1985.
- The Awakening of the Sleeper: Persian Gulfs, 1988.
- *El perro del hortelano*: Luis de Pablo, 1963; Pedro Estevan and Suso Saiz, 1989.
- *El rufan castrucho* Mariano Diaz, 1991.
- *El villano en su rincon* Manuel Parada, 1950; Matilde Salvador, 1962[165] .
- *Fuenteovejuna*[166] : Manuel Parada, 1944 and 1962, Jose Tejera, 1984; Tomas

---

[161] About the poem "Pues andais en las palmas" from *Pastores de Belen.*

[162] It is interesting to recall here a work by the Russian composer Aram Ilyich Khachaturian, who wrote in 1940 the incidental music for *The Valencian Widow* (his *op.* 45), from which he composed a suite for orchestra with the same title (op. 45A). Vtfase in this respect SCHWARZ, Boris, "Khachaturian, Aram Ilyich", *The New Grove..., op. cit,* vol. 10, p. 47-48.

[163] We offer here the titles and authors of the music that appear in TINNELL, *Catalogo anotado...,* op. cit., and in PEDRAZA JIMENEZ, Felipe B.; RODRIGUEZ CACERES, Milagros (eds.), *El teatro segun Lope de Vega,* 2 vols., Compania Nacional de Teatro Clasico, Madrid, 2009. We exclude from the list those stagings whose music was not originally written for the occasion.

[164] *El baile del Caballero de Olmedo by Lope de Vega*, six episodes to be danced, with solo, chorus and orchestra accompaniment. To these fragments he adds as a prelude the "Diferencias sobre el Canto del Caballero" by Antonio Cabezon. The autograph manuscript is dated, "4-IX-35". Gil Fombellida *(Rivas Cherif margarita Xirgu,..., op, cit,* p. 324) reports on the 1934 performances of *El caballero de Olmedo* by the Melia-Cebrian company, and Michael D. McDagha (McDAGIA, Michael D., *The theatre in Madrid during the Second Republic: a checklist*, Grant & Cutler, London, 1979, p. 72) notes a premiere of the same play, with the same company at the Teatro Benavente, on 21 June 1935. Given the dates, Casal Chapi's score may be a later revision of the music used in those theatrical performances. See also ALVAREZ CANIBANO, Antonio; CANO, Jose Ignacio; GONZALEZ RIBOT, Mª Jose (eds.), *Rtmo para el espacio. Los compositores espanoles y el ballet del siglo XX*, Centro de Documentacion de Musica y Danza, Madrid, 1998, p. 43.

[165] SEGUI, Salvador, *Matilde Salvador,* Fundacion Autor, Madrid, 2000, pp. 76, 77.

[166] The *Diccionario panhispanico de dudas*, RAE, 2005, in the entry "Fuente Obejuna" clarifies that it is "the official name of this municipality in the province of Cordoba [...]. The spellings with *v (Fuente Ovejuna, Fuenteovejuna)* come from a period of graphic hesitation in which it was common to find the same word written sometimes with *b* and sometimes with *v*. In fact, in the famous work by Lope de Vega which bears the name of this town, the writer from Madrid wrote *Fuente Ovejuna,* which has also been transcribed *Fuenteovejuna,* in a single word". Real Academia Espanola, *Diccionariopanhispanico de dudas* [online], <http://buscon.rae.es/dpdI/> [accessed 20-11-2011]. Given that the two forms *Fuente Ovejuna* and *Fuenteovejuna* have been used interchangeably as the title of different editions and works based on Lope's comedy, we will henceforth follow the

Bohorquez, 1993.

- *La bella malmaridada* Manuel Parada, 1947; Manuel Blancafort, 1962; Jose Luis Valderrama, 1991.
- *La dama boba (The Lady* Federico Garcia Lorca, 1935[167] ; Fernando Moraleda, 1951; Carmelo Bernaola, 1979; Pedro Luis Domingo, 1990; J. M. Diaz-Canel, 1998.
- *La discreta enamorada*: Manuel Parada, 1945.
- *La Dorotea* Alfredo Carrion, 1983.
- *La estrella de Sevilla*: Fernando Moraleda, 1957; Luis de Pablo, 1970; Jose Garcia Roman, 1998.
- *La moza del cantaro*, Manuel Parada, 1952.
- *La noche toledana*: Julio Gergely, 1990.
- *The Andalusian Queen*: Rafael Riquelme, 1989.
- *The Valencian widow:* Matilde Salvador, 1962[168] ; Angel Holgado, 1992.
- *The Return from Egypt*: Manuel de Falla, 1935.
- Las bizamas de Belisa: Manuel Parada, 1941.
- Los locos de Valencia: Jose Nieto, 1986.
- Los melindres de Belisa: Eduardo Vasco, 1992.
- The Seven Infantes de Lara: Carmelo Bernaola, 1966.
- *Peribanez y el comendador de Ocana* Manuel Parada, 1942; Jaume Pahissa, 1962; Eliseo Parra, 2002.
- *To fight to the death*: Gustavo Ros, 1989.
- *Santiago el verde:* Antonio Ramirez Angel, 1953.

Soundtracks are another compositional format of which some examples remain. In the cinematographic medium: *Fuenteovejuna (*Antonio Roman, 1947) with music by Manuel Parada, *La moza del Cantaro (*Florian Rey, 1953) by Juan Solano, *Fuenteovejuna (*Juan Guerrero Zamora, 1970) by Luis de Pablo, and *El perro del hortelano (*Pilar Miro, 1996) by Jose Nieto. Teddy Bautista wrote the music for the television production of *La viuda valenciana (*1983), directed by Francisco Regueiro for TVE.

Although the text written by librettists Romero and Fernandez-Shaw is a very free version inspired by *La discreta enamorada*, we would like to mention the two feature films with the music of the lyric comedy *Dona Francisquita* by Amadeo Vives, one of the most notable successes of Spanish lyric theatre in the 20th century, which was taken to the big screen on two occasions, in 1934 directed by Hans Behrend, and in 1952 directed by Ladislao Vajda[169] . The zarzuela had seen the light of day in 1923 and its great success led to these two versions, the first on the eve of the third centenary of the death of Lope de Vega[170] . Other comedies by Fenix saw their zarzuela adaptation[171] [172] : *El domine Lucas* by Barbieri, based on the play of the same name by Lope; *La*

form used by the most prestigious editions of the same, those of McGrady (which is the one we take as our reference), Juan Maria Marin and that of Rinaldo Froldi: all three note *Fuente Ovejuna.* We will respect the other form when it is part of a title so assigned by the respective author.

[167] See: GIL FOMBELLIDA, Mª . Carmen, p. 306.

[168] SEGUI, Salvador, *Matilde Salvador,* Fundacion Autor, Madrid, 2000, p. 78.

[169] Ramon Navarrete analyses these two film versions, together with one of *El huesped del sevilano* by Jacinto Guerrero, this one inspired by *La ilustre fregona* by Cervantes. NAVARRETE, Ramon, "Los clasicos, la zarzuela y el cine", *XXIV y XXV Jornadas de Teatro del Siglo de Oro*, Instituto de Estudios Almerienses, Almena, 2011, pp. 127-139.

[170] On the second of the adaptations, see PEREZ BOWIE, Jose Antonio, "La función parodica de las estrategias metaficcionales. Apuntes sobre la adaptacion cinematografica de la zarzuela *Dona Francisquita* (Ladislao Vajda, 1952)", *Anales de Lteratura Espanola,* no. 19, 2007, pp. 189-204. On the adaptation of Lope's comedy to zarzuela format there is another work: FERNANDEZ SAN EMETERIO, Gerardo, "La herencia lopesca en el teatro musical espanol: *La discreta enamorada y Dona Francisquita*", in *Lope de Vega: comedia urbana y comedia palatina. Actas XVIII jornadas de teatro clasico. Almagro, July 1995*, Almagro, 1996, pp. 157-171.

[171] See FLOREZ ASENSIO, Maria Asuncion, "Lope *libretista* de zarzuela", *Revista de Musicologa,* XXI, p. 95.

[172] The relation between both works is studied by Florez Asensio in the aforementioned article. *Ibid.,* p. 93-112.

*vilana (*1927), based on *Peribanez y el Comendador de Ocana,* by Amadeo Vives; *La rosa del azafran (*1930) by Jacinto Guerrero, based on *Elperro del hortelano" and Elhio fingido (*1964) by Joaquin Rodrigo, based on *De cuando aca nos vino* and *Los ramilletes de Madrid*; *Fuenteovejuna (*1980) by Mariano Moreno Buendia; and the most recent, *San Isidro labrador (*1986) by Valentin Ruiz Lopez.

The operatic genre has two works that base their libretto on *Fuente Ovejuna.* One is written in French by Salvador Bacarisse, his *Font-aux-cabres*[173] (1956), the other unfortunately unfinished by the composer Francisco Escudero, with the same title as the comedy (1967-)[174] .

Musical creations in the ballet discipline[175] that draw on Lope de Vega are rare. Outside Spain, *Fuente Ovejuna* was used as the plot for the ballet *Laurencia,* written by Alexander Krein, which premiered at the Kirov Theatre, Leningrad, in 1939, with choreography by Vakhtang Chabukiani[176] . In our country, the only case is the flamenco dance show choreographed by Antonio Gades based on the plot of *Fuente Ovejuna (*1994), with a libretto by Jose Manuel Caballero Bonald, using music by various flamenco composers and artists. Part of the music was written by Anton Garcia Abril for the occasion, together with fragments by Moussorgsky, Antonio Gades, Faustino Nunez, Juan Antonio Zafra and baroque music[177] .

1935: THE THIRD CENTENARY OF LOPE DE VEGA AND THE PRIZE NATIONAL MUSIC

Three hundred years after the death of Lope de Vega, numerous official and private institutions are preparing to celebrate the event and commemorate his figure and his work. The events that take place throughout Spain and abroad are numerous and varied, and the concern for the study of his creations is shown in the large number of publications that have appeared around this event. The first decades of the twentieth century saw, in addition to this, other celebrations that stimulated the interest of writers and scholars in the enormous literary work of our Golden Age. In the following sections, we will study the musical consequences of the centenary of the centenary of the birth of Cervantes, Gongora and the publication of Don Quixote, with emphasis on the production of concert songs, also compared with the celebrations of the anniversaries of Cervantes, Gongora and the publication of Don Quixote.

The close precedents of the celebration of the 3rd centenary of the death of Cervantes in 1916 and of Gongora in 1927, of crucial literary importance, did not have the same repercussions in terms of

---

[173] The library of the Fundacion Juan March conserves various materials such as the libretto by Jean Camp, the score, reduction for piano and voice, as well as a recording from the French Radio Television.

[174] LARRINAGA CUADRA, Itziar, "El proceso de creacion de *Fuenteovejuna*, la opera inacabada de Francisco Escudero", *Eusko Ikaskuntza,* n° 17, 2010, pp. 497-556.

[175] Joaquin de Entrambasaguas, in a newspaper article in 1962, to which he gives the misleading title of "Lope de Vega author of "ballet"", gives some examples of Lope's use of dance and dance in its two senses, the purely choreographic and those dances that contain plot references, as well as the use of specific choreographic indications, affirming with a certain lightness, perhaps out of a need for journalistic impact, that these manifestations are "the precedent of what is modernly understood as "ballet". ENTRAMBASAGUAS, Joaquin de, "Lope de Vega autor de "ballets", *ABC,* 8-4-1962 [article in the special issue that *ABC* dedicated to the IV centenary of the birth of Lope de Vega].

[17.] Ballet in three acts with libretto by E. Mandelberg and scenography by S. Virsaladze. First performed on 22 March 1939. Created at the request of the Soviet government, it was very popular and was staged many times in the Soviet Union and Eastern Europe. In 2010 it was revived after fifty years in a new production by the Mikhailovsky Ballet. See: CRAINE Debra; MACKRELL, Judith, "Laurencia", *The Oxford Dictionary of Dance,* Oxford University Press Inc. Oxford Reference Online. Oxford University Press. University of Valencia. <http://www.oxfordreference.com/views/ENTRY.html?subview=Main&entry=

t74.e1456> [accessed: 13-2-2012].

[177] First performed at the Geneva Opera, it was later given in Spain at the Teatro de la Maestranza. BAYO, Javier, *Diccionario biografco de la danza,* Libreria Esteban Sanz, Madrid, 1997, p. 134; ALVAREZ CANIBANO, Antonio; RIBOT, Maria Jose, *Ritmo para el espacio: los compositores espanoles y el ballet en el siglo XX*, Centro de Documentacion de Musica y Danza, Madrid, 1998, p. 47. There is a commercial DVD of the performances of this show at the Teatro Real in Madrid in 2011 (Teatro Real label).

the composition of liederistic works, as a musical sublimation of poetic language.
As will be seen below, music in general had a notable, though uneven, development in Cervantes' and Gongor's celebrations in comparison with those of Lope. While in the case of Cervantes the greatest impetus was seen in orchestral works and in the genre of the symphonic poem, in the vocal repertoire the balance is highly positive for Lope de Vega. This, compared to Cervantes, is understandable, since the poetic work, from which the repertoire for voice and piano is basically nourished, is incomparable between the two writers, as far as quantity and dedication are concerned. The same is not true of Gongora, a poet about whom only two works of this genre were composed in the year of his centenary.
The first half of the 20th century was particularly intense in terms of Cervantes celebrations. The production of works inspired by Don Quixote is abundant in the first half of the century, an influence due to the celebrations of the four anniversaries of the author and his work. Among these numerous musical fruits, however, not so numerous are the compositions that take the text directly from Cervantes[178] . In 1905 the third centenary of the publication of the first part of Don Quixote was celebrated, and for this purpose the Junta National del Centenario was set up to promote and coordinate the activities that took place, in which Adela Presas sees a clear political intention in the use of this date as an element of national reaffirmation[179] . The atmosphere was already prepared, as the interest shown by the writers and intellectuals of the generation of '98 in the preceding years was that of a collective feeling of exaltation[180] . Most of the musical works written in Spain focused on the zarzuela genre, on the symphonic genre with a programmatic character, a genre in which Richard Strauss played a pioneering role with his *Don Quixote, Fantastic Variations on a Cabaleresque Theme* of 1896, and especially in the composition of laudatory hymns to Cervantes[181] . Only one of these works was originally written for voice and piano, the *Canto a Atisidora* by Benito Garcia de la Parra[182] . Of particular note are the orchestral works *Los galeotes* by Tomas Breton, the *Andante sinfonico* by Angel Mora Vadillo, winner of the competition organised for the celebration of the III centenary, *La cueva de Montesinos* by Camilo Perez Monllor, *La vela de las armas* by Amadeo Vives, *El caballero de los espejos* by Manuel Nieto, and the stage works *Don Quijote de la Mancha* by Teodoro San Jose, *[Gloria a Cervantes!* by Jose Verdu, and *Atisidora* by Rafael Taboada. The play *Don Quixote in Aragon*, composed with the collaboration of Borobia y Trullas, Sanjuan, Fernandez Goyena and Gonzalez, was premiered this year in Madrid.
Although the celebration in 1915 of the third centenary of the publication of the second part of the novel had little relevance in terms of musical compositions[183] , it left two songs with lyrics by Cervantes by Amadeo Vives, two of his *Canciones epigramatcas, La buena ventura* and *Madre la mi madre.* The celebration in 1916 of the third centenary, this time of Cervantes' death, was prepared well in advance. As early as 1914, orders and decrees appeared in the *Gaceta de Madrid*

[178] See TINNELL, Roger, *Catalogo anotado..., op. cit,* pp. 190-209. The catalogue offered is extensive but there are many works whose text is adapted or reworked from Cervantes.
[179] PRESAS, Adela, "1905: la trascendencia musical del III centenario", *Cervantes y el Quijote en la musica: estudios sobre la recepcion de un mito*, Centro Estudios Cervantinos, Madrid, 2007, p. 285.
[180] The writings of Unamuno, Azon'ii, Ganivet, Maeztu, Baroja, among others, advocated the presence of Don Quixote as a symbol of national identity. LOLO, Begona, "Interpretaciones del ideal cervantino en la musica del siglo XX (1905-1925)", *Visiones del Quijote en la musica del siglo XX*, Begona Lolo (ed.), Centro de Estudios Cervantinos, Madrid, 2010, p. 86-87.
[181] PRESAS, Adela, "1905: la trascendencia...", *op. cit,* pp. 305-307. The author gives a complete list of the works composed that year related to Don Quixote.
[182] Besides this song, a reduction for voice and piano, or piano solo, of *Altisidora*, serenata burlesca, by Rafael Taboada y Mantilla, Madrid/Bilbao, Casa Dotesio, [1905] is preserved. The text is not by Cervantes himself, but by Ricardo Taboada Steger.
[183] Begona Lolo gives news of two unique works of lyric theatre, the zarzuela *La hisula Barataria* by Arturo Udaeta and the revue *La Patria de Cervantes y Zorrilla* by Luis Foglietti, as well as the symphonic poem *Una aventura de Don Quijote* by Jesus Guridi. LOLO, Begona, "Interpretaciones del ideal ceivaiiliiio...", *op. cit,* p. 95-96.

creating the Junta in charge of "preparing and directing the solemnities, festivities and other events to commemorate the third centenary of the death of D. Miguel de Cervantes Saavedra", announcing different projects or calling literary competitions[184] . Already in 1916, the RAE instituted and announced the Cervantes Prize[185] , "a national and five-yearly competition", which in its first edition was unsuccessful. At official request only the composition of a hymn to Cervantes was promoted[186] , "written in unison, in an extension of the voice appropriate to be sung by the people in the festivities to be held, the accompaniment will be written for band, subject to the usual template in those of our Army". The winning work was the *Hymn to Cervantes* by Julio Gomez[187] .

In the years immediately after 1916 some works inspired by Cervantes were composed, such as the symphonic poems *Don Quixote de la Mancha*, by Emilio Serrano, *La primera salida de Don Quijote*, by A. M. Pompey, and *Don Quixote velando las armas* by Espla, or *El Retablo de Maese Pedro,* by Falla, but only one work for voice and piano, the melody *Dulcinea* by Jose Luis Lloret[188] .

Nor did the celebration of the IV Centenary of the birth of Cervantes in 1947 mean a substantial advance in the composition of works for voice and piano. The call for a competition between musicians and writers, promoted by the Executive Commission of the IV Centenary[189] , warned that the musical compositions had to comply with "a vocal or instrumental work based on the Cervantes texts that are attached to the call. The sung part may be solo or multi-voice, with instrumental accompaniment by a large orchestra". The texts that were attached to this call for entries were those beginning with the verses "Arboles, hierbas y plantas", "Madre, la mi madre" and "Marinero soy de amor". The previous year, 1946, saw the composition of two works that anticipated the celebration, the orchestral overture by Jose Maria Pages *Las bodas de Camacho* and the soundtrack for the feature film *Dulcinea* written by Manuel Parada. In 1947, Rodolfo Halffter's *Tres epitafios* para coro, Bal y Gay's *Don Quijote*, Gerardo Gombau's *Don Quijote velando las armas*, Salvador Bacarisse's *Preludio sobre la primera salida de Don Quijote* y *Soneto a Dulcinea del Toboso,* and Carlos Chavez Ramirez's *Don Quijote were* composed. Other instrumental works composed also this year are the one for a BBC broadcast with the title *Don Quixote* by Monica Lazareno[190] and the ballet *La pastora Marcela* by Manuel Martinez Chulillas.

En 1948, como consecuencia de la celebracion del ano anterior, todavia se compuso *Ausencias de Dulcinea,* de Joaquin Rodrigo[191] *, La ruta de Don Quijote,* de Rodriguez Albert, la musica de la pelicula *Don Quijote* de R. Gil composed by Ernesto Halffter, the *Cuatro letrillas de Cervantes* for choir by Adolfo Salazar, as well as the compositions by Goffredo Petrassi, the ballet *Ritratto di Don Chisciotte*, or the music written by E. Lehmberg for the film by Flavio Calzavara[192] .

The National Music Competition of 1927 did not facilitate the development of the genre either by favouring in its two modalities the composition of works inspired by poems by

---

[184] *Gaceta de Madrid*, 23-4-1914, Royal Decree appointing the Board. Various projects are announced, none of them of a musical nature. In the *Gaceta de Madrid*, 4-11-1915, a literary competition is announced with three prizes.

[185] *Gaceta de Madrid*, 23-4-1916: the RAE founds and announces a national, five-yearly competition, "Premio Cervantes", to commemorate the third centenary of Cervantes' death, with the theme "Vocabulario general de Cervantes" (Cervantes' general vocabulary). When it was unsuccessful that year, the RAE announced it again with the same slogan in 1923 (*Gaceta de Madrid,* 27-5-1923).

[186] *Gaceta de Madrid*, 29-7-1915, Royal Order.

[187] MARTINEZ DEL FRESNO, Beatriz, *Julio Gomez, op. cit.,* p. 162. TINNELL, Roger, *Catalogo anotado..., op. cit.*, p. 201.

[188] This is the title noted by Querol: QUEROL, Miquel, *La musica en..., op. cit,* pp. 209-210. Begona Lolo notes it with the title *Ceivantina (*LOLO, Begona, "Interpretaciones del ideal cervantino.", *op. cit,* p. 96).

[189] Order of 4 July 1947 (*BOE*, 13-7-1947).

[190] TINNELL, Roger, *Catalogo anotado..., op. cit,* p. 202.

[191] This work was awarded the 1948 National Prize. The format of the work and the texts used coincide with those requested in the 1947 call for entries, which we have noted above.

[192] QUEROL GAVALDA, Miquel, *La musica en., op. cit,* pp. 209-210.

Gongora written for orchestra or solo piano[193] . The prize-winning works were *Gongoriana* by Manuel Palau[194] , and the *Seis pequenas composiciones para orquesta y pequeno coro*[195] by Conrado del Campo, inspired by "Romances" by the Cordovan poet. The orchestral suite in six movements, inspired in Gongorian poems, *Homenaje a Gongora,* by Fernando
Remacha, written that year, coincides in format and theme with the requirements of the National Competition, although there is no documentation to ensure that this work was submitted to the competition. Adolfo Salazar composed his *Zarabanda* for instrumental ensemble also in 1927[196] . *Soneto a Cordoba* by Manuel de Falla and *Soledades* by Oscar Espla, this original for voice and orchestra although later adapted by the composer for piano, are the only works of the genre written that year with text by Gongora[197] . A few years earlier, in 1914, Enrique Granados composed two songs with lyrics by Gongora: *Llorad corazon* and *Serranas de Cuenca.* In 1925 Eduardo Lopez-Chavarri used a poem for one of his *Seis canciones espanolas* of 1925, as did Sabino Ruiz Jalon in *Las flores del romero*, all of them for voice and piano[198] .
27 August 1935 marked the three hundredth anniversary of Lope's death, which took place in Madrid in 1635. The celebration of the tercentenary of his death had a wide repercussion on Spanish cultural life that year. Numerous events were held, including theatrical performances, poetry recitals, conferences, new Lope editions and publications, and literary competitions throughout Spain, South America, and in some European cities such as London, Cambridge, Hamburg, Amsterdam, Poitiers, Paris, Lisbon and Strasbourg. He also arrived in Algiers, Havana, and New York, where a tribute event was organised at the
Columbia University promoted by the Spanish embassy. The magazine *"Fenix",* which appeared in six bimonthly issues during 1935, brought together Lope's studies and initiatives, events, publications and performances both nationally and internationally, "with the aim of restoring to Lope the prestige and leadership he enjoyed in his egregious century"[199 200] .
This invaluable document, which gives us an idea of the extent and importance of the celebration, reflects, however, how little importance music had in Lope's memory. With the exception of the consequences of the announcement of the National Music Competition, which we will deal with later, we can conclude, after observing in detail the news that *Fenix* gives of musical events related to the centenary celebrations, that with few exceptions, music played a merely ornamental role. The following is a list of the news items that appear in the magazine:

1. No. 1, February:

a. Pag. 152: Representation of *Peribanez y el Comendador de Ocana* with musical illustrations by J. Bal y Gay. Capitol Theatre, 25 January 1935.

b. Pag. 154: Performance of *The Knight of Olmedo* at Cambridge University, with 17th century musical illustrations performed on the harpsichord.

2. No. 2, April:

a. Pag. 287: Performance of *La discreta enamorada* by the Asociacion de Antiguos Alumnos del Instituto Cervantes, at the Teatro Cervantes in Madrid, in which "in the intermission several dances of the XVI and XVII centuries were performed".

b. Pag. 287: On April 24, act in the theatre Romea of Murcia, organized by the University, in

---

[193] The publication of the rules and the call for applications was published in *Gaceta de Madrid*, num. 27, 27-01-1927, pp. 566-567, signed in Madrid on 26 January 1927 by Callejo (sic), Director General of Fine Arts.
[194] First National Music Prize 1927. *Madrid Gazette,* 15-12-1927.
[195] Music for child or mezzo-soprano voice, choir and orchestra. Second National Prize 1927. *Gaceta de Madrid,* 15-12-1927. There is a current edition: Madrid, Barcelona, Editorial de Musica Espanola Contemporanea, 2002.
[196] TINNELL, Roger, *Catalogo anotado..., op. cit.,* p. 276.
[197] *Ibid.,* pp. 271-276.
[198] *Ibid.,* p. 274-276.
[199] HERRERO, Miguel; ENTRAMBASAGUAS, Joaquin de, (dirs.), *Fenix, revista del tricentenano de Lope de Vega, 1635-1935,* Numeros 1-6, Grafica Universal, Madrid, 1935.
[200] GARCIA SANTO-TOMAS, Enrique, La creacion del "Fenix". Recepcion cntica y representation canonica del teatro de Lope de Vega, Gredos, Madrid, 2000, p. 362.

which are interpreted, together with a conference and a scenic representation, "a symphony by the quartet of Mr. Salas", a song of the time of Lope de Vega sung by Mrs. Martinez Cano, several musical pieces executed by the Tuna Estudiantil Murciana, and "beautiful compositions" sung by the Masa Coral of the class of choral singing of the Institute Nacional de Segunda Ensenanza.

3. No. 3, June:

a. Pag. 442: In Granada, performance by students of the University, of *La vuelta de Egpto* and *La moza del cantaro,* "with musical direction by the great Manuel de falla and Valentin Ruiz Aznar".

b. Page 443: A lecture given by Paul Valery at the Sorbonne was followed by a performance by the Spanish guitarist Emilio Pujol, a disciple of Tarrega, playing several musical works.

c. Pag. 443: In an act of homage of the France-Spain Committee in Paris, the Masa Coral of students interpreted tonadillas of the 15th and 16th centuries, adapted by Heri Collet. Then the pianist Cras and the cellist Sener played music by Nin, Falla, Granados and others, and "Senorita Maria Cid sang modern coplas".

d. Pag. 657: Publication of the *Cancionero teatral* with prologue and notes by Robles Pazos, Baltimore, 1935.

4. No. 4, August:

a. Pag. 574: Three extraordinary broadcasts of Radio Espana on 25, 26 and 27 August. The station's orchestra performed "a rich collection of songs by Cabezon and several anonymous authors of Lope's time", together with recitations of verses and dissertations by "masters of the pen".

b. Pag. 576: In Leon, staging of the auto sacramental *La siega,* with music, "notabilisima muestra de canciones de la mejor estirpe espanola del siglo XVI", by the maestro de capilla de la catedral leonesa, D. Manuel Uriarte.

c. Pag. 576: On 31 August, in the Summer Courses of the Junta Central de Accion Catolica, they held a session in the Pereda Theatre in which Fr. Nemesio Otano premiered "a composition, in the style of the time, with the lyrics of the famous sonnet by Lope *Que tengo yo, que mi amistadprocuras".*

d. Pag. 577: In Vega de Carriedo, his parents' home town, a solemn funeral was held in memory of Lope, in which a choir, directed by D. Teodoro Hernandez, beneficiary of the cathedral, "sang masterfully Haller's mass and Perosi's responsory for three voices, the musical part being in charge of the learned national maestro, Senor Arruga".

5. No. 6, December:

a. Pag. 763: As a culmination of the tribute at the Centro de Estudios Historicos[201] , the group Cantores Clasicos de Madrid "then offered some musical examples of Lope de Vega's lyrics, composed by various masters of the time".

Not all the musical manifestations that took place this year are included here, as will be seen later on. We can see that the composition by P. Nemesio Otano and the interpretation of the songs rescued by Bal y Gay by the Cantores Clasicos de Madrid are the only ones directly related to Lope's poetry, the rest being limited to serving as mere musical illustrations of an ornamental nature.

The government of the Republic, at the request of the Ministry of Public Instruction, created the *Junta de iniciativas del Tricentenario de Lope de Vega* which was in charge of organising the official events[202] . The multitude of official initiatives such as the restoration of Lope's house

[201] The newspaper *El Sol* of 11-12-1935, p. 5, publishes a detailed review signed by Ad. S. [Adolfo Salazar].

[202] This Board was not constituted until 16 April of that year. It was initially composed of Ramon Menendez Pidal, director of the Spanish Academy, as president, Rafael Salazar Alonso, mayor of Madrid, Miguel Artigas, director of the National Library, and Josë F. Montesinos, of the Centro de Estudios Historicos, as secretary. Its mission was to propose and gather initiatives for the celebration of the anniversary *(Gaceta de Madrid. Diario Ofcial de la Republica,* num. 108, de 18/04/1935, pp. 570, Order signed in Madrid on 16 April 1935 by Ramon Prieto,

initiated at the request of the Spanish Academy[203] , the publication of a series of commemorative stamps[204] , the holding of an official gala performance in the Spanish Theatre with the attendance of the authorities of the Republic[205] and the announcement of the National Competition of
The events of the Bellas Artes, which will be dealt with later, are a small sample of a long list of events promoted by all kinds of public and private institutions[206] , and a demonstration of the wide interest in the celebration.
From the beginning of the 20th century, the figure of the stage director who gives his vision of the theatrical work, as in the case of Cipriano Rivas Cherif or Federico Garcia Lorca in another field, began to take centre stage. At the same time, the revalorisation of classical theatre, especially towards the end of Primo de Rivera's dictatorship, took on nationalist overtones, claiming itself as a solution to the crisis of the Spanish stage[207] . The political implications are present, also in classical theatre, in such an ideologically convulsive historical moment[208] . As could not be otherwise, in 1935 the Spanish stage was invaded by the dramatic works of Lope. Performances were staged all over Spain. It must be understood that Lope's recovery in 1935 came at a time of intense intellectual activity, and his figure summoned reflections on his theatre, on his person, but also on a Spanish reality that was more problematic and confrontational than ever[209] .
Only in Madrid this year Peribanez y el Comendador de Ocana, El acero de Madrid, La corona merecida, La dama boba, Fuente Ovejuna, San Isidro labrador, El villano en su rincon, El caballero de Olmedo, El degollado, La locura por la honra, and La moza del cantaro[210] . Federico Garcia Lorca, with his theatre group La Barraca, toured four titles: Fuente Ovejuna, the most performed play that year, El caballero de Olmedo, La dama boba and Las almenas de Toro[211] . He

---

Subsecretario del Ministerio de Instruccion Publica. Also reported in *Fenix,* n° 2, April, p. 281). *La Vanguardia* of 19-5-1935, p. 25, *ABC* of the same day, p. 45, and El Sol of 21-5-1935, p. 3, report Menendez Pidal's resignation as president because of the suppression of the economic allocation initially planned for the Junta. Prior to these dates, *ABC* of 9-3-1935, p. 20, chronicles a second meeting of the Board attended by Eduardo Chincharro, director general of BBAA, Rafael Salazar Alonso, Mayor of Madrid, Eduardo Marquina, for the Society of Authors, Miguel Artigas, Enrique Borras and Luis Gabaldon, without mentioning Menendez Pidal. Probably from the beginning of the year the Junta functioned informally until the official appointment on 16 April. In Seville, a committee in homage to Lope de Vega was also set up.

[203] *Fenix* magazine reports on the beginning of the restoration in the February issue, p. 148. The government approves a budget, without auction procedure, on 6 December 35 (*Gaceta de Madrid: Diario Oficial de la Republica* num. 360, of 26/12/1935, p. 2588 to 2589). *ABC* offers a full report on 8-5-1935, p. 6.

[204] Order ordering the Fabrica Nacional de Moneda y Timbre to proceed with the production of a series of postage stamps of 15, 30, 50 cëntimos and one peseta, commemorating the date of the death of Lope de Vega (*Gaceta de Madrid: Diario Ofcial de la Republca* num. 22, 22/01/1935, p. 640). This is also reported in *El Sol,* 16-1-1935, p. 1.

[205] 25 October 1935, gala performance at the Teatro Espanol organised by the Junta, attended by the President of the Republic, the President of the Government and other officials. In addition to various speeches and recitations of poetry, the group Cantores Clasicos Espanoles performs works by Lope in music of his time, probably transcriptions by Jesus Bal. Perez Casas, with the Filarmonica, perform Mozart's *Snoina in G minor. ABC* of 24-10-1935, p. 35, publishes an advertisement, Union Radio broadcasts it live (see: *ABC,* 25-10-1935, p.42; *E Sol,* 25-10-1935, p. 2). *ABC* of 26-10-1935, p. 51, and *El Sol* of the same day, p. 2, publish a review of the event without mentioning the participation of the Cantores Clasicos.

[206] The broad programme of initiatives planned, but not all of them realised, by the Sociedad de Autores Espanoles, published on 26 December 1934, is certainly ambitious. It is collected by *Fnix,* February 1, p. 148-149. The interesting proposal of Piedad de Salas to make a biographical film on Lope de Vega was not completed (*El Sol,* 12-1-35, p. 2).

[207] GARCIA SANTO-TOMAS, Enrique, *La creation del "Fnni", op. cit.,* pp. 322-323.

[208] Diego San Jose went so far as to write that the state did not sufficiently promote its cultural heritage because "in many of those glorious works there are great political teachings that should not be aired". Quoted by GARCIA SANTO-TOMAS, Enrique, *La creation del "Fnni", op. cit,* p. 325. In section 4.2.2 of this thesis we deal with the ideological use of Lope in these years.

[209] *Ibid.,* p. 343.

[210] *Ibid.,* p. 343. Garcia Santo-Tomas also gives the dates of the premieres and comments on the performances given in the 1920s and 1930s (pp. 326-368). The review *Fnix* also gives news of the performances given, not only in Madrid.

[211] The staging of *Las almenas de Toro* is only reported by Ian Gibson in *Federico Garcia Lorca,* Barcelona, Gnjalbo, 1987, quoted by DIEZ DE REVENGA, Francisco Javier, "El *Arte nuevo de hacer comedias* y la

also took part in the performances that Margarita Xirgu's company gave at the Teatro Espanol of Fuente Ovejuna and La dama boba. The music included in some of these performances will be discussed later.

The numerous studies published in previous years, especially those of prestigious researchers Rudolph Schevill and Hugo Rennert, have ordered and fixed many data on Lope that will open up avenues of investigation in later works such as those of Karl Vossler, Marcelino Menendez y Pelayo, Jose Fernandez Montesinos or Americo Castro[212] . These studies only confirm and increase the fascination for his literary work, his life events and his intense sentimental life.

The repercussion of the celebration of Lope's death in the Spanish musical environment is quite minor in comparison with that which it had in literary, scientific and theatrical circles, but in any case important, and noteworthy. The inclusion of music in some acts is frequent and varied. Sometimes it is directly related to the texts, sometimes it serves as a recreation of the musical atmosphere of the time. The newspapers in Madrid publish reviews of different acts that include some kind of musical performance, generally works or melodies from Lope's time in different arrangements, although compositions that are not directly related to our poet are also used. On 11th April 1935, an artistic and literary tribute was held at the Casa de Valencia, and after a conference on Lope's stay in Valencia, the Choir of the Toledo Institute performed choral works inspired by passages from Lope's works[213] . On 12 June of that year Manuel de Falla prepared and conducted a choir in the performances of two of Lope's autos sacramentales in Granada[214] . On 18 June a literary-musical evening organised by the Cabildo of Madrid Cathedral is held in the Salon Marla Cristina, in which works from the Codice de Medinaceli and the Codice Colonial by Fray Gregorio Dezuola are sung in chorus[215] . On 25, 26 and 27 August, Radio Espana broadcast two radio broadcasts in which the *Diferencias sobre el canto del caballero* de Cabezon was performed, interspersed with poetic and dramatic recitals, together with several anonymous performers *(Arrojome las naranjitas, Mananicas Hondas, Como retumban los remos, La verde primavera, Oh, que bien que baila Gi), Entre dos alamos verdes* by Juan Blas de Castro and *Madre, la mi Madre* by Pedro Ruimonte, all of them in anonymous orchestral arrangements and sung by Rosita Hermosilla[216] . Of other musical manifestations included in various events, we report later when we talk about the official gala performance at the Teatro Espanol and the revue *Fenix.* In these cases it is generally a question of instrumental and vocal musical illustrations from all periods, with a predominance of those from the sixteenth and seventeenth centuries.

Enrique Casal Chapi was one of the musicians who contributed most to the creation of music based on Lope's plays. Apart from the five songs with piano that we will study in due course, his work as musical director of the Teatro Escuela de Arte allowed him to come into contact with the staging of comedies by Lope and to compose incidental music for some of them. This is the case of the one written for *El villano en su rincon* in the performances of the Xirgu-Borras compama at the Teatro Espanol[217] , the aforementioned *Cancion madrigalesca* for the comedy *El acero de Madrid,* for three equal voices with flute and guitar accompaniment, dated 26 January 1935[218] , and *El baile del Caballero de Olmedo*, incidental music composed of six episodes to be danced

---

generation del 27: lilologia y escena", *El Arte nuevo de hacer comedias y la escena, XXXII Jornadas de teatro clasico,* Almagro, 2009, pp. 151-169.

[212] GARCIA SANTO-TOMAS, Enrique, *La creation del "Fnni", op. cit.,* p. 344.

[213] *ABC*, 12-5-1935, p. 35

[214] *La Vanguardia*, 13-6-1935, p. 23

[215] *ABC*, 19-6-1935, p. 21.

[216] *El Sol*, 21-8-1935, p. 2.

[217] Review in *ABC*, 4-6-1935, p. 45.

[218] There are two autograph manuscripts in the BNE with the call numbers M.CASALCHAPI

3>and
M.CASALCHAPI4, the latter signed and dated.

with solo accompaniment, chorus and orchestra[219] , as well as his participation in the musical direction of the performances of *La dama boba* with musical adaptations by Garcia Lorca[220] .
A composition by P. Nemesio Otano in four voices on the rhyme *Que tengo yo que mi a mis tad procuras*[21] , according to the magazine Fenix "in the style of the time", was premiered in Santander on 31 August at a memorial service as part of the Summer Courses of the Junta Central de Accion Catolica[221 222] .
The conferences given by Miguel Salvador y Carreras, "Alusiones musicales de Lope en *La Dorotea*", and Conrado del Campo, "La musica en la epoca de Lope de Vega", are works that complete the Lope studies from the point of view of music[223] . However, the most important and transcendental musicological research is that carried out by Jesus Bal and Gay[224] . Bal published his timely work *Treinta canciones de Lope de Vega*[225] , in the *Residencia* magazine, a publication of the Residencia de Estudiantes, as an extraordinary issue. In addition to the scores of the 30 polyphonic works by masters of the sixteenth and seventeenth centuries, there are introductory pages by Menendez Pidal, the transcriber's comments and the volume closes with five unpublished poems by Juan Ramon Jimenez entitled *Ramo a Lope.* The research and editing work had repercussions on Spanish musical life, as these works were performed at different events, always by the vocal quartet Cantores Clasicos Espanoles[226] . Another important contribution was that of another key figure in these years, Eduardo Martinez Torner, who in 1935 gave a conference on several occasions with the title "La musica en la epoca de Lope de Vega", the elaboration of which was included in the work of the Centro de Estudios Historicos. This lecture was repeated in the context of the Pedagogical Missions, given in front of the microphones of Union Radio and in different cultural centres, such as the Ateneo de Madrid, the headquarters of the Centro de Estudios Historicos, the Residencia de Estudiantes, the Instituto Escuela, and the Club Femenino[227] .

---

[219] Autograph manuscript dated 4 September 1935. BNE signature M.CASALCHAPI 3 (the BNE gives the same signature for the *Cancion madrigalesca.* See previous note).
[220] GIL FOMBELLIDA, M.ª del Carmen, *Rivas Cheri, Margarita Xirgu y el teatro de la II Repiiblica,* Fundamentos, Madrid, 2003, pp. 257-259 and 311-315.
[221] OTANO EGUINO, Nemesio, *Que tengo yo,* for four solo voices in classical polyphonic style, Tesoro Sacro Musical, 1957. Nemesio Otano lived between 1880 and 1956.
[222] *Fenx,* n° 4, p.576.
[223] The lectures were given on 30 January 1936 at the headquarters of the Real Academia de Bellas Artes de San Fernando. Conrado del Campo's lecture was illustrated with musical examples by the quartet Cantores Clasicos Espanoles, with works by Victoria and Morales, and by the guitarist Regino Sainz de la Maza, with works by Millan, Mudarra and Gaspar Sanz. See advertisement in *ABC,* 30-1-1936, p. 40, and the notice of 31-1-1936, p. 27.
[224] Between 2005 and 2006 an exhibition of Bal's life and work was presented in Lugo, Santiago de Compostela and Madrid, and a book-catalogue was published: VILLANUEVA, Carlos (dir.), *Jesus Baly Gay: tientosy silencios 1905-1993,* Residencia de Estudiantes, Madrid, 2005.
[225] BAL Y GAY, Jesus, "Treinta canciones de Lope de Vega, puestas en musica por Guerrero, Orlando de Lasso, Palomares, Romero, Company, etc. y transcritas por Jesus Bal. With some unpublished pages by Ramon Menendez Pidal and Juan Ramon Jimenez", *Residencia,* extraordinary issue, Madrid, 1935. The presentation of this publication took place in the auditorium of the Residencia, together with the performance of a selection of the works by the quartet Cantores Clasicos Espanoles in a concert on 14 May of that year. See review in *ABC*, 15-5-1935, p. 52.

[22,]Performance of *Peribanez* on 25-1-1935, together with other popular songs for the wedding song and the *Trebole* (*El Sol*, 26-1-35, p. 2). Performed in Cordoba on 27 August in a performance of *Fuente Ovejuna* (*ABC*, 27-8-1935, p. 25). Concert in the Holiday Courses of the Centro de Estudios Historicos (*ABC*, 19-7-1935, p. 39). Homage at the Centro de Estudios Historicos on 31-12-1935: after two
dissertations by Menendez Pidal and Sanchez Canton on *El arte nuevo de hacer comedias* and some biographical notes respectively, the group Cantores Clasicos Espanoles offered several pieces composed by masters of Lope's time (chronicle of the event in *ABC*, 1-1-1936, p. 75).
[227] MALLO DEL CAMPO, Maria Luisa, *Torner mas alia del fokore,* Universidad de Oviedo, Oviedo, 1980, pp. 71-72. Mallo also reports on Torner's other activities related to Lope and music, carried out in later years, such as the lecture at the BBC in London, entitled *Antologa de villancicos,* with examples of St. Teresa, Lope, Gil Vicente and Gongora (p. 147). Ad. S. [Adolfo Salazar] signs an article praising Torner's studies presented at the event at the Centro de Estudios Historicos with the intervention of the Cantores Clasicos Castellanos who perform the

The most important event for our work was the announcement of the National Fine Arts Competition. As had been the custom in previous years, the *Gaceta de Madrid: Diario Ofcial de la Republica,* in its number 213 of 1 August 1935, published an Order with the rules and regulations for the Literature, Painting, Engraving, Music and Architecture Competitions of that year, dated 30 July, and stipulated that their publication would serve as a call for entries[228] . The general rules set out the conditions of the competition: the artists had to be Spanish, Spanish-American or Filipino residents of the Peninsula, Balearic and Canary Islands, except for those who had won prizes in previous similar competitions; the jury was asked that, in order to encourage artists and writers, it should, if it did not find absolute merit, "keep to the relative merit of the works submitted so that no competition would remain deserted or without awarding a prize". They were also empowered to propose that the prize be lower than that announced in the announcement "if in their opinion there was no work worthy of the totality of the prizes", as well as to "advise that the prizes be transferred from one theme to another - when there are several in the competition - if in one of them no work worthy of a prize was found and, on the other hand, in another, more than one stood out". The rules for the presentation and return of entries end the rules at[229] .

The order defines the themes of the competition in each artistic speciality. For the Music Competition, two themes or modalities are established:

a) A suite for orchestra in the style and character of Spanish music in Lope de Vega's ëpoca, the composer being free to choose the instrumental elements used in the score according to his ideas and expressive purposes.

b) A group of at least four songs for one voice with piano or guitar accompaniment, on poems by Lope de Vega chosen at the contestant's personal discretion from among the immortal creations of the glorious poet[230] .

The prizes stipulated are one of 4,000 pesetas for the first category and another of 1,000 pesetas for the second, and the deadline for submitting works is from 20 to 30 September of the same year. Although the order states that the prize-winning works belong to the corresponding authors, they are obliged to leave a copy with the secretary of the National Competitions of the Ministry of Public Instruction and Fine Arts, and the State reserves the right to publish them if it deems it appropriate for their dissemination. After the publication of the competition rules, the Director General of Fine Arts, in a new Order of 19 September[231] , rectified one of the rules, allowing authors who had not won first prizes in the three previous competitions to submit their works.

The jury for the Music competition was chaired by Joaquin Turina, with Emilio Serrano, Benito Garcia de la Parra and Eduardo Martinez Torner acting as members, and Nicanor Hevia[232] as secretary of the National Competitions. The jury's minutes were signed on 23 December and state:

1°. That the amount of 4,000 pesetas allocated for the prize for theme A) be transferred to theme B), of which 1,000 pesetas will be awarded, as a reward, to each of the works marked with the numbers 1, 3 and 10, signed by Mr Josë Maria Guervos, Mr Angel Mingote and Mr Francisco Esbri, respectively.

2°. That the prize of 1,000 pesetas indicated for theme B) be awarded to work number 11, signed by Mr. Julio Gomez[233] .

Two important doubts arise from the jury's decision. We do not know whether the decision not to award any prize in category "a" was due to a lack of entries or to a lack of quality. The other is that according to the distribution of the economic prizes according to the two categories, it is not clear in the decision whether this distribution is due to the need to justify administratively the economic distribution of the prizes, understanding that the four prizes awarded are *ex aequo*, or whether

---

polyphonic works published in the magazine *Residencia*. *El Sol*, 11-12-1935, p. 4.

[228] *El Sol*, 2-8-1935, p. 5, is the only Madrid newspaper to report the call.

[229] *Madrid Gazette. Diario Oficial de la Republica*, num. 213, of 01-08-1935, pp. 1079-1081, signed in Madrid on 30 July 1935 by Joaquin Dualde, Director General of Fine Arts.

[230] Idem.

[231] *Gaceta de Madrid. Diario Ofcial de la Republica,* num. 268, 25-09-1935, pp. 2345-2346, signed in Madrid on 19 September 1935 by Rafael Gonzalez Cobos, Director General of Fine Arts.

[232] *Gaceta de Madrid. Diario oficial de la Republica*. n° 362 de 28-12-1935, pag. 2646, signed in Madrid on 27 December 1935. Manuel Becerra, Undersecretary of the Ministry.

[233] ^dem.

there is a gradation in them by giving Julio Gomez the economic reward of category B), corresponding to the works for voice and piano[234] . The jury affirms that "it has the power to transfer the prize from one theme to another if in one there is no work that in its opinion deserves it and in the other it finds more than one work worthy of reward"[235] , a consideration that does not clarify the doubts that we raise.

From the minutes we can deduce, since Julio Gomez's was numbered 11, that at least eleven works were submitted to the competition. Unfortunately only the winning songs by Gomez, Guervos and Mingote are preserved today, those by Francisco Esbri being lost, and the names and works of the rest of the candidates being unknown[236] . We could suppose that the collections of songs by Enrique Casal Chapi, Jose Maria Guervos and Fernando Moraleda, which we present in chapter V and in annexes II and III, could have been submitted to the competition, given that they meet the requirements of the competition rules, although we have found no evidence that this is the case. The *Cnco canciones* de Guervos do not bear the exact date of composition, but the *Cuatro canciones con textos de Lope de Vega* by Moraleda are dated, according to the manuscript, September 1935, and the two collections by Casal, composed between 21 and 29 September 1935, are also dated within the deadline for the submission of originals, although this does not guarantee that they were submitted. What does seem clear is that Joaquin Turina's *Homenaje a Lope de Vega*, premiered at the concert in homage to Lope de Vega at the Madrid Conservatory, which we report below, could not be submitted to the competition because the composer himself was president of the jury, as we have already seen, which disqualified him from competing.

One of the last acts of homage to Lope was organised by the Conservatorio de Musica y Declamacion de Madrid. On Thursday 12 December 1935, in a matinee performance, the Madrid Conservatory made its contribution to the tercentenary by preparing and presenting to the public gathered in the Teatro Espanol a show in which several works of our interest were performed[237] . In addition to the recital of poems by Lope offered by three students of each of the declamation teachers, compositions by Jose Maria Guervos, Joaquin Turina and Conrado del Campo[238] were presented. From Guervos, Mercedes Garcia Lopez[239] , first prize in singing at the Conservatory, performed three songs accompanied by the composer himself: *Lo fngido verdadero, Blanca coge Lucinda las azucenas* and *Cancion de siega*[240] . Turina made known, from the piano, his three

---

[234] On 8 January 1936 *ABC* gives the news of the awarding of the prizes for the National Music Competition. From the editorial staff we interpret that the first prize was awarded to Julio Gomez and the second prize was shared between Guervos, Mingote and Esbry (sic) *(ABC,* 8-1-1936, p. 49). Likewise, *ABC,* in the daily images section, published a photo of Mingote with the caption: "Don Angel Mingote Lorente, inspired composer, who in the national competition on the occasion of the tercentenary of Lope de Vega, has won the National Prize for his music for songs from the "Fenix de los Ingenios"", which contributes to the confusion in the order of the prizes *(ABC,* 5-11936, p. 30). Nor does *El Sol (*31-12-1935, p. 5), which reports in a review the awarding of the National Fine Arts Competitions: "In the Music Competition, one thousand pesetas were awarded to each of the works presented by Mr Josë Maria Guervos, Mr Angel Mingote and Mr Francisco Esbri', with another prize of one thousand pesetas, marked for theme B, being awarded to Mr Julio Gomez". This same text appears in *El Heraldo de Madrid,* 31-12-1935, p. 2, and in *La Voz*, 31-12-1935, p. 2.

[235] Idem.

[236] Enquiries to discover these authors and rescue their works have been unsuccessful. In addition to all the archives and libraries consulted, the searches for the scores and the minutes of the jury meetings in the General Archives of the Administration and the Archives of the Ministry of Culture, as already reported in Chapter I, have also been unsuccessful.

[237] The show was broadcast by Union Radio. See *ABC*, 12-12-1935, p. 57.

[238] *ABC,* 13-12-1935, p. 44. A detailed chronicle of the event is given. Julio Gomez writes a review of the performance in *El Liberal on* the same day. *El Heraldo de Madrid,* 13-12-1935, p. 15, gives a chronicle of the event. *La Libertad*, 14-12-1935, p. 7, publishes a review which also includes information about Torner's lecture at the Centro de Estudios Historicos.

[239] GUERVOS, Jose Maria, *Cinco canciones,* UME, Madrid, 1936. Guervos dedicated these three songs to him, as indicated in the score published by the UME.

[240] Belonging to the cycle *Five songs*, awarded in the National Competition. We assume that these three songs will be performed in this concert.

songs op. 90, *Homenaje a Lope de Vega*, sung by Rosita Hermosilla, who dedicated them[241] , winner of the Lucrecia Arana Singing Competition.

The second part of the festival was occupied by a "Retablo en verso sobre la vida de Lope de Vega compuesto en dos estampas por los versos de Diego San Jose, y la musica del maestro Conrado del Campo"[242] , with the title *Una dama se vende a quien la quierl*[243] . As in the rest of the matine, the performers were various students and ensembles from the Conservatory. The work, performed with costumes and sets[244] , consisted of two prints in verse[245] that commented on an amorous episode in Lope's life, that of his love affair with Elena Osorio. Solo singers, choir and corps de ballet, all of them pupils of the centre prepared by the teachers of the different disciplines, took part in the performance. The orchestral part was performed by teachers from the Sinfonica and Filarmonica orchestras.

In the altarpiece by Conrado del Campo there are several characters: Madre Claudia, Ginesa, Aldara, Leonarda, Ines, Elena, Ana, Perronet, Lope de Vega, Dos mozos, Media Capa, Mari Blanca, Un Autor, Rodrigo de Saavedra, as well as 4 Comediantas, 3 Comediantes, 2 Alguaciles, and Mozas and Mozos who form the chorus. It is scored for orchestra, with harp, percussion and guitar. The musical numbers, whose numbering has been changed in red pencil from the original, include a prelude, three songs, a chacona, a zarabanda and a gallarda bailada.

Between the two pictures of the altarpiece the tenor Miguel Fleta, accompanied on the piano, performed a song, *Tan vivo esta en mi alma,* also by Conrado del Campo, with a text taken from *La Dorotea*. According to *ABC* and *El Heraldo de Madrid*, this song was sung backstage[246] . The fact that it was not orchestrated and was inserted between the two prints could be due to the fact that it was a last-minute personal contribution of the famous tenor to the act, after the composition of the retablo, inserting the song in the middle of the two parts because of the relation of the verses to the plot that unfolds.

The song *Coplas del pastor enamorado* by Joaquin Rodrigo, which we will study in due course, is an important contribution as it is one of the most performed works, together with the songs by Turina, of those composed this year.

1962: THE 400TH ANNIVERSARY OF THE BIRTH OF LOPE DE LOPE DE VEGA

The celebration of the fourth centenary of Lope's birth in 1962 did not have the same repercussion as the tercentenary of his death, neither from the musical point of view nor from the attention paid by public or private institutions. In the field we are interested in, the 1962 National Fine Arts Competition in the Music section, announced by Order of the Directorate General of Fine Arts signed on 14 June 1962[247] , could not function as a stimulus for the composition of music inspired

[241] This is how it appears in the heading of the collection, in the UME edition.

[242] *ABC*, 13-12-1935, p. 44.

[243] In the programme, a copy of which is preserved in the library of the FJM (call number M-Pro-1079), the title reads "...a quien la quiere", an error that the following day's *ABC* review picked up, as opposed to the first line of the libel written by Lope against Elena Osorio and her family. The *Anuario del Real Conservatoiio Superior de Musica y Declamacion de Madrid, 1935-1939,* Madrid, 1940, pp. 14-18, includes the programme of the performance, identical to the hand programme.

[244] *ABC,* 3-12-1935, p. 5. A group photo of the musicians, dancers and actors who took part is published.

[245] Julio Gomez says in his review in *El Liberal:* "Our illustrious companion Diego San Josë was the one who sustained most of the day with his literary mastery and his profuse knowledge of the classics. He has composed a tableau in gallant verses in the most stale national style on the episode of Lope de Vega's love affair with Elena Osorio". *El Liberal*, 13-12-1935.

[246] This circumstance is not mentioned by Julio Gomez in the review he published the following day in *El Liberal.* If so, it could be because the stage was occupied with sets and *props* for the stage performance of *Una dama se vende a quien la quiera.*

[247] Order published in the *BOE*, 17-7-1935, p. 9982-9983. The prize money was 14,000 pesetas.

by Lope's work, as it did in 1935, since the theme of the competition was not sensitive to the celebration that year: "composition of chamber music to be performed by a quartet". The National Music Prize of the previous year, serving as a gateway to the celebration of the IV Centenary, was awarded to Rafael Rodriguez Albert for his work *Fanl.asia en triptico on a drama by Lope de Vega, an* orchestral work based on *El mejor alcalde, el rey,* written in 1961. Curiously, this year's call for entries did take into account the celebration of the year in question in advance, with the announcement of the Music Competition with the slogan "Tres piezas breves ce orquesta como interludios a un drama de Lope"[248] , perhaps with the idea that the winning orchestral piece could be used as music for a staging the following year, which did not happen[249] .

Of the works written on the composer's own initiative for the centenary, we only have references to a *Homenatge a Lope de Vega*[250] by Josep Casanovas i Puig, the only work for voice and piano composed this year, untraceable until now[251] . The interest of this composition comes from the commentary by Celsa Alonso, Tomas Marco and Antonio Fernandez-Cid, informing that it is an atonal work, one of the two composed with this technique of those presented in the catalogue[252] .

The celebration of the fourth centenary is used by some composers to publish, either in a new edition or in a new one, songs written in the past. This is the case of the *Romance del conde Ocana* by Joaquin Rodrigo written in 1947 and published for the first time this year of the fourth centenary. Also appearing are the *Seis villancicos de Lope de Vega* by Joan Llongueres, composed in 1942, which had already been published previously in Barcelona by Union Musical-Casa Werner[253] . Two collections, by Rafael Rodriguez Albert and Gracia Tarrago, entitled *Cuatro canciones sobre textos de Lope de Vega* and *Cinco canciones del siglo XVII*, respectively, were published a year later. The songs for soprano and guitar by Rodriguez Albert had been composed for the celebration of the tercentenary in 1935, and had already been published that same year[254] , and were now republished by the UME in 1963. Tarrago's songs were also published this year[255] , and for their composition he based himself on existing melodies by the poet's contemporaries: Jose Marin, Mateo Romero, Juan del Vado and two anonymous[256] .

Apart from this handful of musical works generated around the IV Centenary, music concerts motivated by this celebration were few and far between. We have only been able to gather information about one session in the Aula de Cultura, a concert by the soprano Marta Santaolalla

---

[248] The announcement appears in the *BOE* of 26-7-1961. The *BOE* does not mention the award of the prize. *ABC* gives the news on 17 February 1962, *La Vanguardia* on 20 January.

[249] It was adapted years later for ballet by the composer himself and Guillermo Fernandez-Shaw. Although the work was not premiered at the time, a recording by the JONDE conducted by Jose Antonio Pascual is now available. Catalogue of Contemporary Composers of the Fundacion Autor [online] <http://www.catalogodecompositores.com> [accessed 30-10-2011]. The data of this catalogue have been taken from: VEGA SANCHEZ, Jose de la, *Rafael Rodriguez Albert. Complete catalogue of his works,* ONCE, Madrid, 1987.

[250] We know of his existence from the commentaries on Casanovas and his songs by Celsa Alonso *(Diccionario de la Musica Espanola e Hispanoamericana,* vol. 3, p. 17), Tomas Marco (*Historia de la Musica espanola. 6. Siglo X,* Alianza, Madrid, 1983, p. 205) and Fernandez-Cid *(La musica espanola en el siglo XX,* Juan March/Rioduero, Madrid, 1973, p.221).

[251] It has not been possible to locate the composer's personal archive, nor is this work to be found in any of the libraries and archives consulted for the preparation of the catalogue. The search in the Arxiu Nacional de Catalunya has been fruitless. Nor does it appear in the *Fons Anna Ricci* of the Biblioteca de Catalunya, being this singer the habitual interpreter in these years of vocal works by Casanovas and of the whole of the Spanish and Catalan musical avant-garde in particular.

[252] The other is *Al entierro de Cristo*, by Francisco Escudero, dated 1974, of which the published score is preserved (Alpuerto, Madrid, 1975) and two RNE recordings: one by Atsuko Kudo and Alejandro Zabala, dated 18-8-1992, from a concert at the San Sebastian Musical Fortnight, and the other by Pura M. Martinez and Gerardo Lopez Laguna, dated 27-8-2002, also from the same festival.

[253] The date of this edition is unknown.

[254] The 1935 edition does not mention the publisher. EMU republished them in 1981.

[255] In addition to 1963, EMU reissued them in 1971.

[256] These are the melodies('A quien contare mis quejas? by Mateo Romero, Al son de los arroyuelos by Jose Marin, Molinillo que mueles amores by Juan del Vado, and the anonymous jOh, que bien baila Gil! and En esta larga ausencia.

and the harpist M. del Carmen Alvira, with explanations about the "musical outline" of the IV Centenary.[a] del Carmen Alvira, with explanations on the "musical outline of Lope"[257] , the performance of the song *Pastorcito Santo* sung by Isabel Penagos in a concert in homage to Joaquin Rodrigo[258] , a series of concerts organised by the Madrid City Council in the Teatro Espanol to celebrate the IV Centenary, with the Orquesta Arriaga conducted by Julian Garcia de la Vega, in which curiously the only works truly related to Lope were Eduard Toldra's songs *Cantarcillo* and *Madre, unos ojuelos vi*, sung by the soprano Victoria Munoz[259] . Finally, there was Pan's premiere of Salvador Bacarisse's *Font-aux-cabres*, an opera written in 1956, adaptation of *Fuente Ovejuna.* Tony Aubin conducted the soloists, chorus and orchestra of the RTF on 28 December 1962 .[260]

As had already happened in 1935, the national government, through the Ministry of National Education, promoted the creation of a Board responsible for organising the events of the IV Centenary of the birth of Lope de Vega, made up of heads of different public and academic bodies of the State, under the Presidency of the Minister of Education himself. This Board being eminently representative, a Permanent Executive Commission was created, chaired by the Undersecretary of National Education, for the direct and immediate organisation of the events[261] .

The impulse to theatrical performances of Lope's works this year, described as "authentically disappointing" by Andres Pelaez Martin when referring to the productions motivated by the celebration[262] , does not go beyond three or four titles in the theatres of the capital, with carefully staged productions and a sufficient number of performances, to which are added occasional initiatives, which Pelaez describes as "well-intentioned", but of lesser importance. Among the former are those offered at the Teatro Espanol and the Teatro Maria Guerrero, among the latter are productions by student or second-rate companies:

1. *La bella malmaridada* by the Cia. Teatro Popular Espanol, at the Goya Theatre in Madrid; staged by Jose Luis Alonso at the Maria Guerrero and at the Santander Festival.
2. *Fuente Ovejuna:* Teatro Espanol, in a production by Jose Tamayo; in the town of Fuente Obejuna; at the Salamanca Festival.
3. *El perro del hortelano*: Teatro Espanol de Madrid.
4. *El caballero de Olmedo:* in June it is performed in the main square of Madrid together with *La ninez de Sal Isidro;* in Olmedo; by the pupils Institute). Cardenal Cisneros on the feast of St. Thomas Aquinas; reading in the Aula de Teatro del Servicio de Educacion y Cultura del Movimiento.
5. *El acero de Madrid*: in the Certamen Nacional de Teatro held in Murcia, the TEU de Madrid wins the prize, with subsequent performances in Madrid.
6. *Los guanches de Tenerife o la conquista de Tenerife*: Teatro Guimera de Santa Cruz de Tenerife; reading at the Hogar Canario de Madrid.
7. *El galan de la membrilla* Manzanares, Almagro and Teatro Maria Guerrero, for the TEU of Madrid.
8. *Porfar hasl.a morin* by a company from Uruguay who came to Madrid after performing it in Paris.

---

[257] Federico Sopena wrote a review of this informative concert in *ABC* on 8 May.
[258] *ABC*, 24-11-1962.
[259] Federico Sopena wrote a musical review and critique of these concerts (*ABC,* 5-12-1962, p. 79) in which he took the opportunity to suggest the need to organise an "academic session where study and music would have a special solemnity" to celebrate the quadricentenary, a session which never took place. A programme of this concert is preserved in the FJM. Perhaps the inclusion of these two songs is due to Toldra's recent death, as will be discussed later.
[260] *ABC*, 29-12-1962.
[261] Order of the Ministry of National Education, dated 22-12-1961, *BOE*, 3-2-1962.
[262] PELAEZ MARTIN. Andres, "Lope de Vega en los teatros nacionales y festivales de Espana", *Actas del XVIIIjornadas de teatro Clasico de Almagro,* ed. by Felipe B. Pedraza and Rafael Gonzalez Canal, 1995, p. 94.
Pedraza and Rafael Gonzalez Canal, 1995, p. 94.

9. *La siega*, auto sacramental: in June in the Plaza Mayor in Madrid.
Some performances of international importance were prepared abroad, such as the production of *Fuente Ovejuna* that Jose Tamayo presented in the theatre-auditorium of the Library of Congress in Washington, in an English translation of *El caballero de Olmedo*, "Knight from Olmedo", offering several performances in November and December. The same director presented *Fuente Ovejuna* at the opening of the Venice Biennale. Others, of lesser repercussion, were presented as acts in homage to Lope: in San Juan de Puerto Rico *Peribanez y el comendador de Ocana* was performed, in Tetuan El *caballero de Olmedo,* and in Ceuta, as part of the Festivals of Spain in July, *E anzuelo de Fenisa.* Other initiatives related to the IV Centenary, these of an academic nature, took place in Cairo, where students performed a reduced version of *El caballero de Olmedo*; in Oxford, where The Spanish Society staged *Fuente Ovejuna*; at the University of Manchester, where students from that university performed *Porfiar hasta morir*; and in Tiflis, the city from which *ABC* of 16-9-1962 reported on preparations for a performance of the same title. Finally, Radio-Television Italiana programmed a television version of *Peribanez y el comendador de Ocana*[263] .
From the information given in the catalogue of Matilde Salvador's works, we know that in 1962 she composed the incidental music for the performances of two comedies by Lope. These performances were staged at the Instituto de Ensenanza Media Luis Vives and at the Claustro de la Universidad de Valencia. On 11th April, the PREU students of the secondary schools of Valencia Luis Vives and San Vicente Ferrer, directed by Carola Reig, staged *El viilano en su rincon,* with incidental music for soprano, two guitars and choir. On July 1st of the same year, the Teatro de Camara del CEM, directed by Antonio Diaz Zamora, performed *La viuda valenciana,* this time with music for solo voice and guitar[264] . Another work of incidental music was prepared by Gustavo Pittaluga for the performances of *Los guanches de Tenerife y la conquista de Canarias* at the Teatro Guimera in Santa Cruz de Tenerife and in other theatres on the islands organised and staged by the CEM.
supported by various official bodies[265] . We also know that Anton Garcia Abril composed the music that was played at the performances that Jose Tamayo gave of the English translation of *El caballero de Olmedo* in Washington, D.C. mentioned above.
A curious musical show related to Lope, programmed especially for the Christmas season, is announced in Madrid as *Pastores de Belen* ("shepherds who sing and dance") of which the author of the music is unknown. The show includes this performance followed by Gian Carlo Menotti's one-act opera *Ahmal y los Reyes Magos*[266] , given by the Sinfonica de Madrid conducted by Alberto Blancafort, with Angel F. Montesinos as stage director, various soloists, the RNE choir and the Grupo de Teatro Los Titeres de la FE y las JONS[267] .
Lectures by prestigious literary personalities such as Joaquin de Entrambasaguas, perhaps the most active this year, Rafael Balbin Lucas, Angel Valbuena Prats and Eberhard Muller-Brochat, Pedro Rocamora, Jose Hierro, Jose Maria Peman, Felipe Ximenez de Sandoval, or from the stage, such as Modesto Higueras, took place both in the capital and in other cities, even abroad. In addition to these events, there were literary prizes related to the IV Centenary, such as the Justa Poetica en Honor de Lope de Vega in Madrid, the Premios de la Diputacion de Murcia, the poetry prize in Arcos de la Frontera with the theme Lope de Vega and the literary competition in Fuente Obejuna.

---

[263] *ABC*, 14-6-1962.
[264] Of these works, two manuscript drafts are preserved at the Institut Valencia de la Musica. The composer's inventory is in the process of being compiled.
[265] *ABC*, 5-12-1962.
[266] It is actually entitled *Amah and the Night Visitors [Ahmaly los visitantes noctiunos].* It was Julio Gomez who translated Menotti's opera. He was commissioned to do so in 1960. See: MARTINEZ DEL FRESNO, Beatriz, *Julio Gomez. Una epoca..., op. cit.*, p. 477.
[267] It is performed between 28 December and 13 January 1963. The show is advertised in several Madrid newspapers.

A bibliographical exhibition was also presented at the BNE, showing different manuscripts and editions of Lope's works. Finally, the playwright Alfonso Paso premiered one of his plays, *El mejormozo de Espana, un (da en la vida de Lope de Vega)*, at the Teatro Alcazar in Madrid, taking advantage of the momentum of the event[268] .
A mournful event has come to cloud this celebration. It is the death of the composer Eduard Toldra, who died in Barcelona on 31 May 1962. He was one of the leading composers of songs with piano in Spain, author of two works with text by Lope, perhaps the most fortunate ones written in our country, *Madre, unos ojuelos* vi *and Cantarcillo*[26] .
[269] In the catalogue (Annex) we note the details of these songs.

[268] Wilfried Floeck speaks of a "historical" work, thus, in inverted commas, in which Paso himself favoured being compared, for his theatrical fecundity, with Lope himself. FLOECK, Wilfried, *Teatro espanol contemporaneo: autoresy tendencias,* Kassel, Reichenberger, 1995, p. 100.

Part IV

SPANISH SONGS FOR VOICE AND PIANO WITH LYRICS BY LOPE DE VEGA

In this chapter we will study the 109 works included in our catalogue of songs written on Lope de Vega's lyrics[270] . If in this chapter we present the details of each of the songs, here we will study transversally different aspects that will give us the necessary overview. On the one hand, we will observe the order and temporal distribution of composition, the influence of the historical periods and the prevailing ideologies. On the other hand, we will look at the lyrics used in the songs, their origin, the most commonly used poems, the type of lyrics according to their subject or the poetic forms that support them. We will also study the different musical procedures and styles with which composers approach the poetic text, especially with regard to the formal relations between music and poetry, or the tonal and harmonic approaches, as well as the influence of the text in the choice of elements of musical representation that can relate the musical construction to the semantic content of the lyrics. Finally, we will investigate other questions related to scores, song collections, recordings, premieres or dedications.

TEMPORAL DISTRIBUTION OF THE COMPOSITIONS

Lope de Vega's texts have been used to compose songs for voice and piano since the middle of the nineteenth century, but it has been during the twentieth century when more works have been written, having at our disposal several compositions from the present century. The oldest known song for voice and piano with lyrics by Lope is *La barca de Amor* by Manuel Garcia[271] . Obviously we do not consider the works written in the 18th century published by Bal y Gay or those collected by Querol in his *Cancionero de Lope de Vega*, as they are compositions that are not adapted to the musical genre we are dealing with.

The most recent, the two songs by Voro Garcia Fernandez written in 2011, released in April of the same year.

The songs follow one after the other throughout the 20th century and up to the present day with an uninterrupted rhythm of composition, the number of works written in each year oscillating between one and five, approximately. The exceptions come, in a negative sense, from the scarce production in the 19th century, and in a positive sense, from the particularity of 1935, the year of the celebration of the III centenary of the death of the *Phoenix* (see Graph I).

Without considering the tercentenary year, the years in which the production increases discretely, as in 1942, 1986, and to a lesser extent 1998 or 2004, are because there are collections by a single composer, as in the case of Joan Llongueres, Jose Maria Benavente, Antonio Barrera, Gonzalo Diaz Yerro and Eduardo Rincon respectively. However, we note the exception of the year 1944, in which five works are composed, and these correspond to three different composers: Arturo Menendez Aleyxandre, Salvador Bacarisse, Joan Maria Thomas Sabater.

In order to check in more detail the rhythm of composition of the works in our catalogue, we present Graph II, in which the scale distributes proportionally all the years included in the interval so that the years in which no songs with lyrics by Lope were written can also be appreciated. In this way we can clearly see that, together with the 28 songs of 1935, the period of time in which

[270] In Annex i.

[271] Manuel del Populo Vicente Garcia (Seville, 1775 - Paris, 1832), the famed Spanish tenor, singing master and composer of great international impact in the early decades of the 19th century. The premieres of Rossini's *Il barbiere di Siviglia* and *Otello* are considered the pinnacle of his tenor career. In addition to operas, he composed a large number of chamber songs, both with piano and guitar accompaniment. His daughters Maria Malibran and Pauline Viardot-Garcia inherited their father's fame in the bel canto repertoire. See ROMERO FERRER, Alberto; MORENO MENUBAR, Andres (eds.), *Manuel Garcia, de la tonadila escenica a la opera (1775-1832)*, Universidad de Cadiz, Cadiz, 2006.

there is the greatest compositional intensity is the post-war years, from 1939 to 1956, with 38 works, which represent 62% of the total.

Figure 1: Songs composed each year.

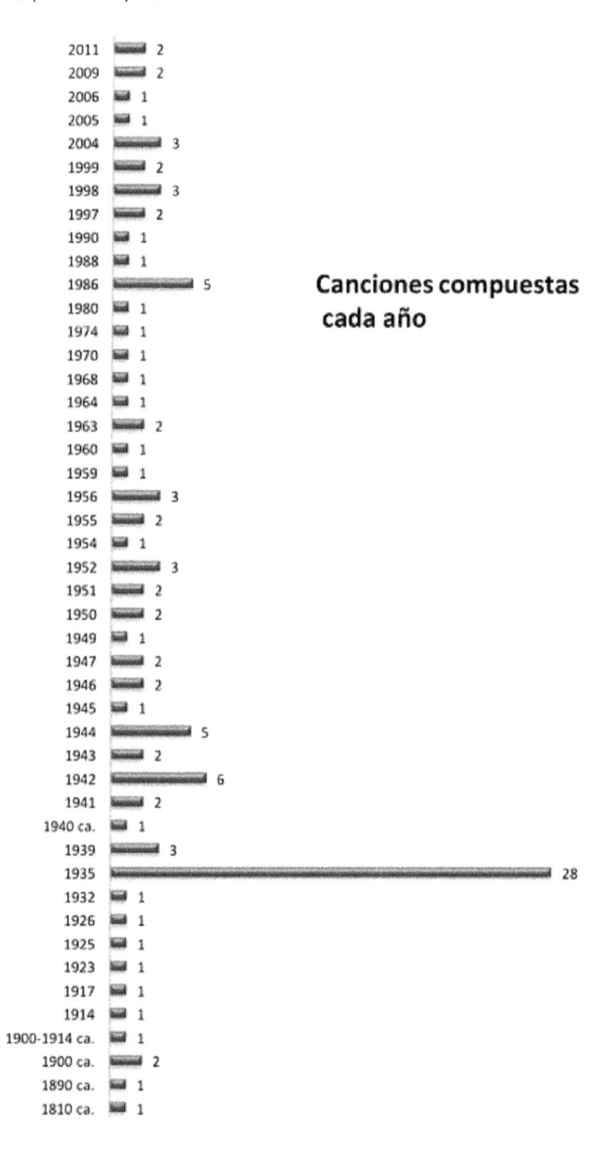

Figure 2: Pace of songwriting.

Grouping the data by decade[272] we see that in the 30s, 40s and 50s most of the songs are composed, 64%.

Figure 3: Songs composed in each decade.

Songs composed in each decade

[272] The two songs composed in April 2011, the most recent songs in our catalogue, are included in the

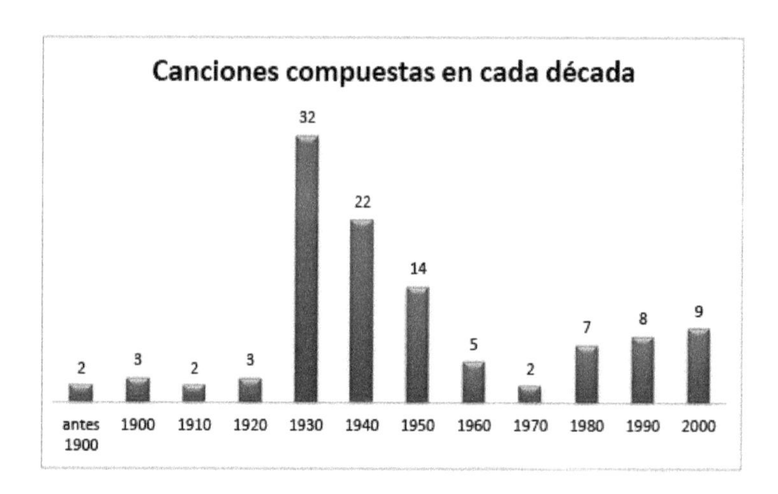

In view of the influences of certain political, social or ideological events, we now propose another grouping of the works we are studying. The main socio-historical milestones of the 20th century in Spain are mainly marked by the establishment of the Second Republic, the Civil War, the post-war Francoist period and the democratic period that began in 1975. To these historical periods we will add two other milestones related to Lope de Vega which are fundamental in our research, the years of the celebration of the III Centenary of his death in 1935 and the IV Centenary of his birth in 1962, so that we will have an overall view in which we integrate political-social events with other purely literary or musical ones. Here we divide the period of the Franco regime in two, taking the date of the IV centenary (1962) as a dividing line, as it practically coincides with the period of the opening of the regime in the early sixties.

Figure 4: Songs composed by historical periods.

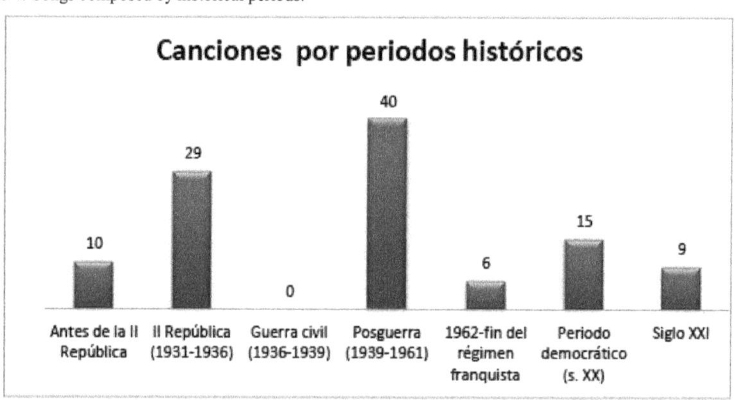

The following data can be extracted from the above graph:

a) Before the Second Republic, in a period of approximately 120 years, only 10 songs were composed.

b) The 28 songs of the III centenary are included in the period of the Republic, with only one, Menendez Aleyxandre's song *Lucinda,* composed for no apparent reason. This song has come down to us as a result of revisions in 1943 and the definitive one in 1982, and it seems to us as legitimate to ascribe it to the aforementioned group as to the songs of the democratic period.

c) No works are recorded for the period of the Civil War. The three songs by Matilde Salvador, dated between June and July 1939, are included in the following stage.

d) The post-war period (1939-1961) is the most fruitful, with 40 songs, especially if we compare it with a period of similar duration, such as the democratic period of the 20th century (1975-2000), which only presents 14 compositions.

e) The influence of the 4th centenary celebration in 1962 is quite irrelevant as far as songwriting is concerned.

THE LYRICS OF THE SONGS

ORIGIN OF THE LETTERS

Of all the lyrics in the catalogue, the most abundant are those known as "letras para cantar" (lyrics for singing)[273] , although not all belong to the dramatic work. The case of *Pastores de Belen* is particular, as it contains abundant lyrical fragments that Lope puts into the mouths of some of the characters in the novel. Since it is not a dramatic text and, therefore, does not contain stage directions, we can deduce from the text that precedes these interventions the references to the character who sings them.

The same happens with *La Dorotea*, a play also in prose from which several fragments in verse are extracted and set to music, and which are sung on stage by the corresponding character. The inclusion of lyrical interventions with music is a fundamental element in the theatre of the Golden Age and in Lope's in particular, as we have already seen in previous chapters, a procedure that Fenix usually uses in these two works not intended for the stage.

Figure 5: Origin of the letters.

Origin of the letters

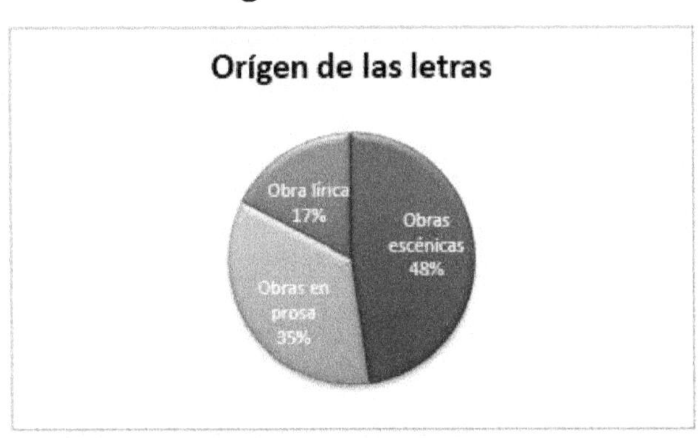

Within the scenic works we include the lyrics of fragments of comedies, whether they are lyrics for singing or monologues, and of an auto sacramental. In the group of lyrics corresponding to prose works we find fragments of *La Arcadia, La Dorotea* and *Pastores de Belen.* In these three cases, the fragments we are dealing with are poems that Lope inserts into stories of a novel type that one of the characters sings. Considering the function they have in Lope's works, the texts set to music in most of the songs we have catalogued have their origin in lyrics for singing, according to the usual denomination of our poet's time:

Table 1: Number of songs composed according to the origin of the lyrics.

			N° Songs		
Lyrics to sing	Theatre	Comedies	44	45	83

[273] In expression of the poet's time. first decade of the 21st century.

		Cars	1		
	Prose work	La Dorotea	14	38	
		Shepherds of Bethlehem	23		
		The Arcadia	1		
Theatrical monologues			7		
Work Erica			19		

Following this grouping, we show in the following table the complete list of Lope's works from which lyrics are taken, followed by the number of songs composed from that work and indicating the fragments taken and the number of songs composed from each fragment. The order in the table allows us to see which are the lyrics most used by the composers and which of Lope's works are most represented in the songs. The lyric about which most songs have been written is "Madre, unos ojuelos vi", a poem sung by Dorotea in the play of the same name. It is followed by "Las pajas del pesebre" from *Pastores de Belen*, "Blanca me era yo" from *El gran duque de Moscovia* and "Mananicas floridas" from *El cardenal de Belen.* All four arc in the poetic form of a carol.

Table 2: Number of songs composed from each of Lope's plays and the fragments taken from them.

	Works by Lope		Fragment	
	Tftulo obra Lope	Number of songs	1st verse	Number of songs
Theatre	Peribanez and the Commander of Ocana	6	Dente congratulations	2
			Tr'bole, jay Jesus, like guele!	2
			Cogiome a tu puerta el toro	2
	The Cardinal of Bethlehem	5	Flowering mannikins	5
	The Grand Duke of Muscovy and persecuted emperor	5	White was me	5
	The Knight of Olmedo	5	That he was killed at night	3
			I saw the most beautiful labrador	1
			Oh, rigorous state	1
	The villain, in his corner	4	On the mountain alone	4
	The good guard	3	Wash me in the Tagus	2
			Green pleasant riverbanks	1
	Fuente Ovejuna	3	Al val de Fuente Ovejuna	2
			Welcome	1
	The discreet lover	2	When I look at you so beautiful	2
	The school dummy	2	Naranjitas me tira la nina	2
	The porcelains of Murcia	1	Morenica they adore me	1
	The Aldeguela	1	They skipped my eyes	1
	Pedro Carbonero	1	Beautiful little rivers	1
	The battlements of Toro	1	Candle that the castle candles	1
	Thc human seraphim	1	Sweet Jesus, I was blind	1
	If only women could not see!...	1	He who does not know about love, lives among wild animals	1
	The Knight of Illescas	1	White takes Lucinda	1
	The flowers of Don Juan and the rich and the poor exchanged	1	They leave Valencia	1
	The villain of Getafe	1	A lady sent me	1

	La burgalesa de Lerma	1	No longer catch' verbena	1
	The Star of Seville	1	If with my wishes	1
	Asturian celebrities	1	Pariome mi madre	1
	The Dina robbery	1	In the mananicas	1
	The tamed Arauco	1	Piraguamonte, piraguamonte, piragua	1
	The pretended true	1	Not to be, Lucinda, your beautiful	1
	The slave of her lover	1	How short-lived are the joys	1
	The Ruisenor of Seville	1	Si os parti'redes al alba	1

Table 3: Number of songs composed from each of Lope's prose and lyric works with the fragments taken from them.

	Works by Lope		Fragment	
	Titulo obra Lope	Number of songs	1st verse	Number of songs
Prose works	Shepherds of BelCn	23	The straws in the manger	6
			Zagalejo of pearls	4
			Well, you are in Las Palmas	4
			No llorCis, my eyes	3
			Of a beautiful Virgin	2
			Where are you going, zagala	1
			Let's go to Belcn, Pascual	1
			Today the ice is born	1
			A la dina dana	1
	La Dorotea	15	Mother, I saw some eyelets	8
			Poor nacelle mla	3
			No llorcis, ojuelos	2
			So alive in my soul	1
			To my solitudes I go	1
	The Arcadia	1	O precious freedom	1
Lyric work	Sacred rhymes	10	(■Quc have I, that thou seekest my friendship?	3
			The evening darkens	2
			Shepherd, who with your loving whistles	2
			To the arms of Mary	1
			When I stop to contemplate my state	1
			How many times, Lord, have you called me	1
			Hincado is on his knees	1
	Rhymes	5	These the willows are and Csta the spring	1
			Daughter of time, who in the golden century	1
			I was giving sustenance to a little bird one day	1
			To go and to stay, and by staying to leave	1

			Night, the maker of hoaxes	1
	Loose poems274	3	Oh, bitter loneliness	1

274 The three poems come from the following collections: *Romancero general* de 1604 (one of the 28 romances dedicated to Filis, "Ay, amargas soledades"), the BNE manuscript MSS/3985 which belonged to the Duke of Uceda (¡Ay, zagales!, lo que veo"), and from the *Codice Agustin Duran* ("Celos, que no me matais"). The information concerning each of the songs and lyrics is detailed in our catalogue.

			Oh, my friends, what I see!	1
			Jealousy, don't kill me	1
	Rimas divinas y humanas del licenciado Tome de Burguillos (Divine and human rhymes by Tome de Burguillos)	1	Drop in, Pascual	1

TYPEFACES

In order to classify the songs according to the subject to which the lyrics refer, we have defined some general groupings where we place them according to the main subject they deal with. In addition to the two characteristic themes of Fenix, love and religion, we have added other no less infrequent themes[274] .

Table 4: Number of songs composed according to the subject to which they refer.

	Number of songs
Loving	40
Christmas	30
Sacred	13
Jobs	5
Various	8
Nature	5
Festivas	3
Jocosas	3
Vital state	2
Sacred decontextualised	1

Within the group of love songs we find lyrics with a popular flavour, such as those beginning with "Piraguamonte, piragua", "Saltearonme los ojos", "Trebole, ¡ay Jesus, como guele!", "Cogiome a tu puerta el toro", "Riberitas hermosas", "Por el montecico sola", "Ya no cogere verbena", "Al val de Fuente Ovejuna" and "Naranjitas me tira la nina", and others of a more cultured poetic elaboration, such as "Madre, unos ojuelos vi", "No lloreis, ojuelos", "Cuando tan hermosa os miro", "Blancas coge Lucinda", "Ay, rigoro estado", "Que poco duran las dichas", "Tan vivo esta en mi alma", "Yo vi la mas hermosa labradora", "Celos, que no me matais", "Si con mis deseos", "No ser, Lucinda, tus bellas", "Quien no sabe de amor, vive entre fieras", "Velador que el castillo velas", "Si os partieredes al alba", "Ay, amargas soledades". The poems "Ir y quedarse, y con quedar partirse" and "A mis soledades voy" are grouped here in a typology that we call of vital state, as they express feelings of suffering due to absence and loneliness respectively. Although the origin could well be amorous, thus decontextualised, they lose that character.

274 The thematic classification is taken from D^EZ DE REVENGA, Francisco Javier, *Teato de Lope de Vegay lrica traditional,* Universidad de Murcia, Murcia, 1983. The difficulty to which we allude is reflected in the different typological assignment that Pedraza uses when studying the lyric in Lope's theatre. The differences are usually due to the poet's own thematic richness. See PEDRAZA JIMENEZ, Felipe B., *El universo poetico de Lope de Vega,* Laberinto, Madrid, 2003, pp. 241-246.

There are two festive lyrics, the wedding song of *Peribanez and the Commander of Ocana,* "Dente parabienes", and the song welcoming the Commander in *Fuente Ovejuna,* "Sea bien venido". Those classified as jocosas are "Lavareme en el Tajo", "Una dama me mando", to which we could add, because of their double entendre and popular wit, "Trebole, jay Jesus, como guele!", "Cogiome a tu puerta el toro" or "Naranjitas me tira la nina", already included in the group of the amorosas.

Those that refer to natural elements are the maya "En las mananicas", a song of San Juan, "Salen de Valencia", the sonnets "Noche, fabricadora de embelecos" and "Estos los sauces son y esta la fuente" which speak of the night and the mutability of Nature and the human heart respectively. The sonnet "Daba sustento a un pajarillo un dla", which we include in this group, could also be associated with love lyrics, since in addition to referring to Lucinda, the poetic name he gave to Micaela de Lujan, the text plays with the double meaning of the little bird that goes and returns to its cage as a transcript of the lover who abandons and then returns to his beloved, moved by her tears.

Of those with a sacred theme, those dealing with Christmas stand out for their number. Except for "Morenica me adoran" from *Los porceles de Murcia* and "Mananicas floridas" from *El cardenal de Belen* and "Dejate caer, Pascual" from the *Rimas divinas y humanas del licenciado Tome de Burguiilos,* all the others have lyrics from *Pastores de Belen, a* work par excellence centred on the mysteries of the Nativity of the Lord in the form of a pastoral novel, and which contains abundant lyrics sung by the shepherds who appear as characters in the novel.

The distinction between sacred and profane lyrics, apparently simple, requires some considerations. The case of Joaquin Rodrigo's song *Coplas del pastor enamorado,* with the fragment from *La buena guarda* "Verdes riberas amenas" is paradigmatic, as it is a text apparently profane but with a sacred subject if we consider it in its scenic context. This monologue, as explained in its place, expresses the symbolism of the parable of the Good Shepherd, but decontextualised it loses this character to become a profane text. For this reason, and considering that the songs are presented to the listener outside their literary context, we attend exclusively to the semantic content of their text, without taking into account the meaning that the words may have within the work from which they are extracted.

Table 5: Number of sacred and secular songs.

Sacred	43
Profane	65
Sacred decontextualised	1

In the history of Spain in the 20th century, the influence of religion or its negation has been particularly intense and even virulent in some historical periods. From the above table it seems interesting to consider the years of composition of the songs with sacred lyrics and relate it to the historical periods we have taken in the previous section in order to be able to observe the possible influence of the political, social and cultural environment in which they were written on the choice of the texts due to their subject matter.

Table 6: Number of sacred and secular songs composed in the different historical periods.

	Sacred	Profane
Before the Second Republic	0	10
II Republic (1931-1936)	6*	22*
Civil War (1936-1939)	0	0
Post-war period (1939-1961)	22	19
1962 - end of Franco's regime	5	1
Democratic period (20th c.)	6	9
21st Century	5	4

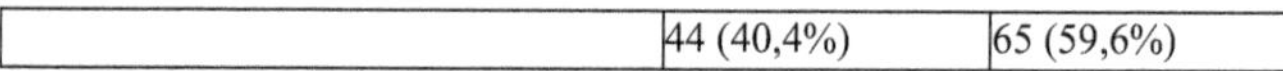

	44 (40,4%)	65 (59,6%)

It is clear from the above table that the highest number of songs with sacred lyrics corresponds to the period of the Franco regime. The figure is most notable in the years of National Catholicism, the post-war period up to the opening of the regime in the 1960s. Even so, from 1962 until the end of the regime, even with a lower number of compositions, the balance is highly favourable to sacred lyrics. The percentage of songs with sacred lyrics composed in these thirty-six years of the Francoist period (1939-1975) is 61% of all those composed in more than a century, which leads us to conclude that the concentration of sacred songs in this period at least coincides with the ideological approaches of the regime, although it is no less certain that 20 were written with secular lyrics. As a counterbalance, the time of the II Republic has an opposite tendency, with the election by composers of a majority of profane lyrics.

The ideological use made of Lope de Vega's work from the 1930s onwards, especially the revaluation that the third centenary brought about, may lie at the root of the percentages we have just presented. The strong political polarisation that took place in Spain in those years meant that *Fuente Ovejuna* was taken as the paradigm of the work that synthesised the ideological essence of both political camps. The character of an open work, in the concept expressed by Umberto Eco, in which there is no single way in its reception, but multiple spaces and cultural discourses[275] , makes the left and the right highlight and appropriate certain values inherent to the work.

The interpretation of Garcia Lorca's *Fuente Ovejuna* was controversial at the time and is the clearest example of how the radicalisation of the ideological positions of the final stage of the Second Republic invaded the cultural life of the pals[276] . Francisco Florit Duran, in his study on the ideological use of Lope in 1935, concludes:

Although it is true that some of the numerous studies that came to light on the occasion of the tercentenary, or in the years before or after, attempted to reach a reasoned and objective understanding of Lope's image, it is no less true that the publishing scene of that time abounds in works that offer a markedly subjective and politicised reading of our poet. Thus, if one reads carefully a good part of the works, whether books, articles or conferences, a landscape emerges before us in which Lope appears anililelically and contradictorily outlined, a two-faced silhouette, with no middle ground, where sometimes the Phoenix is the champion of an imperial and national-Catholic Spain, and at other times, on the other hand, Lope is the popular and revolutionary poet, a transcript of a people oppressed and subjugated by the new feudal lords. This paradoxical and politicised image of the Phoenix could only emerge in a climate such as the one that prevailed in Spain in 1935, because only eight years earlier, on the occasion of Gongora's tercentenary, a similar attitude could not be found with the Cordovan poet[277 278] .

In this version of *Fuente Ovejuna*, the final scene of the kings was eliminated and the social character of the play was emphasised, which "privileged the social struggle between the lord and his vassals" [279]:

From the other side, the Falange, also turned *Fuenteovejuna* into a play that symbolised their national-Catholic ideology, accusing the left of appropriating the Lopesque drama[279] .

Other opinions brought the play ideologically closer to the Falangist camp, such as the one summarised a few years later by Esteban Calle, who saw in *Fuente Ovejuna* the emblem of the

---

275 GARCIA SANTO-TOMAS, Enrique, *La creation del "Feni", op. cit.,* p. 341.

2" Garcia Lorca's version, premiered at the Teatro Principal in Valencia in July 1933, is collected in BYRD, Suzanne W., La Fuente Ovejuna de Federico Garcia Lorca, Pliegos, Madrid, 2003: BYRD, Suzanne W., *La Fuente Ovejuna de Federico Garcia Lorca,* Pliegos, Madrid, 2003. Byrd reports that various folkloric music and dances were interspersed in the wedding scene, accompanied by vihuela, guitar and land. These are "Sal a bailar, buena moza", an Asturian folk dance, and "Las agachadas", an Andalusian dance with music harmonised and arranged by Garcia Lorca himself. These fragments were additions not derived from Lope's verses (see p. 16). Two other interpolated musical pieces were the "Sea bienvenido el Comendadore" and the "Romance de Fuente Ovejuna" sung by the chorus and accompanied by instruments. The authorship of these two melodies is unknown, although they are presumably by Garcia Lorca. The scores are included in this same edition: pp. 39, 80-82.

277 FLORIT DURAN, Francisco, "La recepcion de Lope en 1935: ideologia y literatura", *Anuario de Lope,* VI, 2000, pp. 107-124. In the article, the author gives an account of the tendentiousness of many of the writings that were published at that time.

278 GARCIA SANTO-TOMAS, Enrique, *La creacion del "Fnnix", op. cit,* p. 350.

279 FLORIT DURAN, Francisco, *op. cit,* p. 110.

yoke and arrows, and that the play dramatises "the realisation of social justice by liberating the common state from the barbarous feudal regime and placing it under the sceptre of the social state"[280] . Felipe Lluch Garin, who proposed in 1935 the recovery of Lope's religious plays as a "return to our classical and catholic scene", the opinions of Julian Pemartm appealing to Lope's theatre as a reflection of the principles of fascist totalitarianism, or the defence by Joaquin de Entrambasaguas of the Fenix plays in which he saw a historical conception that would be assumed by the Franco regime[281] , fostered the atmosphere that would be installed in the post-war period. The activities of the Teatro Nacional de Falange, active during the war, and the work of some theatre directors linked to Catholic traditionalism, such as Luis Escobar, Huberto Perez de la Osa and Felipe Lluch, found in the auto sacramental the theatrical spectacle of choice[282] .
The consequences of this partisan use of Lope were logically extended in the post-war period, and were combined with other events that found fertile ground in the dominant political ideology. In addition to the ideological approaches of the regime, the increase in interest in the composition of religious works, liturgical or otherwise, was favoured in the post-war years by the flourishing of the so-called *Motu proprio* Generation, *a* generation of musicians of which we have already spoken in chapter III.
Of the most outstanding composers of the *Motu proprio* movement we have only one case in our catalogue, that of the Mallorcan Joan Maria Thomas, who, curiously enough, set to music in 1944 two secular poems by *Peribanez y el comendador de Ocana.* Another musician we could ascribe to the movement, and present in the catalogue, is Angel Larroca, chapel master of the Cathedral of Murcia, who wrote towards 1940-1945 two sacred works *La oración de Cristo en el Huerto (*"Hincado esta de rodillas") and *Plegaria a Cristo crucifcado (*"Pastor, que con tus silbos amorosos").
Where these types of works stand out is in other musical genres and other types of instrumental formations linked to liturgical and church music, such as works for one or several voices with organ or harmonium, and choral compositions with or without accompaniment. Of this type there are works with sacred lyrics of Lope by minor composers such as Jose Manuel Adran, Gregorio Arciniega, G. Calzolari, Arturo Duo Vital, Victorina Falco de Pablo, Jose Font Roger, Francisco Laporta, Rafael Lozano, Jose Luis Rubio Pulido, Eduardo Torres and Jose Alfonso. In chapter III we have referred to religious works of other musical genres.

Table 7: Years of composition of texts that are set to music on at least three occasions.

First verse	N° songs	Anos de composition
"Mother, I saw some eyelets"	8	antes1900-1900-1923-1925-1935-1941-1944-1950
"The straws in the manger	6	1935-1935-1942-1957-1963-2009
"White was me"	5	1935-1935-1935-1938-1986
"Flowering mananicas".	5	1947-1955-1963-1990-2004
"Well, you're in the palms".	4	1941-1952-1954-2006
"On the mountain alone".	4	1939-1944-1950-1955
"Zagalejo of pearls	4	1942-1952-1959-1970
"That he was killed at night"	3	1944-1951-1986
"('What have I that you seek my friendship?"	3	1935-1999-2004
"Don't cry, my eyes"	3	1946-1956-1960

[280] Quoted by GARCIA SANTO-TOMAS, Enrique, *La creacion del "Fnnix", op. cit,* p. 355.
[281] HUERTA CALVO, Javier, "Clasicos cara al sol, I", *XXIVy XXVJornadas de Teatro del Siglo de Oro,* Institute of Almerian Studies, Almena, 2011, pp. 219-220.
[282] *Ibid.*, p. 232.

The table above shows that there do not seem to be any letters that come into fashion at any particular time. The most frequently used text, "Madre, unos ojuelos vi", from *La Dorotea, is* not used again after 1950; also, "Por el montecico sola", from *El vilano, en su rincon,* is only used in the first half of the 20th century, between 1939 and 1955. The carols "Zagalejo de perlas" and "No lloreis, mis ojos", both from *Pastores de Belen,* with 4 and 3 songs respectively, focus on the period 19421970.
Of the fragment from *Pastores de Belen* "Las pajas del pesebre", and of "Mananicas floridas", from *El cardenal de Belen,* both of which are also very popular in choral music, we find compositions spread over the broad period 1935-2009, as is the case with "Que de noche le mataron", although in a shorter period, up to 1986. The sonnet "^Que tengo yo, que mi amistad procuras?" is the one with the greatest disparity, with one case from 1935 and two others from the 21st century.
In the choice of vocal repertoire or the preparation of recital programmes, singers have sometimes taken into consideration the masculine or feminine character of the lyrics of the songs. In the catalogue we present here, 9 lyrics are clearly masculine (11 songs), 6 are feminine (14 songs) and 47 are indistinct for both sexes (89 songs). Obviously the consideration of this factor is strictly personal. If within the vocal genre that concerns us, outside the theatrical field, we consider the singer as a reciter of the verses, not as an actor who plays a character, even if he gives the dramatic vision required by the text, this distinction may be accessory.

TYPES OF VERSE. METRICA

It is impossible to know whether the choice of a text to compose a song is influenced by the type of verse. That the poetic form influences the musical form is evident, as we studied when analysing and comparing both factors in the songs of 1935. Statistically, the poetic form of the carol in its different variants is in the majority in the songs in our catalogue, 55%.

Table 8: Number of songs according to the poetic stanza of the lyrics.

	Number of songs
Christmas carol	60
Sonnet	14
Romance	10
Romancillo	8
Seguidilla	7
Date	3
Redondilla	3
Broken foot couplets	1
Silva	1
Song	1
Chained thirds	1

The metrical variety and the recurrence of the refrain offered by the villancico form make this poetic structure one of the most widely used, both by Lope in the songs inserted in his comedies and prose works and by composers when writing songs. In these cases, the refrain allows the use of a recurring musical element that structurally orders the song, at the same time as it provides a return of the most characteristic melodic material of the piece, formally uniting the work. For their part, the stanzas fulfil the explanatory function of the development of the action in some cases, of the exposition of poetic ideas in others. Within the basic scheme of refrain-stanza alternations, there are several forms of versification, combining different strophic structures, as can be seen in the following table:

Table 9: Forms of versification in the refrain-stanza type.

Number of	Number of

	songs	letters
irregular chorus, foot with redondilla	15	8
refrain and foot with redondillas	9	2
estribillo seguidilla, foot with redondilla	7	2
refrain and foot with seguidillas	5	2
irregular date	6	1
refrain seguidilla, foot and general rhyme of romancillo	6	2
romancillo form and rhyme	8	5
broken foot verses	4	1
romance form and rhyme	1	1

The most common forms of villancico are those constructed with the canonical form of estribillo and foot, the latter consisting of mudanza, enlace and verso de vuelta. Variations occur in the type of verse on which these elements are based. In the 24 lyrics that follow this structure, the redondilla is the form that appears most frequently: we find it in the majority of the carols, usually in the foot part (12 cases) as well as in the refrain (2 cases). The seguidilla is used as a refrain (4 cases) and also in the foot (2 cases). But the most common refrains in the lyrics are those that do not correspond to a pre-existing structure. In the 8 cases where this is the case, we find combinations of three lines (5), two (2) and four (1), the last two being paired by rhyme:

a. 8/a/8b/8b: "Si os partieredes al alba": "If you leave at dawn".
b. 8-/8a/8a: "I will no longer fuck verbena".
c. 8-/5a/8a "Cogiome a tu puerta el toro".
d. 6-/6a/9a: "White was me".
e. 9-/10a/10a: "Candlelight that the castle candles".
f. 8a/5a: "Jealousy, don't kill me".
g. 10-/10-: "Trebole, jay Jesus, como guele!"
h. 8a/6a/6b/8b: "When I look at you so beautifully".

The irregularity of these refrains also affects, as we can appreciate, the syllabic computation, which in the songs will need the necessary adjustments to balance the musical phrasing. The particularities of some of them will be studied in detail in the analyses of the songs of 1935. The next type in number of cases is the villancico, which organises its elements on the basis of the romaiicillo, as far as syllables and rhyme are concerned. There are five lyrics: "Donde vais, zagala", "Hoy al hielo nace", "Naranjitas me tira la nina", "No lloreis, mis ojos" and "Saltearonme los ojos".

The choice of a major or minor-art poem has a decisive influence on the organisation of the phrases and semi-phrases, as the number of syllables in the verse generates more or less extensive musical periods. Only 15 of the songs are composed on major-art verse: the 14 sonnets set to music by Salvador Bacarisse, Vi'ctor Carbajo Cardenas, Enrique Casal Chapi, Gonzalo Diaz Yerro (4), Voro Garcia Fernandez, Julio Gomez, Angel Larroca, Arturo Menendez Aleyxandre, Miquel Ortega, Eduardo Rincon, and only one with chained tercets, *Dulasimo Senor, yo estaba ciego,* also by Eduardo Rincon. On the other hand, the combination of major and minor art is found in two songs that set to music a silva, *Si con mis deseos* by Turina, and a regular song, *La Libertad* by Bernardino Valle, the well-known "Oh libertad preciosa".

USE OF LETTERS

The lyrics of songs are generally taken by the composers in their entirety, whether they are single poems or fragments of a larger work. However, this is not always the case, as there are cases in which the composer intervenes by altering the original fragment in one way or another. The usual interventions are:

1. Changes in the order of the stanzas:

a. Antonio Barrera, in *Seguidilla*, belonging to his collection *Canciones del Siglo de Oro*, changes the order of the stanzas with respect to the original text of the comedy. In it the musicians intervene alternating the three stanzas with interventions by Dª Clara, Damas 1ª and 2ª , Galan 1° and 2°, beginning with "Lavareme en el Tajo..." (third stanza in the song), then following the other two stanzas in the same order as the song "Que no quiero bonetes" and "Si te echares al agua" (first and second in the song respectively).

b. Antonio Mingote, in *Copla,* in which he sets to music the well-known "Madre unos ojuelos vi", inverts the order of the two stanzas with respect to Lope's text. Similarly, Antoni Parera Fons, in Palmas de Belen, does not use the refrain of the poem, but only sets the stanzas to music, but in a different order than usual, changing the second, "El Nino divino", for the third, "Rigurosos hielos", and vice versa.

2. Omissions:

a. Omission of stanzas: omissions are the most frequent intervention of composers in the original text, in many cases because the poetic fragments used are too long for the format of a song with piano. In *La barca de Amor,* Manuel Garcia uses in this song only the first of the four stanzas that form the "Indian" scene of *El Arauco domado.* Asins Arbo only takes two stanzas of the ten that make up *Las pajas del pesebre,* and omits the refrain at the beginning of *Donde vais que hace fro?* Vicente Miguel only writes the first 4 stanzas of "Las pajas del pesebre" in his *Tonadila navidena.* Bernardino Valle chooses 6 of the 9 stanzas (1-4-5-7-8 and 9) that make up the poem *La Libertad*, while he uses the first ten of "Pobre barquilla mia" in *La barquila.* In *Danza giana,* Jose Maria Benavente takes 10 and then 8 of the 116 lines of Elifilia's "A la dina dana" in *Pastores de Belen.* Both Granados and Mercedes Carol omit the second verse of "No lloreis ojuelos" from *La Dorotea.* Llongueres, in *Dejate caer Pascual,* omits 90 verses, using only the first and last of the 10 stanzas. Fernando Moraleda omits the last verse of *Dicha*, and in *Pobre barquila mi'a* he takes the first four of the 11 stanzas. Palau takes the first 4 stanzas of "Las pajas del pesebre" in his *Villancico*. Eduardo Rincon in *Diici'sinio Jesus* takes stanzas 3, 5, 6 and 8 of the 10 chained tercets in the poem. Matilde Salvador takes the second intervention of the musicians "Naranjitas me tira la nina", in her song *Valenciana*, omitting the first intervention "Claros aires de Valencia".

Turina, in *Si con mis deseos,* puts music to the first 11 verses of Estrella's performance in *La Estrella de Sevila.*

b. Mixture of stanzas: Enrique Truan omits a verse and return of the refrain in *No lloreis mis ojos,* and in *Mananicas foridas* he mixes two verses from two different works: the first verse is from the auto *El nombre de Jesus* ", and the second, from which he takes the title, from *Pastores de Belen.*

c. Omission of speeches by another character in the comedy: another common and logical procedure is to omit speeches by characters in the comedy that are interspersed or alternate with the poem sung or recited by another character. From *La Dorotea,* Casares, Cotarelo and Toldra take from the fragment "Coma un manso arroyuelo" the carol that is interspersed, "Madre, unos ojuelos vi", which Lope, through the dialogue between the protagonist, Don Bela and Gerarda, separates the refrain and the verses. The same happens in "Salen de Valencia noche de San Juan" from the comedy *Las flores de don Juan*, a fragment used by Gustavo Duran for his *Seguidillas de la noche de San Juan*, eliminating the dialogue of the characters which alternates with the interventions of the musicians.

d. Omission of single lines of verse: this is the case of Joaquin Rodrigo in *Coplas del pastor enamorado*, where he omits an intermediate line and the three final lines of the intervention of the Pastor in *La buena guarda.* Similarly, in *Al entierro de Cristo*, Francisco Escudero sets to music the first 56 lines of the 96 lines of the complete romance. Within the group of those set to music, he omits stanzas 3, 10 and 11, the first line of the second stanza, half of the first line of the sixth stanza, and repeats a word from the first line of the eighth stanza.

3. Added:

a. Stanzas or verses that are not by Lope: Nin-Culmell adds two stanzas that are not by the poet in *Lavareme en el Tajo, they* are stanzas 3ª and 5ª of the song[283] [284] . The second verse of *Por el montecico sola* by Juan Altisent is not by Lope, nor from *El villano en su rincon,* from which the first verse is taken, nor from any other work, so we suppose that it is the composer's own invention. Garcia de la Parra adds a second verse to the refrain "Naranjitas tiraba la nina / en Valencia por Navidad / pues a fe que si las tira / se les van a volver azar"[285] . In the first stanza he had already added a first verse "Donde van los suspiros" to the final three lines of the first intervention of the musicians in *El bobo del colegio* "Claros aires de Valencia / Que dais a la mar embates".

b. Exclamations: addition of exclamations at the end of a song or section. Mingote in *Canto de un mal nacer* and Turina in *Al val de Fuente Ovejuna* and *Si con mis deseos,* add an interjection "Ah" at the end of the piece, while Matilde Salvador in *Castellana* does so at the beginning of each verse and at the end of the song.

Occasionally the composer or a second person makes a free arrangement of Lope's text. All these cases have been excluded from the catalogue for obvious reasons, we are only interested in Lope's lyrics. The *Romance del comendador de Ocaiia* by Joaquin Rodrigo is the best known case. The lyrics of this work, written for voice and orchestra as well as for voice and piano, are a free adaptation by Joaquin de Entrambasaguas.

Changes of words with respect to Lope's original are frequent. The most common cause is transcription error or the use of editions or anthologies with errata. Even so, it is possible that the composer's intervention is at the origin of some changes, as is the case with Salvador Bacarisse in the song *Por el montecico,* where he changes "enamorada" for "abandonada", or that of Turina's *Cuando tan hermosa os miro* in whose last verse we read "suspiro por mi deseo" instead of "suspira por mi el deseo" which we find in Lope. In this same poem Jose Maria Franco Bordons in *A...l.i,* writes the last line as in Lope, but changes the first line, "cuando tu hermosura miro" and modifies the penultimate "si no te veo" instead of "y cuando no os veo", because he changes the treatment, the voseo for the tuteo.

MUSICAL ELEMENTS

VOCAL EXTENSION

We will consider here the amplitude of the melodic line of the voice, rather than the tessituras in which the songs move, since, as has happened in our case, the transport of the songs to adapt to the different vocal categories relativises the concept of tessitura. From the reduced sixth range of Manuel Garaa's *La barca de Amor*, to the compromised seventeenth minor required by Francisco Escudero in his atonal piece *Al entierro de Cristo*, we find all kinds of extensions. The following graph shows that the range with the highest number of cases (52%) is from the octave to the eleventh:

Figure 6: Melodic extension of the vocal part of the songs.

Vocal extension

[283] "Alegria zagales / valles y montes, / que el zagal de Maria / ya tiene nombre". ALIN, Jos6 Maria, *Cancionero teairal..., op. cit*, p. 414.

[284] "No corrais vientecillos / con tanta prisa / porque al son de las aguas / duerme mi nina", and "Mariquita me llaman / los carreteros, / mariquita me llaman, / voyme con ellos". These verses could be by Garcia Lorca, since Nin-Culmell, as he himself notes in the preface to Max Eschig's 1998 edition, an edition which was never published, takes the lyrics for his *Canciones de La Barraca* from a notebook by Federico preserved by Luis Saenz de la Calzada and Angel Barja with pieces sung in the company's performances. See the observations on this song in our catalogue, Appendix I.

[285] The text of the refrain is also modified by Garcia de la Parra with respect to Lope: "Naranjitas me tira la nina / En Valencia por Navidad; / Pues a fe que si se las tiro, / Que se le han de volver azahar".

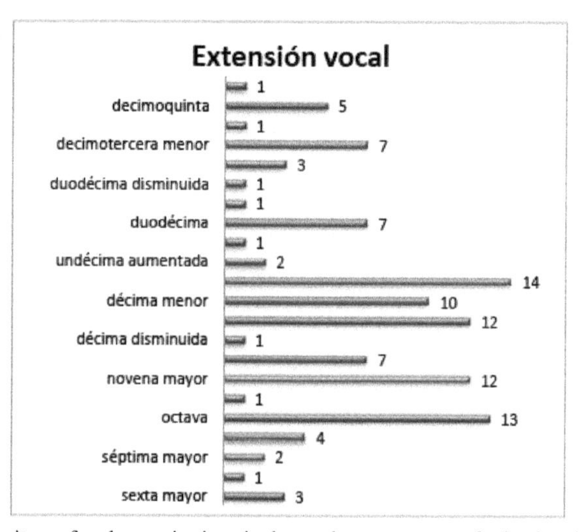

The absolute tessitura of each song is given in the catalogue as a way of orienting the reader to the vocal requirements of each work. This indication can give us an idea of the vocal category for which they were written, as in very few cases is it stated in the score. 20 songs are annotated with the voice type for which the composer wrote them: 3 for soprano *(Al entero de Cristo* by Francisco Escudero; *A la muerte de Jesus* by Jose Luis Iturralde; *Por el montecico sola* by Manuel Palau), 3 for mezzo-soprano (*Tres poemas religiosos* by Eduardo Rincon), 2 for countertenor (*A mis soledades voy* and *A la noche* by Voro Garcia), 1 for tenor *(Celos, que no me matais* by Julio Gomez), 9 for baritone *(Mananicas de mayo* and *Tonadila navidena* by Vicente Miguel, *Soneto* by Miquel Ortega, *Cuatro sonetos* by Diaz Yerro, *La Verdad* and*('Qi.ic tengo yo que mi amistadprocuras?* by Julio Gomez), 2 as a soprano and mezzo-soprano duo *(Ausencia* by Victor Carbajo, *Copla by* Salvador Bacarisse). In addition to these, 3 note the possibility of being sung by soprano or tenor *(Plegaria a Cristo crucfcado* and *La oracion de Cristo en el Huerto* by Larroca and *Madre, unos ojuelos vi* by Menendez Aleyxandre), in 4 others there is confusion as to the vocal type according to the various manuscripts which have been preserved of them (*Castellana, Gallega* y *Levantna* by Matilde Salvador and *A...t by* Jose Maria Franco). In 5 songs the composer opts for the aseptic and obvious "voice and piano", which is really the destiny of this type of work, given the possibilities of transporting them and of interpreting male or female texts by singers of either sex indistinctly.

SHADE

The tonal treatment of most of the songs, 86 cases (80%), follows the procedures of traditional tonality, with the stylistic differences of each composer. In 10 songs the tonality is enriched with different harmonic and modulatory resources that broaden the possibilities of the composition, even though the tonal centre is clarified at the points that each composer considers appropriate. The years of composition of these works to which we refer here show that the recourse to extending the limits of tonality extends in the songs that we catalogue from 1935, the year in which we find songs by Casal Chapi, del Campo and Turina in which harmonic, modal and formal procedures are used that go beyond the strict tonal ambit without abandoning its coordinates, to those composed in the 21st century, such as the *Tres poemas religiosos* by Eduardo Rincon *(*2004) or the two songs by Vicente Miguel Peris (2009), including the songs by Matilde Salvador in 1939, the sonnet *Quien no sabe de amor set to* music by Salvador Bacarisse in 1943, or the songs by Manuel Palau (1951) and Jose Peris (1955).

Arturo Menendez Aleyxandre in his song *Lucinda,* and Joaquin Rodrigo in *Coplas del pastor enamorado*, work with several tonal centres without any of them being the main one, generating an intended effect of ambiguity. While Rodrigo's work was composed in its entirety in 1935, Menendez's was composed in 1932, although it underwent two subsequent revisions by its creator, in 1943 and 1982, without us being able to know the extent to which these revisions affected the final result. A similar approach is that of Victor Carbajo Cardenas with *Ausencia (*1999), a duo for soprano and mezzo-soprano in which he employs a diatonic language organised by sections without supports or defined tonal relationships.
Another of the resources used in the 20th century to weaken and/or extend the possibilities of tonal language is the use of modal organisations. In the catalogue there are 9 songs that resort to this procedure, five based on the Phrygian mode, *Riberitas hermosas* by Jose Maria Guervos, *Cancion de siega* by Antonio Barrera, *Celos, que no me matais* by Julio Gomez, and the sonnets by Enrique Casal Chapi and Miquel Ortega. The latter two go beyond the tonal-modal organisation with the use of different harmonic and modulatory resources that enrich and at the same time weaken the tonal hierarchy. It is worth remembering that the composition of these two songs, those of Casal and Ortega, are separated by a period of 70 years, from 1935 to 2005. On the other hand Gonzalo Diaz Yerro writes his *Cuatro sonetos*, from 1998-1999, using complex special modes generated by the composer himself[286] .
The free use of sounds without following a defined system of tonal relationships is present in three works. Francisco Escudero wrote *Al entierro de Cristo* in 1974, for soprano voice and piano, developing a complicated and demanding score for both voice and piano. The vocal register is the widest of all, a seventeenth that goes from A2 to C5, and the piano is deployed in three staves without compass indications in wide intervalic leaps that include *clusters and* other non-conventional graphic resources. Voro Garcia Fernandez's works *A la noche* and *A mis soledades voy (*both from 2011), with highly virtuosic writing and abundant phonetic effects, are also atonal in their approach. It should also be remembered that in 1962 the Catalan composer and critic Josep Casanovas i Puig wrote a work in atonal style which has not been located.

MUSICAL WORKS

TITLES. COLLECTIONS

The titles that composers give to songs are usually related to the verses of the text. We group the following cases:

1. Title outside the text: out of a total of 68 (62%)

a. 38 songs take the first verse in full

b. 12 of a part of the first verse

c. 21 use another verse or part of a verse, different from the first one

2. Taken from a title by Lope: in three songs the composer uses the same title given by Lope to his poem, *A la muerte de Jesus* de Iturralde, *Al entierro de Cristo* de Escudero and *A la noche* de Garcia Fernandez. *Lo fingido verdadero* de Guervos coincides with the title of the comedy from which it is taken.

3. Taken from the comedy to which the fragment belongs: *Foli'a yparabien de unos recien casados* de Thomas, from the internal title with which Lope heads the refrain at the wedding of *Peribanez and the Comendador de Ocana.*

4. Title invented by the composer, although related to the text: in 36 songs (33%) the composer invents a title which, although evidently related to the lyrics, is not taken directly from them.

5. Title invented by the composer, unrelated to the text: 33 songs (30%)

a. Poetic or musical expressions (Trova, Cancion, Cantarcillo, Copla, Coplas, Danza, Cancion de amor, Seguidillas, Elegia, Leyenda, Plegaria, Tonadilla and Villancico.

[286] This is how Diaz Yerro himself describes them in an e-mail communication with the author of this work [15-6-2001].

b. Denominations that have nothing to do with the text but with the musical style, such as *Gaita and Guitara* de Thomas, *Castellana, Galega and Valenciana*[287] by Matilde Salvador.

A particular case is the carol with the text "Blanca me era yo / cuando entre en la siega...", set to music by five composers, Casal Chapi, Guervos, Mingote, Barrera and Matilde Salvador. Four of them are almost coincident: *Cancion de siega, Cantar de siega, Cantar moreno de siega*, and the other that has nothing to do with the verses: la *Castellana* de Salvador. Only 13 (12%) songs have subtitles. Four of them coincide with the first verse, four others add redundant expressions such as "Cancion", "Cancion llrica", "Cancion espanola" and "Tonadilla espanola", "Villancico" or "Soliloquio". Two refer to Spanish regions, "Castilla la vieja" and "Levantina", and in one we find a subtitle in the form of a dedication with the title of the first verse: "A la muerte de Cristo nuestro Senor" (To the death of Christ our Lord).

The groups of songs[288] formed entirely from texts by Lope are the following:

Table 10: Collections of songs with texts by Lope de Vega.

<table>
<tr><th>Author</th><th colspan="2">Songs</th><th>Group's title</th></tr>
<tr><td>Joan Llongueres</td><td colspan="2">6</td><td>Six carols by Lope de Vega</td></tr>
<tr><td>Angel Mingote</td><td colspan="2">6</td><td>Canciones espanolas con textos de Lope de Vega (Spanish songs with texts by Lope de Vega)</td></tr>
<tr><td>Antonio Barrera</td><td colspan="2">5</td><td>Songs of the Golden Age</td></tr>
<tr><td>Josd Maria Benavente</td><td colspan="2">5</td><td>Christmas T'riplico by Lope de Vega</td></tr>
<tr><td>Josd Maria Guervos</td><td colspan="2">5</td><td>Five songs</td></tr>
<tr><td>Gonzalo Diaz Yerro</td><td colspan="2">4</td><td>Four sonnets</td></tr>
<tr><td>Julio Gomez</td><td colspan="2">4</td><td>Cuatro poesias liricas de Lope de Vega (Four lyric poems by Lope de Vega)</td></tr>
<tr><td>Fernando Moraleda</td><td colspan="2">4</td><td>Four songs with texts by Lope de Vega</td></tr>
<tr><td>Eduardo Rincon</td><td colspan="2">3</td><td>Three religious poems</td></tr>
<tr><td>Enrique Truan</td><td colspan="2">3</td><td>Three Christmas carols by Lope de Vega</td></tr>
<tr><td>Joaquin Turina</td><td colspan="2">3</td><td>Homage to Lope de Vega</td></tr>
<tr><td rowspan="2">Enrique Casal C 'liapi</td><td rowspan="2">5</td><td>3</td><td>Three songs by Lope de Vega</td></tr>
<tr><td>2</td><td>Two fragments of the Knight of Olmedo</td></tr>
<tr><td>Salvador Bacarisse</td><td colspan="2">2</td><td>Two cantares by Lope de Vega</td></tr>
</table>

In total there are 55 songs (50.5%) which form part of collections of songs, all of them with texts by Lope. There are 32 single songs (29.5%), and the rest, 22 (20%), belong to collections in which texts by various poets are set to music. Among these, the groups of Joan Altisent, Miguel Asins Arbo, Salvador Bacarisse, Voro Garcia Fernandez, Enrique Granados, Manuel Palau, Matilde Salvador, Joan Maria Thomas and Eduard Toldra use texts by other Golden Age poets alongside

[287] These titles referring to a Spanish region, a manifestation of nationalist assumptions, were very frequent in the first half of the 20th century, perhaps following the model of the titles given by Falla to his *Siete canciones espanolas, a* reference cycle for so many Spanish composers. Matilde Salvador herself dedicates her collection of songs, written in 1939, to "Don Manuel". The manuscript is preserved in the Instituto Valenciano de la Musica, and Salvador's work is in the process of being inventoried.

[288] We would like to note here the difficulty of speaking of a song-cycle as the concept is very broad and sometimes confusing. *The New Grove*, in the voice "song-cycle", refers to "a composition of vocal music that is made up of a group of individually complete songs, for solo or ensemble voices, with or without instrumental accompaniment. It may relate a series of events or series of impressions, or it may simply be a group of songs unified to the composer's taste. The texts may be from a single author or from several sources. In the generally accepted sense, a song cycle is a 19th century form, belonging primarily to the German Lied tradition. In any case, it has predecessors" (PEAKE, Luise Eitel, "Song-cycle", *The New Grove..., op. cit.*, vol. 17, pp. 521-422). Ruth O. Bingham exposes the difficulty of defining it and the breadth of meaning of the tërmino in: BINGHAM, Ruth O., "The early nineteenth-century song cycle", *The Cambridge Companion...*, *op. cit*, pp. 104-107. We therefore opt for the aseptic term "group of songs", unless the composer specifies otherwise.

those of Lope, while the rest, those of Benito Garcia de la Parra, Joaquin Nin-Culmell, Mercedes Carol, Jose Maria Franco, Francisco Cotarelo, Jose Luis Iturralde and Vicente Miguel and Joaquin Rodrigo, combine ancient poems with their contemporaries.

The two songs by Conrado del Campo, *Tan vivo esta en mi alma* and *Cancion de la pastora Finarda*, are the only cases in the catalogue inserted as interludes in symphonic works, although written for voice and piano. The former from the stage tableau *Una dama se vende a quien la quiera (*1935), the latter from the "evocaciones sinfonicas" entitled *Figuras de Belen (*1946).

MOTIVATIONS, ORDERS, DEDICATIONS

Of all the songs presented in the catalogue, 67 (62%) do not have a motivation stated by the composer in the score. Among the remaining songs that do, there is a large group whose composition was a consequence of the National Fine Arts Competition of 1935: Gomez, Guervos and Mingote (15 songs), and those supposedly written for this occasion by Casal Chapi and Moraleda (8 songs), a total of 23, to which should be added those by Francisco Esbri awarded in the National Competition that have not been located. Turina's triptych *Homenaje a Lope de Vega* and Conrado del Campo's song *Tan vivo esta en mi alma* were written for the Madrid Conservatory's concert-homage to Lope de Vega at the Teatro Espanol in Madrid in December 1935. Another song written for a concert was *Ay amargas soledades.* This anonymous 17th century melody from the Turin songbook[289] , was adapted and performed on piano by Felix Lavilla for a recital with other songs with lyrics by Lope de Vega which he gave accompanying the tenor Manuel Cid at the Teatro Espanol in Madrid[290] . Voro Garaa Fernandez composed his cycle *De el alma*, which includes *A la noche* and *A mis soledades voy*, commissioned by the Festival Festclasica in commemoration of the 400th anniversary of the death of T. L. De Victoria. Josep Casanovas' *Homenatge a Lope de Vega*, from 1962, now lost, was presumably written for the 4th centenary of the poet's birth.

There are several cases of academic works. Jose Peris Lacasa composed and premiered *Pobre barquilla mia* in 1952 and *Mananicas foridas* in 1955, as well as Jose Maria Benavente his *Triptco navideno de Lope de Vega,* from 1956, all of them "school exercises" at the Real Conservatorio Superior de Musica de Madrid[291] . From the academic year 1998-99 are the four sonnets by Di'az Yerro, written and premiered, also as composition class works, at the Universitat fur Musik und Darstellende Kunst in Vienna.

The *Canciones de la Barraca,* by Joaquin Nin-Culmell, two of which have lyrics by Lope and another by Tirso de Molina, although erroneously attributed to our poet by the composer, were written to set to music a notebook kept by Luis Saenz de la Calzada and Angel Barja with pieces sung in the performances of the theatre company *La Barraca* directed by Federico Garcia Lorca, to the memory of whom they are dedicated, together with the members of the theatre group and Tierry Mobilion, a friend of the composer.

Only one song is commissioned by RNE: *A enterro de Cristo* by Francisco Escudero.

Thirty of the songs are annotated with a dedication at the head of the score. Most of these are

---

[289] See QUEROL, Miquel, Cancionero musical de Lope de Vega, II. Poesias sueltas, op. cit. p. 5.

[290] The exact date and purpose of this recital are uncertain. The documentation with the details of this concert have been lost due to the fire that in 1975 destroyed, in addition to the building, the entire documentary archive. The tenor Manuel Cid, the vocal protagonist of the recital, in a telephone conversation with the author of this work (25-11-2011), informs us that the concert included works with lyrics by Lope, among them the aforementioned *Ay amargas soledades*, the two *Lieder* by Hugo Wolf, *Die ihr schwebet* and *Weint nicht, ihr Augelein*, the Brahms song *Geistliches wiegenlied,* performed with viola and piano, as in the original score, as well as other compositions by musicians of Lope's time such as Monteverdi, together with other songs with lyrics by Bertold Brecht. The reason for this concert is also unclear. It seems to have been a complementary activity to a production of a comedy by Lope de Vega. Cid also explains that the anonymous melody *Ay amargas soledades* was a favourite of Lavilla, who in those years often performed it in an arrangement, not to his liking, by Jose Maria Goma, and that Lavilla wrote it especially for this recital. The current illness of Felix Lavilla prevents us from knowing more details and contrasting the information offered by Manuel Cid.

[291] MARTINEZ DEL FRESNO, Beatriz, *Julio Gomez. Una epoca..., op. cit,* p. 509-512.

dedicated to the singers who premiered them, such as the four sonnets that Diaz Yerro dedicates to the baritone Alfredo Garcia, the *Dos cantares de Lope de Vega* by Bacarisse to the soprano Amparito Peris, who premiered and recorded them in Paris, *Lo fingido verdadero, Blancas coge Lucinda las azucenas* and *Cancion de siega,* by Guervos to Mercedes Garcia Lopez, *Copla de Anlano* by Moreno Torroba, dedicated to the Russian soprano Dagmara Renina, very active in Madrid in the twenties, *Soneto* by Miquel Ortega to the baritone Federico Gallar, *Ay, amargas soledades* by Felix Lavilla to tenor Manuel Cid, *Madre, unos ojuelos vi* by Toldra to soprano Mercedes Plantada, *Homenaje a Lope de Vega* by Turina to soprano Rosita Hermosilla, *Cancion de vela* by Matilde Salvador to the famous soprano Victoria de los Angeles, although she was not the one who premiered it, the Valencian soprano Emilia Munoz did it in the orchestral version, and finally *Los ojos verdes* by Julio Perez Aguirre, to the internationally successful baritone at the end of the 19th and beginning of the 20th century Ramon Blanchart.

Jose Maria Guervos dedicated three of his *Cinco canciones* to other teaching colleagues at the Conservatorio in Madrid: *Lo fingido verdadero* to the violinist Antonio Fernandez Bordas, *Trebole* to the Harmony professor Benito Garcia de la Parra, and *Blancas coge Lucinda las azucenas* to the aforementioned singing teacher Mercedes Garcia Lopez, who premiered it together with two other songs from the cycle, *Lo fingido verdadero* and *Cantar de siega*. The recipients of the other two remaining songs were two relatives, his sister Carmen, *Cantar de siega*, and his niece Florinda, *Riberitas hermosas*. In the same way, Fernando Colodro dedicated *Mananicas floridas* to his niece Laura, Conrado del Campo the *Cancion de la pastora Finarda* to his daughter Elsa and Voro Garcia to his wife.

Joaquin Rodrigo paid tribute to his friendship with the Spanish diplomat in Paris Aurelio Vinas by dedicating *Coplas del pastor enamorado*, and one of his most famous hits in the vocal genre, the entranable *Pastorcito Santo* to another great family friend, Dr. Jack Schermant. The personal friendship with the director of the Pontifical Institute of Sacred Music Valentin Miserachs, who acted as transmitter, was the link that made Vicente Miguel Peris dedicate *Tonadila navidena,* based on the poem "Las pajas del pesebre", to Pope Benedict XVI.

In 1939 Matilde Salvador wrote her *Six Spanish Songs*, dedicating them to Manuel de Falla, to whom she sent them with the intention of making his music known to him. She received a letter from Manuel with encouraging comments, although the trip to Argentina and the subsequent death of Falla frustrated the beginning of their professional relationship and friendship[292] . Three of the six songs, *Valenciana, Castellana, Gallega,* have lyrics by Lope, the rest have lyrics by Gil Vicente and anonymously. In this song cycle the composer from Castellón follows, like so many other composers of her time and later, the model set by Falla in his *Siete canciones populares espanolas*.

RECORDINGS. PREMIERES

The currently available recordings of songs with lyrics by Lope do not give a broad representation of the titles and composers. The 198 recordings of which we are aware in our catalogue are spread over 31 titles, so there are still 76 that are unrecorded.

Table 11: Letters with sound registers.

Title	Composer	No. of recordings
Mother, I saw some eyelets	Eduard Toldra	39
Holy Shepherd	Joaquin Rodrigo	37
Coplas del pastor enamorado		19
Cantarcillo	Eduard Toldra	19
Don't cry, you little eyes	Enrique Granados	13
When I look at you so beautiful	Joaquin Turina	13

[292] SOLBES, Rosa, Matilde Salvador, converses amb una compositora apassionada, Tandem, Castello, 2007,

Al val de Fuente Ovejuna		9
If with my wishes		9
At the burial of Christ	Francisco Escudero	4
Wash me in the Tagus	Joaquin Nin-Culmell	4
Wash me in the Tagus		3
St. John's Eve	Pascual Rodriguez	2
Oh, bitter loneliness	Felix Lavilla	2
Welcome	Joaqum Nin-Culmell	2
On the mountain alone	Salvador Bacarisse	1
That he was killed at night		1
Cantarcillo	Mercedes Carol	1
Sonnet	Enrique Casal Chap!	1
Romancillo		1
Seguidillas of the night of San Juan	Gustavo Duran	1
Christmas carol	Julio Gomez	1
Beautiful little rivers	Jose Marla Guervos	1
At the death of Jesus	Jose Luis Iturralde	1
Sonnet	Miquel Ortega i Pujol	1
On the mountain alone	Manuel Palau	1
Flowering mannikins	Jose Peris Lacasa	1
Most sweet Lord, I was blind	Eduardo Rincon	1
Flowering mannikins		1
What do I have that you seek my friendship?		1
Guitar	Joan Maria Thomas	1
Flowering mannikins	Enrique Truan	1

The table above shows that the eight most frequently recorded songs, those by Toldra, Rodrigo, Granados and Turina, account for 75% of the records available to date. Among them there are two songs, *Madre, unos ojuelos v* by Toldra and *Pastorate Santo* by Rodrigo, which stand out notably from the rest, with 39%. Of all the recordings currently available, 117 are Radio National de Espana takes preserved in their sound archive, 69 are modern recordings or remasterings on CD, 8 are preserved on LP or cassette, and 1 on tape.

We only know of the release of 36 of the 109 songs. Among these, we know of the premiere of *Celos, que no me matais* by Julio Gomez but not the date. Comparing the list of songs premiered in public concert with the previous table of recordings, we have to add to this number those that have at least been premiered directly in a recording.

ATTRIBUTED, EXCLUDED AND LOST

Although we have not included in the catalogue the songs with lyrics attributed to Lope, we would like to give notice of them in order to avoid future confusion, since by mistake they appear in the score or in the catalogue cards of the archives or libraries where these songs are preserved.

1. The oldest is by J. Ramon Gomis[293] , entitled *Yo.... ¿para que naci?* with a poem by Fray Pedro de los Reyes[294] [295] [296] , published by Almagro y Cia. around 1900. The score includes the

[293] Born in 1856, died in 1939. A copy of the score is in the BNE.

[294] Edward M. Wilson in an article on the religious poetry of Miguel Barrios tells us: "His poem *Real consideration del hombre* is the gloss of an *octave* which begins: "Yo,('para que naci? Para salvarme..."' According to Lope de Vega, this stanza was written by Fray Pedro de los Reyes; it has been learned off by heart by thousands of Spanish Roman-Catholic children ." [His poem *Real consideracion del hombre* is a gloss on an octave which begins: "Yo,(q>para que naci? para salvarme." [I, what was I born for? to save myself]. According

subtitle "Pensamiento de Lope de Vega".

2. Emilio Lopez de Saa Paramo composed in December 1979 the song *La nina blanccE,* whose text he attributes to Lope. The expression "nina blanca" or "blanca nina" appears in some works by Lope and his contemporaries. We find it in the song "*E Arauco domado* Jerizaua piragua" (Manuel Garcia wrote a song with this text around 1818), in *Pastores de Belen, Rimas sacras* and *La madre de la mejor*[9]. Margit Frenk finds "Que despertad, la nina blanca,..." in Velez de Guevara and in Lope's *El labrador de Tormes*, as well as in Madrigal's Romancero[297], which gives us an idea of the popularity of the expression, but in none of the cases mentioned does the text coincide with that of Lopez de Saa's song[298].

3. Joaquin Nin-Culmell composed the song "La Mari-Juana"[299] wrongly attributing the lyrics to Lope de Vega: "La Mari-Juana, la que cantaba, / bebia vino, se emborrachaba / y a su nino tetica le daba". These lyrics coincide exactly with those written down in a notebook that Garcia Lorca wrote with some of the lyrics of the songs he devised for La Barraca[300]. Garcia Lorca, with his company, performed Tirso de Molina's *El burlador de Sevilla* in Santander and Zamora. For the wedding scene of Aminta and Batricio he staged a popular wedding with music[301], including a song with the same text as Nin's song.

The work *Romance del comendador de Ocana* was originally written by Joaquin Rodrigo for soprano and orchestra in 1947. There is a version for voice and piano by the composer himself, but the text is not entirely by Lope. Joaquin de Entrambasaguas reworks several fragments of *Peribanez,* using as a basis the verses of Casilda's intervention in Act II, "Labrador de lejas tierras,..." (vv. 1554-1617) and of the song sung by a reaper towards the end of the same act (vv. 1918-1929), which contains the romance considered to be the germ of the tragicomedy[302]:

More I want Peribanez
with its cape the pardilla,
that to the Commander of Ocana
with his own garrisoned.

Entrambasaguas's intervention in Lope's original is remarkable, changing places, cutting and

---

to Lope, this couplet was written by Fray Pedro de los Reyes, and has been learnt by heart by thousands of Spanish Catholic children.... (translation by the author)]. WILSON, Edward M., "Miguel de Barrios and Spanish religious poetry", *Bulletin of Hispanic Studies,* 40, 1963, p. 177.

[295] The handwritten score is preserved in the FJM library under the call number M-2544-B. Composed in December 1979, it is subtitled "cancion lirica" and is dedicated "A mi hija Iris". There is a 1982 recording on a Columbia LP, CS 8589, sung by Dolores Cava, with the composer himself at the piano.

[296] CORDE recovers 6 cases of "blanca nina" and 22 of "nina blanca" by different authors between 1550 and 1650. Real Academia Espanola, Corpus Diacronico del Espanol [online], <http://corpus.rae.es/cordenet.html> [accessed: 6-10-2011].

[297] FRENK, Margit, *New corpus*, *op. cit.* p. 738.

[298] "(T)o where does the white girl go in the morning / If the snow has set on the mountain / When the white girl goes up to the mountains / In streams the snow flees in envy / Don't run in such a hurry / Because to the sound of the waters the girl sleeps / The girl sleeps, jjAy!

[299] *La Mari-Juana,* No. 2 of *Canciones de La Barraca,* by Joaquin Nin-Culmell [iredita].

[300] Mentioned above, it is the one preserved by Luis Saenz de la Calzada and Angel Barja, with which Nin-Culmell composed the *Canciones de La Barraca.*

[301] AUCLAIR, Marcelle, *Vida y Muerte de Garcia Lorca,* Era, Mexico, 1972, p. 258. The author reports that "for the wedding of Aminta and Batricio the violins played with a devilish rhythm, the dances were inspired by Andalusian dances and the songs bordered on the picaresque: "La Marijuana, la que cantaba / Bebia su vino, se emborrachaba, / y a su nino tetica le daba. / She went to the orchard / to cut sprigs of verbena / and you go out, and you go out, / and you go out, I want to see you / jumping and jumping...". Luis Saenz de la C alzada, recounting the wedding of Aminta and Batricio from *El Burlador de Sevilla* in Lorca's staging, recalls: "This time we had violin accompaniment, as Carmelo Risoto and Mario Etcheverri knew how to play such instruments. Songs and dances. [.]"; and also: "La Marijuana / la que cantaba / bebia vino / siempre bailaba / y a su nino tëtica le daba. And the dancers took turns. And you go out, I want to see her / jump and leap and walk in the air [.]". SAENZ DE LA CALZADA, Luis, "*La Barraca*, Teatro Universitario", *Revista de Occidente*, Madrid, 1976, p.80-81.

[302] BLECUA, Alberto; SALVADOR, Gerardo, prologue to the edition of *Peribanez y el comendador de Ocana*, Prolope, part IV, vol. I, p. 415.

adding verses, changing, adding or altering the position of some words, which is why we took the decision to exclude it from the catalogue. We also exclude the versions for voice and piano of the arias from the zarzuela *El hijo fingido* which Rodrigo wrote between 1955 and 1960, as they are also adaptations by Victoria Kamhi and Jesus de Arozamena from reworked fragments of the comedies*(D)c cuando aca nos vino?* and *Los ramilletes de Madrid.*

The following songs have not been located in any of the numerous archives and libraries reviewed for the preparation of the catalogue. We know of their existence from references to them in some published catalogues of composers such as those of the SGAE, the catalogues published with the works published or premiered in Spain used to compile the catalogue[303] , as well as comments in manuals and studies on the history of Spanish music or monographs of composers, and as many books and articles as we have consulted. As we do not have the scores to extract the necessary data from them, we have excluded them from the catalogue.

1. Miguel Asins Arbo: *Aegres pastores.* According to the SGAE catalogue[304] it is from 1963, and belongs to the collection *Cuatro villancicos sobre textos antiguos*, which includes: I. Alegres mudanzas (text by Joaquin de Hinojosa, II. Alegres mudanzas (text by Joaquin de Hinojosa), II. Alegres pastores (Lope de Vega), III. Este nino se lleva la flor (text by Jose de Valdivieso), IV. Mananicas floridas (Lope de Vega). The doctoral thesis of Jose Miguel Sanz Garcia[305] , "Miguel Asins Arbo: Musica y cinematografia. Analisis musico-visual de sus composiciones en la filmografia de Luis Garcia Berlanga", includes a catalogue of the composer in which it is said that the score is in the SGAE, however it does not appear registered in this Society. Neither this song nor the collection to which it supposedly belongs can be found in the Miguel Asins Arbo Archive, belonging to the Valencian Library, where the composer's family archive has been deposited.
2. Josep Casanovas Puig: *Homenatge a Lope de Vega.* Written in 1962, in the year of the IV Centenary, we do not know if the text of the song is by Lope or if it is a text by another pen written in his homage. Unfortunately we have not been able to locate the score, being a work of importance both for the date of composition and for being a composition that follows the principles of atonality, an infrequent characteristic in our catalogue.
3. Luis Coello: *Cancion de Cuna.* This is an academic work from Julio Gomez's composition class at the Madrid Conservatory. Premiered in a concert of composition students on 17-12-1956[306 307] .
4. Arturo Duo Vital: *Alamos delprado*[M] .
5. Francisco Esbri: collection of songs with texts by Lope de Vega awarded in the National Competition of 1935[308] .
6. Ernesto Halffter: *Efectos de amor*, from 1940. Unfinished song, part of an unfinished composition project entitled *Cinco canciones de amor*, from 1940, consisting of *Efectos de amor*

---

303 Essentially: ACKER, Yolanda; ALFONSO, M.ª de los Angeles; ORTEGA, Judith; PEREZ CASTILLO, Belen (eds.), *Archivo historico de la Union Musical Espanola, partituras, metodos, librettos y libros*, Instituto Complutense de Ciencias Musicales (ICCMU), Madrid, 2000; GOSALVEZ LARA, Carlos Jose, *La edicion musical espanola hasta 1936*, AEDOM, Madrid, 1995; GUTIERREZ DORADO, Pilar; MARCOS PATINO, Cristina (Coords.), *20 anos de estrenos de musica: 1985-2004* (CD-ROM), Centro de Documentation de Musica y Danza, Madrid, 2004; IGLESIAS, Nieves (dir.), *La musica en el Boletin de la Propiedad Intelectual 1847-1915*, Biblioteca Nacional, Madrid, 1997.

304 ACKER, Yolanda, SUAREZ-PAJARES, Javier, *Miguel Asms Arbo,* SGAE, Madrid, 1995.

303 SANZ GARCIA, Jose Miguel, Miguel Asins Arbo: Musica y cinematografia. Analisis musico-visual de sus composiciones en la filmografia de Luis Garcia Berlanga, Tesis doctoral, Universitat de Valencia, Valencia, 2008, p. 692.

306 As mentioned above, Martinez del Fresno annotates the programmes of all the academic concerts given by Julio Gomez's students at the Madrid Conservatory. MARTINEZ DEL FRESNO, Beatriz, *Julio Gomez. Una epoca..., op. cit.,* p. 509-512.

307 Work from 1951. It has not been possible to locate it. The catalogue of this composer's works warns that it is out of the catalogue: LASTRA CALERA, Julia, *Arturo Dlio Vital,* Catalogos de compositores, Fundacion Autor, Madrid, 1999, p. 88: TINNELL, Roger, *Catalogo anotado, op. cit.* p.494.

308 See section 3.2.4 of Chapter III.

(Lope de Vega), *Cancion de Dorotea (*Cervantes) and *Tres redondillas* (Camoens)[309] .
7. Anton Garcia Abril: *Mananicas foridas.* According to a conversation with the composer, this song was an academic work from Julio Gomez's composition class at the Madrid Conservatory. He does not keep it in his personal archive[310] .
8. Fernando Moraleda Bellver: *Soneto,* from 1935. It is no longer extant. It was part of *Cuatro canciones con textos de Lope de Vega,* together with *Chanzoneta, Dicha* and *Pobre barqula mia.* From the date and place of composition, indicated next to the composer's signature at the end of the handwritten copy of the three surviving ones, "Madrid, September 1935", from the number of works in the group, and from the author of the lyrics, it could be a group of songs written for the National Fine Arts Competition[311] . The three songs that have survived bear indications in red pencil at the head of each: *Chanzoneta,* "n° 9", *Dicha,* "N° 10/ copiar en parte de apuntar", and *Pobre barqula mia,* "n° 9", which leads us to suppose that Moraleda may have subsequently used these pieces in some of the numerous theatrical performances for which he was responsible for the incidental music due to his professional relationships with different companies and theatres in Madrid. It could be that *Soneto* was lost when he took out the sheets on which it was written for the rehearsals or performance of a hypothetical performance in which it was used. In all probability Moraleda took the texts of the first three songs from an anthology of poems by authors of the Golden Age published in 1917[312] . This includes eleven poems by Lope de Vega, some of which are titled by the editor. Two of them, *Dicha and Chanzoneta, are* set to music by Moraleda, who titles them in the same way, from which we deduce that the composer took the lyrics from the anthology, as these titles are not by Lope and are not found in any other collection. It is quite possible that the one entitled *Soneto,* untraceable at the moment, was one of the five poems in this poetic form collected there, which begin with "Agradar al discrete, al mas mirado", "No es tan robusta sobre el alta sierra", "Rompe una pena el agua cuando estriba", "Halla con lengua, lagrimas y ruego" or "Ya solo de mi engano me sustento". The fourth song of the group, *Pobre barquila mi'a, a* fragment of *La Dorotea,* is not in this anthology, and is the only one that has the title of the first verse, written between brackets.
9. Jose Munoz Molleda: *No lloreis Virgenpiadosa.* The SGAE catalogue states that the score is preserved in the family archive[313] . However, the score is not among those catalogued by Gemma

---

[309] ACKER, Yolanda, "Ernesto Halffter: a study of years 1905-1946", *Revista de musicologa,* Vol. 17, N° 1-2, 1994, p. 168. See also GAN QUESADA, German, "Variaciones sobre el tema cervantino en la musica de la familia Halffter", *Cervantes y el Quijote en la musica estudios sobre la recepcion de un mito,* Lolo, Begona (ed.), Centro Estudios Cervantinos, Madrid, 2007, pp. 387-388.
[310] Fernando Cabanas notes the title as *Mananicas de mayo,* for soprano and piano, from 1955, warning that it is out of the catalogue. CABANAS ALEMAN, Fernando J., *Anton Garcia Abril. Sonidos en lbertad,* ICCMU, Madrid, 1993, p. 167.
[311] We follow here the arguments put forward, in relation to the National Competition, in the study of Casal Chapi's songs.
[312] *Poesias ineditas de Herrera el Divino, Quevedo, Lope de Vega, Argensola (Lupercio), Gongora, Marques de Urena y Samaniego, Maria Gertrudis Hore, Alvaro Cubillo de Aragon, Juan de Matos Fragoso, Cristobal del Castillejo, Luis Galvez de Montalvo, Zaida poetisa morisca), Tirso de Molna, Baltasar de Acazar,* Editorial America, Madrid, 1917. The introduction to the book states that the poems by Lope de Vega included in the volume are taken from codice 3.985 [BNE, MSS/3985, from the Duque de Uceda]. These are: "Era Ines de Gil querida", the sonnet "Agradar al discreto, al mas mirado", *Dicha':* "jQ.ue poco duran las dichas!", the *Trozo de comedian* "Y en tres noches, Diana", *Clianzoneta'.* "Oh, my fellows! What I see", *Dilinas manos de Cloris.* "Clori, whose white hand", *La puerta del alma':* "Por verte a ti, senora", and the sonnets "No es tan robusta sobre el alta sierra", "Rompe una pena el agua cuando estriba", "Halla con lengua, lagrimas y ruego" and "Ya solo de mi engano me sustento" (pp. 63-84). Those with titles, this is the publisher's title. The 17th-century manuscript, MSS/3985, with the title *Poesias diversas,* comes from the library of the Duke of Uceda, and contains poems by Martin de Urbina, Luis de Ulloa Pereira, Bartolome Leonardo de Argensola, Figueroa, Paravicino, Francisco de la Cueva, Gongora, Fabbio, Lope de Vega, Quevedo, Salinas, Juan de Rojas, Luis de Resa, Esquivel, Fr. Ignacio de Vitoria, Melchor de la Sema... y anonimas. Biblioteca Nacional, *Inventario General de Manuscritos de la BNE,* vol. X, Madrid, 1953-2001, p. 233. [Online version].
[313] GARCIA EST'EFANIA, Alvaro, *Jose Munoz Molleda,* Catalogos de Compositores, Fundacion Autor, Madrid, 2000, p. 33.

Perez Zalduondo in her study of the composer[314], compiled from that archive. Composed in 1978, it was commissioned by RNE, premiered at the Casa de la Radio on 3-3-1978 by Pura Maria Martinez and Rogelio Rodriguez Gavilanes[315]. The work is registered in the SGAE but there is no copy of it, only a few bars of the cipher, as was the custom when it came to small-scale works.

10. Jose Peris Lacasa: *Pobre barquila mi'a.* This song, the result of his academic work with Julio Gomez at the Madrid Conservatory, is not in his personal archive, according to the composer himself,[316]. It was premiered on 21-5-1952 by Teresa Berganza in a concert of academic exercises at the same conservatory.[317]

11. Eduardo Rincon: *Cogiome a tu puerta el toro,* from 1964. The author, in an e-mail conversation, informs us that it is one of the first songs he composed, but it has disappeared.

12. Eduardo Martinez Torner: *La nina a quien dio el angel* and *Psare yo el polvico,* mentioned by Tinnell[318], are not in the Archivo de Musica de Asturias, where his work is preserved.

---

[314] PEREZ ZALDUONDO, Gemma, El compositor Jose Munoz Molleda. De la Generation del 27 al franquismo, Zejel, Almeria, 1989.

[315] There is a recording in the RNE archive. The duration is 6' 10".

[316] Jose Peris Lacasa kindly gave us a copy of another song from his personal archive that we did catalogue, *Mananicas floridas,* also from his student days.

[317] MARTINEZ DEL FRESNO, Beatriz, *Julio Gomez. Una epoca..., op. cit* p. 509-512.

[318] TINNELL, Roger, *Catalogo anotado..., op. cit.,* p. 497.

Sources and Bibliography

LITERARY SOURCES

Poesias ineditas de Herrera el Divino, Quevedo, Lope de Vega, Argensola (Lupercio), Gongora, Marques de Urena y Samaniego, Maria Gertrudis Hore, Alvaro Cubillo de Aragon, Juan de Matos Fragoso, Cristobal del Castillejo, Luis Galvez de Montalvo, Zaida (Moorish poetess), Tirso de Molina, Baltasar de Alcazar, Editorial America, Madrid, 1917.

VEGA CARPIO, Lope Felix de, *La buena guarda,* ed. by Maria del Carmen Artigas, Verbum, Madrid, 2002.

La esclava de su galan, Editorial Estampa, Madrid, 1935.

— --*El caballero de Olmedo*, ed. by Jose Manuel Blecua, Ebro, Zaragoza, 1968.

— --*El caballero de Olmedo*, ed. by Rafael Maestre, Aguaclara, Alicante, 1992.

— --*El caballero de Olmedo*, ed. by Alfredo Hermenegildo, Salamanca, Colegio de Espana, 1992.

— --*El Caballero de Olmedo*, ed. by F. Rico, Catedra, Madrid, 2002.

— --, Coleccion escogida de obras no dramaticas de Frey Lope Felix de Vega Carpio, ed. by Cayetano Rosell, Rivadeneyra, Madrid, 1856.

— --, *Comedias*, ed. by Grupo ProLope, Milenio, Lleida, 1997- [So far the first ten parts have been published].

— --, *La Dorotea*, ed. by Edwin S. Morby, Castalia-University of California Press, Madrid-Berkley, 1968.

— --*La esclava de su galan*, Editorial Estampa, Madrid, 1935.

---*Lo fingido verdadero*, ed. by Mariateresa Cattaneo, Bulzoni Editore, Rome, 1992.

Fuente Ovejuna, ed. by Donald McGrady, Critica, Barcelona, 1993.

---*Fuente Ovejuna*, ed. by Rinaldo Froldi, Madrid, Espasa Calpe, 1995.

Fuente Ovejuna, ed. by Juan Maria Marin, Catedra, Madrid, 1981.

Obras de Lope de Vega publicadas por la Real Academia Espanola, ed. by Marcelino Menendez Pelayo, 15 vols, Rivadeneyra, Madrid, 1890-1913.

Obras de Lope de Vega , ed. by Emilio Cotarelo y Mori, 13 vols., RAE, Tipografia de la "Revista de Arch., Bibl. y Museos", Madrid, 1916-1930.

Shepherds of Bethlehem, ed. by Antonio Carreno, PPU, Barcelona, 1991.

Peribanez y el comendador de Ocana , ed. by Donald McGrady, Critica, Barcelona, 2002.

---*Peribanez y el comendador de Ocana,* ed. by Teresa Ferrer, Biblioteca Virtual Miguel de Cervantes, 2002.

---, *Peribanez y el comendador de Ocana,* ed. by Felipe B. Pedraza, PPU, Barcelona, 1988. Pedraza, PPU, Barcelona, 1988.

Rimas Sacras [facsimile edition], Joaquin de Entrambasaguas (ed.), Consejo Superior de Investigaciones Cientficas, Madrid, 1963.

Rimas , ed. by Jose Manuel Blecua, Planeta, Madrid, 1983.

— --, *Rimas*, ed. by Felipe B. Pedraza, University of Castilla-La Mancha, Cuenca, Cuenca, 2 vols. Pedraza, University of Castilla-La Mancha, Cuenca, 19931994, 2 vols.

Rimas divinas y humanas dellicenciado Tome de Burguiilos, ed. by Macarena Cuinas Gomez, Catedra, Madrid, 2008.

Rimas humanas y otros versos , ed. by Antonio Carreno, Critica, Barcelona, 1998.

— --, *Rimas sacras*, ed. by Antonio Carreno and Antonio Sanchez Jimenez, Iberoamericana-Vervuert, Madrid-Frankfurt am Main, 2007.

MUSICAL SOURCES

HANDWRITTEN SCORES

CAMPO y ZABALETA, Conrado del, *Una dama se vende a quien la quiera*, manuscript score, SGAE, Box 8.51.

GOMEZ GARCIA, Julio, *Cuatro poesias liricas de Lope de Vega,* manuscript, Biblioteca

Nacional de Espana, sig. MP/5352/1.
(Que tengo yo que mi amistad procuras?) , manuscript, Biblioteca Fundacion Juan March, sig. M-766-A.
— --, *La Verdad*, manuscript, Biblioteca Fundacion Juan March, sig. M-767-A.
— --, *Villancico*, manuscript, Biblioteca Fundacion Juan March, sig. M-771-A.
— --, *Villancico*, manuscript, Biblioteca Fundacion Juan March, sig. M-772-A.
— --, *Celos, que no me matais*, manuscript, Biblioteca Fundacion Juan March, sig. M-768-A.
Celos, que no me matais, manuscript, Biblioteca Fundacion Juan March, sig. M-769-A.
— --, *Celos, que no me matais*, manuscript, Biblioteca Fundacion Juan March, sig. M-770-A.
MINGOTE, Angel, *Canciones espanolas con textos de Lope de Vega,* manuscript, Archivo Emilio Reina, Zaragoza, sig. ERG 88 A1.
MORALEDA, Fernando, *Cuatro canciones con textos de Lope de Vega,* manuscript score, Biblioteca Nacional de Espana, sig. M.MORALEDA/9.

EDITED SCORES

ALONSO, Celsa (ed.), Manuel Garcia (1775-1832). Canciones y caprichos liricos, ICCMU, SGAE, Madrid, 1994.
ALTISENT, Joan, Seis canciones inspiradas sobre poesias espanolas de la Edad Media y del Renacimiento, A. Boileau y Bernasconi, Barcelona, 1951.
BARRERA, Antonio, *Canciones del Siglo de Oro*, Real Musical, Madrid, 1986.
CAROL, Mercedes [Mercedes Garcia Lopez], *Cinco canciones [Five songs],* Union Musical Espanola, Madrid, 1964.
CASAL CHAPI, Enrique, *Dos fragmentos del caballero de Olmedo,* Ediciones del Consejo Central de la Musica, Barcelona, 1938.
Tres cantares de Lope de Vega , Ediciones del Consejo Central de la Musica, Barcelona, 1938.
ESCUDERO, Francisco, *Al entierro de Cristo*, Alpuerto, Madrid, 1975.
FALLA, Manuel de, *Siete Canciones populares espanolas,* Ediciones Manuel de Falla, Madrid, 1998.
GARCIA DE LA PARRA y TELLEZ, Benito, *Cancionero espanol, cuaderno primero,* Juan Bta. Pujol Editores, Barcelona, [1943].
GRANADOS, Enric, *Obra completa para voz y piano,* ed. by Manuel Garcia Morante, Trito, Barcelona, 1996.
GUERVOS y MIRA, Jose Maria, *Cinco canciones,* Union Musical Espanola, Madrid, 1936.
LARROCA, Angel, *Plegaria a Cristo crucificado*, Jaime Piles, Valencia, [1940].
LAVILLA, Felix, *Ay, amargas soledades*, Real Musical, Madrid, 1988.
LLONGUERES BADIA, Joan, *Seis villancicos de Lope de Vega*, DINSIC, 2002.
MENENDEZ ALEYXANDRE, Arturo, *Madre, unos ojuelos vi,* Barcelona, Talleres Jose Mora, Barcelona, 1944.
MORENO TORROBA, Federico, *Copla de antano,* Copla de antano, Union Musical Espanola, Madrid, 1923.
PALAU, Manuel, *Seis Lieder (Six Lieder,* Institute). Valenciano de Musicologia, Institution Alfonso el Magnanimo, Piles, Valencia, 1953.
— --, *Villancico*, Piles, Valencia, 1974.
PEREZ AGUIRRE, Julio, *Los ojos verdes*, Sociedad Anonima Casa Dotesio, Barcelona, [1901-1914].
RODRIGO, Joaquin, *Romance del Conde Ocana,* Ediciones Joaquin Rodrigo, Madrid, 1995.
Album centenario canto y piano , Ediciones Joaquin Rodrigo, Madrid, 1999.
— --, Cuatro madrigales amatorios, Chester Music, 2007.
SALVADOR, Matilde, *Cancion de vela,* Piles, Valencia, 1947.
THOMAS, Juan Maria, *Canciones espanolas de instrumentos,* Ediciones Capella Classica,

Mallorca, 1944.
TOLDRA, Eduard, *Seis canciones,* Union Musical Espanola, Madrid, 1992.
TURINA, Joaquin, *Homenaje a Lope de Vega,* Union Musical Espanola, Madrid, 1992.Bibliografia
ACKER, Yolanda, "Ernesto Halffter: a study of years 1905-1946", *Revista de musicologia,* vol. 17, N° 1-2, 1994, pp. 97-176.
ACKER, Yolanda; SUAREZ-PAJARES, Javier, *Miguel Asins Arbo,* SGAE, Madrid, 1995.
ACKER, Yolanda; ALFONSO, Mª de los Angeles; ORTEGA, Judith; PEREZ CASTILLO, Belen (eds.) *Archivo historico de la Union Musical Espanola, partituras, metodos, libretos y libros,* Institute Complutense de Ciencias Musicales (ICCMU), Madrid, 2000.
ALIX, Jose Maria, "Sobre el 'Cancionero' teatral de Lope de Vega: las canciones embebidas y otros problemas", *Lope de Vega y los origenes del teatro espanol: actas del I Congreso Internacional sobre Lope de Vega,* 1981, pp. 533-40.
ALIN, Jose Maria; BARRIO ALONSO, Maria Begona, *Cancionero teatral de Lope de Vega,* Tamesis, London, 1997.
ALMEIDA, Pedro, "Gustavo Duran (1906-1969): Preludio inconcluso de la generation musical de la Republica. Apuntes para una biografia", *Revista de Musicologia,* vol. IX / 2, 1986, pp. 511-42.
ALONSO, Celsa, "Felip Pedrell y la cancion culta con acompanamiento en la Espana decimononica: la dificil convivencia de lo popular y lo culto", *Recerca Musicologica,* XIXII, 1991-1992, pp. 305-328.
La cancion espanola desde la monarqui'a fernandina a la restauracion alfonsina", *La musica espanola en el siglo XIX,* Universidad de Oviedo, 1995.
Canciones y musicos asturianos: entre dos siglos", *Canciones de dentro: musica asturiana para voz y piano,* Caja de Asturias, Fundacion Principe de Asturias, Consejeria de Cultura del Principado de Asturias, Oviedo, 1996, pp. 21-53.
Cancion lrica espanola en el siglo XIX, Institute Complutense de Ciencias Musicales, Madrid, 1998.
La poesi'a prebecqueriana y becqueriana: un fermento del lied espanol", *Homenaje a Jose Maria Martinez Cachero,* Universidad de Oviedo, 2000, pp. 41-61.
(ed.), *Cien anos de cancion lirica espanola (I): 1800-1868,* Institute Complutense de Ciencias Musicales, Madrid, 2001.
ALONSO, Miguel, *Catalogo de obras de Conrado del Campo,* Fundacion Juan March, Centro de Documentacion de la Musica Espanola Contemporanea, Madrid, 1986.
ALVAR, Carlos (dir.), *Gran Enciclopedia Cervantina,* 8 vols., Centro de Estudios Cervantinos, Castalia, Alcala de Henares, 2005- [to date the first 8 volumes of the 10 volumes have been published].
ALVAREZ CANIBANO, Antonio; CANO, Jose Ignacio; GONZALEZ RIBOT, Mª Jose (eds.), *Ritmo para el espacio. Los compositores espanoles y el ballet del siglo XX,* Centro de Documentacion de Musica y Danza, Madrid, 1998.
Anuario del Real Conservatorio Superior de Musica y Declamacion de Madrid, 1935-1939, Talleres Ferga, Madrid, 1940.
AUCLAIR, Marcelle, *Vida y Muerte de Garcia Lorca,* Era, Mexico, 1972.
AVINOA, Xose, "Los congresos del "Motu Proprio" (1907-1928): repercusion e influencias", *Revista de Musicologia,* vol. 27, n° 1, 2004.
BAL y GAY, Jesus, *Treinta canciones de Lope de Vega,* Residencia de Estudiantes, Madrid, 1935.
BAYO, Javier, *Diccionario biografco de la danza,* Libreria Esteban Sanz, Madrid, 1997.
BIBLIOTECA NACIONAL, Inventario General de Manuscritos de la BNE, Madrid, 1953-2001, Madrid, 15 vols [Online version].
BLECUA TEIJEIRO, Jose Manuel, *Linca de Lope de Vega,* Castalia, Madrid, 1981.
---Canciones en el teatro de Lope de Vega", *Anuario Lope de Vega,* IX, 2003, pp. 11174.

BROWN, Jane K., "In the begining was poetry", *The Cambridge Companion to the Lied*, James Parson (ed.), Cambridge University Press, Cambridge, 2004.

BYRD, Suzanne W., *La Fuente Ovejuna de Federico Garci'a Lorca,* Pliegos, Madrid, 2003.

CABALLERO FERNANDEZ-RUFETE, Carmelo, "La musica en el teatro clasico", *Historia del teatro espanol,* Javier Huerta Calvo (dir.), Gredos, Madrid, 2003, vol. 1, "De la Edad Media a los Siglos de Oro", p. 677-715.

CABANAS ALEMAN, Fernando J., *Anton Garci'a Abril. Sonidos en libertad,* ICCMU, Madrid, 1993.

CALMELL, Cesar, *Eduard Toldra,* SGAE, Madrid, 1995.

CAMPANA, Patrizia, "Las canciones de Lope de Vega. Catalogo y apuntes para su estudio", *Anuario de Lope de Vega*, 5, 1999, pp. 43-72.

CARRILLO GUZMAN, Mercedes del Carmen, *La musica incidental en el Teatro Espanol de Madrid (1942-1952y1962-1964),* doctoral thesis, University of Murcia, 2008.

CASARES RODICIO, Emilio (dir. and coord.); FERNANDEZ DE LA CUESTA, Ismael; LOPEZ-CALO, Jose (eds.), *Diccionario de la Musica Espanola e Hispanoamericana,* 10 vols., Fundacion Autor-Sociedad General de Autores y Editores, Madrid, 1999-2002.

CASARES RODICIO, Emilio, *Diccionario de la zarzuela espanola e Hispanoamericana*, 2 vols, ICCMU, Madrid, 2002-2003.

CASTRO, Americo; RENNERT, Hugo A., *Vida de Lope de Vega: (1562-1635)*, ed. by Fernando Lazaro Carreter, Anaya, Salamanca, 1968.

CAUDET, Francisco, *Las cenizas del Fenix. La cultura espanola en los anos 30.* Editorial de la Torre, Madrid, 1993.

CERVANTES, Miguel de, *Don Quijote de la Mancha*, ed. by Francisco Rico, Instituto Cervantes, Critica, 1998.

CHASE, Gilbert, *The music of Spain,* Dover, New York, 1959.

CLARAMONTE, Andres de, *La Estrella de Sevilla,* Madrid, ed. by Alfredo Rodriguez Lopez-Vazquez Catedra, Madrid, 2010.

COOKE, Deryck, I *Saw the World End: A Study of Wagner's Ring*, Clarendon Press, Oxford, 1979. [Audio version: *The Ring of the Nibelung*, CD, Decca, 1968].

CORNEJO, Manuel, "La esclava de su galan, ^comedia de senectute de Lope de Vega?: nuevos datos acerca de las estancias sevillanas del dramaturgo", *Anuario Lope de Vega*, Volume IX, 2003.

COTARELO, Emilio, *La "Estrella de Sevilla", is by Lope de Vega*, Imp. Municipal, Madrid, 1930.

CRAINE Debra; MACKRELL, Judith, "Laurencia", *The Oxford Dictionary of Dance*, Oxford University Press, Oxford, 2010.

CUENCA MUNOZ, Paloma, "La edicion paleografica de textos teatrales antiguos: *La encomienda bien guardada* de Lope de Vega". *III Jornadas Cientfcas Sobre Documentation de Castila e Indias en el siglo XVII,* UCM, Madrid, 2006.

DIEZ DE REVENGA, Francisco Javier, *Teatro de Lope de Vega y lirica traditional,* Universidad de Murcia, Murcia, 1983.

Classic theatre and traditional song", *Cuadernos de Teatro Clasico,* 3, 1989, 29-44.

Blancas coge Lucinda..." amor y lirica traditional en el teatro de Lope", *Amor y erotsmo en el teatro de Lope de Vega: Actas de las XXVJornadas de Teatro Clasico de Almagro, 2002,* ed. by Felipe B. Pedraza Jimenez and Rafael Gonzalez Canal, University of Castilla La Mancha, 2003.
Pedraza Jimenez and Rafael Gonzalez Canal, University of Castilla La Mancha, 2003.

La tradition aurea: sobre la reception del Siglo de Oro en poetas contemporaneos, Biblioteca Nueva, Madrid, 2003.

El Arte nuevo de hacer comedias y la generation del 27: filologia y escena", El Arte nuevo de hacer comedias" y la escena, XXXII Jornadas de teatro clasico, Almagro, 2009.

DRAAYER, Suzanne R., *Art Song Composers of Spain. An Encyclopedia,* Scarecrow Press, Maryland, 2009.

DURAN Agustin, "Poesia popular, drama novelesco", *Obras de Lope de Vega,* ed. by Marcelino Menendez Pelayo, RAE, Vol. 1, Rivadeneyra, Madrid, 1890, pp. 7-16.
--- (ed.), Cancionero y romancero de coplas y canciones de arte menor, letras, letrillas, romances cortos y glosas anteriores al siglo XVIII, pertenecientes a los generosos doctrinal, amatorio, jocoso, satirico, etc., vol. 3 de Coleccion de romances castellanos anteriores al siglo XVIII, Imprenta de E. Aguado, Madrid, 1829.
ENTRAMBASAGUAS, Joaquin de, *Cronos en el metaforismo de Lope de Vega,* [special edition of 50 numbered copies], Madrid, 1935.
---Lope de Vega author of "ballets", *ABC,* 8-4-1962.
ESTEPA, Luis, "Voz femenina: los comienzos de la lirica popular hispanica y su relación con otros géneros literarios", in *Cuadernos de Teatro Clasico*, 3, 1989, p. 13.
Voz femenina: los comienzos de la lirica popular hispanica y su relación con otros géneros literarios" , in *Cuadernos de Teatro Clasico,* 3, 1989.
FERNANDEZ SAN EMETERIO, Gerardo, "La herencia lopesca en el teatro musical espanol: La discreta enamorada y Dona Francisquita", Lope de Vega: comedia urbana y comedia palatina. Actas XVIII jornadas de teatro clasico. Almagro, July 1995, Almagro, 1996, pp. 157-171.
FERNANDEZ-CID, Antonio, *La musica y los musicos de Espana en el siglo XX,* Cultura Hispanica, Madrid, 1963.
Lieder y canciones de Espana. Pequena historia contemporanea de la musica nacional 1900-1963, Editora Nacional, Madrid, 1963.
FISCHER-DIESKAU, Dietrich, Sounds speak, words sound. Historia e interpretacion del canto. Turner, Madrid, 1990.
FLOECK, Wilfried, Teatro espanol contemporaneo: autores y tendencias, Reichenberger, Kassel, 1995.
FLOREZ ASENSIO, Maria Asuncion, "Lope "libretista" de zarzuela", *Revista de Musicologa,* XXI, N° 1, 1998, p. 93-112.
FLORIT DURAN, Francisco, "La recepcion de Lope en 1935: ideologia y literatura", *Anuario de Lope de Vega*, 6, 2000, pp. 107-124.
FRENK ALATORRE, Margit; BICKFORD, John Albert; KRUGER-HICKMAN, Kathryn, *Corpus de la antigua lirica popular hispanica (iiglos XVa XVII),* Castalia, Madrid, 1987.
Nuevo corpus de la antigua lirica popular hispanica, siglos XV a XVII, UNAM, Mexico, 2003.
GAN QUESADA, German, "Variaciones sobre el tema cervantino en la musica de la familia Halffter", *Cervantes y el Quiote en la musica: estudios sobre la recepcion de un mito*, ed. by Begona Lolo, Centro Estudios Cervantinos, Madrid, 2007, pp. 373-398.
GARCIA ESTEFANIA. Alvaro, *Francisco Escudero,* SGAE, Madrid, 1995.
Jose Munoz Molleda , Catalogues of Composers, Fundacion Autor, Madrid, 2000.
GARCIA SANTO-TOMAS, Enrique, La creacion del "Fenix". Recepcion critica y representacion canonica del teatro de Lope de Vega, Gredos, Madrid, 2000.
GASSULL, Eugeni, "La canco de cambra a Catalunya entre 1910 i 1930", *El lied, una important parcel.la de la musica catalana* [Dossier]. *Revista Musical Catalana,* vol. 9, n° 90 (Apr. 1992), p. 31.
GIL FOMBELLIDA, Mª del Carmen, Rivas Cherif, Margarita Xirgu y el teatro de la II Republica, Fundamentos, Madrid, 2003.
GOMEZ AMAT, Carlos, *Historia de la musica espanola 5: Siglo XIX,* Alianza, Madrid, 1984.
GOMEZ RODRIGUEZ, Jose Antonio, *Catalogo de musica: autores y temas asturianos.* Oviedo: Fundacion Principe de Asturias, 1995.
GONZALEZ LAPUENTE, Alberto, *Joaquin Rodngo,* SGAE, Madrid, 1997.
On the centenary of Enrique Casal Chapi", *Scherzo,* n° 245, October, 2009.
GOSALVEZ LARA, Carlos Jose, *La edicion musical espanola hasta 1936,* AEDOM, Madrid,

1995.
GRANDELA DEL Rfo, Ines, "Catalogo de las obras musicales de Carlos Botto Vallarino", *Revista Musical Chilena,* vol. 51, N° 187, Santiago de Chile, 1997.
GRIER, James, *La edicion critica de la musica,* Akal, Madrid, 2008.
GUTIERREZ DORADO, Pilar; MARCOS PATINO, Cristina (Coords.), *20 anos de estrenos de musica: 1985-2004 (*CD-ROM), Centro de Documentation de Musica y Danza, Madrid, 2004.
HEINE, Christiane, "Bacarisse Chinoria, Salvador", *Diccionario espanol e hispanoamericano de la musica*, Emilio Casares Rodicio (dir. y coord.), SGAE, Madrid, 1999-2003, pp. 4-24.
Catalogo de obras de Salvador Bacarisse, Fundacion Juan March, Madrid, 1990.
La relation entre poetas y musicos de la Generation del 27: Rafael Alberti", *Cuadernos de arte de la Universidad de Granada,* no. 26, 1995, pp. 265.96.
HERRERO, Miguel; ENTRAMBASAGUAS, Joaquin de, (dirs.), *Fenix, revista del tricentenario de Lope de Vega, 1635-1935,* Numeros 1-6, Grafica Universal, Madrid, 1935.
HUERTA CALVO, Javier, "Clasicos cara al sol, I", *XXIV y XXV Jornadas de Teatro del Siglo de Oro,* Institute.) de Estudios Almerienses, Almeria, 2011.
IGLESIAS, Antonio, *Escritos de Joaquin Turina,* Alpuerto, Madrid, 1982.
--- (compilation and comments), *Escritos de Julio Gomez*, Alpuerto, Madrid, 1986.
IGLESIAS, Nieves (dir.), *La musica en el Boletn de la Propiedad Intelectual 1847-1915,* Biblioteca Nacional, Madrid, 1997.
KAMHI, Victoria, *De la mano de Joaquin Rodrigo,* Ediciones Joaquin Rodrigo, Madrid, 1995.
KRAVITT, Edward F., *The lied: mirror of late romanticism*, Yale University Press, Michigan, 1998.
LAMBEA, Mariano (ed.), *Revista de Musicologa,* vol. 27, n° 1, 2004 [Actas del Simposio Internacional "El motu proprio de San Pio X y la musica (1903-2003)", Barcelona, 26-28 November 2003].
LARRINAGA CUADRA, Itziar, "El proceso de creacion de Fuenteovejuna, la opera inacabada de Francisco Escudero", *Eusko Ikaskuntza,* n° 17, 2010, pp. 497-556.
LaRUE, Jan, *Analisis del estilo musical*, Idea Books, Barcelona, 2004.
LASTRA CALERA, Julia, *Arturo Duo Vital*, Catalogues of composers, Fundacion Autor, Madrid, 1999.
LEON TELLO, Francisco, "La estetica de la musica vocal de Joaqrnn Rodrigo: catorce canciones para canto y piano", *Cuadernos Hispanoamericanos,* n° 355, 1990, pp. 70-107.
LIANO PEDREIRA, Maria Dolores, Catalogo de partituras del Archivo Canuto Berea en la Biblioteca de la Diputacion de A Coruna, Diputacion Provincial de La Coruna, La Coruna, 1998.
LLORENS, Vicente, *Memorias de una emigration,* Renacimiento, Seville, 2006.
LOLO, Begona (ed.), *Cervantes y el Quiote en la musica. Estudios sobre la reception de un mito*, Centro de Estudios Cervantinos-Ministerio de Educacion y Ciencia, Madrid, 2007.
--- (ed.), *Visiones del Quijote en la musica del siglo XX,* Centro Estudios Cervantinos, Madrid, 2010.
Interpretaciones del ideal cervantino en la musica del siglo XX (1905-1925)", *Visiones del Quijote en la musica del siglo XX*, ed. by Begona Lolo, Centro de Estudios Cervantinos, Madrid, 2010.
LOPEZ ESTRADA, Francisco, "La cancion "Al val de Fuenteovejuna" de la comedia Fuenteovejuna de Lope", *Homenaje a W. L. Fichter*, Castalia, Madrid, 1971, pp. 453-68.
Caracteristicas generales de la Edad Media literaria", *Historia de la Literatura espanola,* Tomo I: *La Edad Media,* Jose Maria Diez Borque (coord.), Taurus, Madrid, 1980.
MALLO DEL CAMPO, Maria Luisa, *Torner mas alla del folklore,* Servicio de Publicaciones Universidad de Oviedo, Oviedo, 1980.
MARCO, Tomas, Historia de la Musica espanola. Siglo X, Alianza, Madrid, 1983.
MARTIN MORENO, Antonio, "Musica, pasion, razon: la teoria de los afectos en el teatro y la musica del Siglo de Oro", *Edad de oro*, vol. 22, 2003.

MARTINEZ COMECHE, Juan Antonio, *Documentation del Siglo de Oro: El Codice Duran*, [s.n.], Madrid, 1997.
MARTINEZ DEL FRESNO, Beatriz, *Catalogo de obras de Julio Gomez,* Fundacion Juan March, Centro de Documentacion de la Musica Espanola Contemporanea, Madrid, 1987.
Nationalismo e internacionalismo en la musica espanola de la primera mitad del siglo XX", *Revista de Musicologa,* no. 1, 1993, pp. 20-37.
---, Catalogue of works by Julio Gomez, Madrid, SGAE, 1997.
---, Julio Gomez, Una epoca de la musica espanola, ICCMU, Madrid, 1999.
La obra de Manuel del Fresno, un capitulo del regionalismo asturiano (1900-1936)", *Homenaje a Juan Una Riu,* vol. 2, Universidad de Oviedo, Oviedo, 1999.
MAYER, Otto, "Nueva musica espanola", *La Vanguardia,* 22-5-1938.
McDAGHA, Michael D., The theatre in Madrid during the Second Republic: a checklist, Grant & Cutler, London, 1979.
MENENDEZ PELAYO, Marcelino, *Estudios sobre el teatro de Lope de Vega,* vol. V, CSIC, Madrid, 1949.
MEYER, Leonard B., *La emotion y elsignificado en la musica,* Alianza, Madrid, 2005.
MOLINA JIMENEZ, Maria Belen, Literatura y Musica en el Siglo de Oro Espanol. Interrelations in the Lyric Theatre, doctoral thesis, University of Murcia, 2007.
MOLINER, Maria, *Diccionario de Uso delEspanol,* 2 vols, Gredos, Madrid, 1998.
MORAN, Alfredo, *Joaqun Turina a traves de sus escritos,* Alianza, Madrid, 1997.
Joaqun Turina , SGAE, Madrid, 1993.
MORENO MENJIBAR, Andres, "Manuel Garcia en la perspectiva", *Manuel Garcia, de la tonadilla escenica a la opera (1775-1832),* Alberto Romero Ferrer, Andres Moreno Menjibar (eds.), Universidad de Cadiz, Cadiz, 2006.
MORGAN, Robert P., *La musica del siglo XX,* Akal, Madrid, 1994.
MORLEY, Griswold; BRUERTON, Courtney, *Cronologa de las comedias de Lope de Vega,* Gredos, Madrid, 1968.
MUNOZ TUNON, Adelaida; ARCE BUENO, Julio; SUAREZ-PAJARES, Javier, *et al., Musica instrumental y vocal. Partituras y materiales del archivo sinfonico.* SGAE, Madrid, 1995.
NAVARRETE, Ramon, "Los clasicos, la zarzuela y el cine", *XXIV y XXV Jornadas de Teatro del Siglo de Oro,* Instituto de Estudios Almerienses, 2011, pp. 127-139.
NOMDEDEU RULL, Antoni, "Por que la Real Academia Espanola es modelo de norma linguistica", *At del XXIII Congresso dell'Association Ispanisti Italiani,* Associazione Ispanisti Italiani e Instituto Cervantes, 2005 pp. 446-460.
OLEZA, Joan, "La traza y los textos. A proposito del autor de La estrella de Sevilla", *Actas del V Congreso de la Asociacion Internacional del Siglo de Oro*, Iberoamericana Vervuert, Munster, 2001, pp. 42-68.
PALACIOS, Maria, La renovacion musical en Madrid durante la dictadura de Primo de Rivera. El grupo de los ocho (1923-1931), SEDEM, Madrid, 2008.
PARSON, James (ed.), *The Cambridge Companion to the Lied,* Cambridge University Press, Cambridge, 2004.
PEDRAZA JIMENEZ, Felipe B., *Lope de Vega*, Teide, Barcelona, 1990.
En torno al teatro del Siglo de Oro, Irene Pardo and Antonio Serrano (eds.), Instituto de Estudios Almerienses, Almeria, 2001, pp. 211-231.
(ed.), Lope de Vega en la Compania Nacional de Teatro Clasico. Ano 2002, Cuadernos de Teatro Clasico, 17, 2003.
El universo poetico de Lope de Vega, Laberinto, Madrid, 2003.
— --, Cervantes y Lope de Vega: historia de una enemistad y otros estudios cervantinos, Octaedro, Barcelona, 2006.
— --, *Lope de Vega, genio y figura*, University of Granada, Granada, 2008.

— --, Lope de Vega. Pasiones, obra y fortuna del "monstruo de la naturaleza", EDAF, Madrid, 2009.
PEDRAZA JIMENEZ, Felipe B.; RODRIGUEZ CACERES, Milagros (eds.), *El teatro segun Lope de Vega,* 2 vols., Compania Nacional de Teatro Clasico, Madrid, 2009.
PEDRELL, Felipe, *Pornuestra musica,* Heinrich and Cª , Barcelona, 1891, pp. 40-41.
PELAEZ MARTIN. Andres, "Lope de Vega en los teatros nacionales y festivales de Espana", *Actas del XVIII jornadas de teatro Clasico de Almagro,* ed. by Felipe B. Pedraza and Rafael Gonzalez Canal, 1995. Pedraza and Rafael Gonzalez Canal, 1995.
PEREZ BOWIE, Jose Antonio, "La función parodica de las estrategias metaficcionales. Apuntes sobre la adaptacion cinematografica de la zarzuela *Dona Francisquita* (Ladislao Vajda, 1952)", *Anales de Literatura Espanola,* n° 19, 2007, pp. 189-204.
PEREZ ZALDUONDO, Gemma, El compositor Jose Munoz Molleda. De la Generacion del 27 al franquismo, Zejel, Almeria, 1989.
PERIS LACASA, Jose, Catalogo del Archivo de Musica del Palacio Real de Madrid, Patrimonio Nacional, Madrid, 1993.
PERSICHETTI, Vincent, *Armona del siglo XX,* Real Musical, Madrid, 1985.
PLIEGO DE ANDRES, Victor, *Manuel Angulo,* Catalogos de compositores espanoles, SGAE, Madrid, 1992.
PRESAS, Adela, "1905: la trascendencia musical del III centenario", in *Cervantes y el Quijote en la musica: estudios sobre la recepcion de un mito,* ed. by Begona Lolo, Centro Estudios Cervantinos, Madrid, 2007.
QUEROL, Miquel, Cancionero musical de Lope de Vega, 3 vols. Poems sung in the novels; II. Poesi'as sueltas puestas en musica; III. Poesi'as cantadas en las comedias, CSIC, Barcelona, 1991.
La musica en la epoca de Cervantes, Centro de Estudios Cervantinos, Madrid, 2005.
QUIRANTE, Luis; RODRIGUEZ. Evangelina; SIRERA, Josep Lluis, *Practiques esceniques de ledatmitjana als segles dor,* Universitat de Valencia, Valencia, 1999.
RATTALINO, Piero, *Historia del piano,* Idea Books, Barcelona, 2005.
REAL ACADEMIA ESPANOLA, *Diccionario de Autoridades,* 1739 [electronic version, <http://buscon.rae.es/ntlle>].
Diccionario de la lengua castellana compuesto por la Real academia Espanola , reduced to one volume for easier use. Third edition, in which all the words of the supplements, which were placed at the end of the editions of the years 1780 and 1783, have been placed in their corresponding places, and new articles have been inserted in the letters D. E. and F., of which a separate supplement will be given. Madrid. Widow of Joaquin Ibarra. 1791. [Digital reproduction at <http://buscon.rae.es/ntlle>].
Diccionario de la Rea Academia , 22ª Edicion, RAE, Madrid, 2001.
Panhispanic Dictionary of Doubts, 2005 (2005): *Diccionario panhispanico de dudas,* Madrid, Real Academia Espanola, Asociacion de Academias de la Lengua Espanola, Santillana, Madrid, 2005. [Electronic version, <http://buscon.rae.es/dpdl>].
Ortografa de la Lengua Espanola , Madrid, Espasa Calpe, 2002.
Ortografa de la Lengua Espanola, Real Academia Espanola, Espasa, Madrid, 2010.
REINA GONZALEZ, Emilio, *Angel Mingote Lorente. Ultimo representante de la tradición musical de Daroca*, Institucion Fernando el Catolico-Centro de estudios Darocenses, Zaragoza, 1986.
---*Catalogue of works by Angel Mingote*, Institucion Fernando el Catolico-Centro de Estudios Darocenses, Daroca, 1997.
RIEMANN, Hugo, "Lied" *Music-Lexikon*, Leipzig, 1992.
RODERO, Leopoldo, *Enrique Truan: vida y obra musical*, Trea, Gijon, 1996.
RODRIGUEZ CUADROS, Evangelina, La técnica del actor espanol en el Barroco: hipotesis y documentos, Castalia, Madrid, 1998.

RODRIGUEZ LOPEZ-VAZQUEZ, Alfredo; RUIZ-FABREGA, Tomas, "En torno al cancionero teatral de Lope", *Lope de Vega y los ongenes del teatro espanol. Actas del Congreso Internacional sobre Lope de Vega*, Edi-6, Madrid, 1981, p. 523-532.

RODRIGUEZ LOPEZ-VAZQUEZ, Alfredo, "La *Estrella de Sevilla* y Claramonte", *Criticon,* no. 21, 1983, pp. 5-31.

RODR^GUEZ-MONINO, Antonio, Manual bibliografico de cancioneros y romanceros impresos durante el siglo XVII, Castalia, Madrid, 1977-1978.

ROMERO FERRER, Alberto; MORENO MENUBAR, Andres (eds.), *Manuel Garcia, de la tonadila escenica a la opera (1775-1832),* Universidad de Cadiz, Cadiz, 2006.

ROSELL, Cayetano, *Coleccion escogida de obras no dramatics de frey Lope Felix de Vega Carpio*, Biblioteca de Autores Espanoles, vol. 38, Rivadeneyra, Madrid, 1856.

RUANO DE LA HAZA, J.M.; ALLEN, John J., Los teatros comerciales del siglo XVII y la escenificacion de la comedia, Castalia, Madrid, 1994.

RUANO DE LA HAZA, Jose Maria, *La puesta en escena en los teatros comerciales del Siglo de Oro*, Editorial Castalia, Madrid, 2000.

RUIZ MONTES, Francisco, *El compositor granadino Jose Maria Guervos y Mira: revision del estado de la cuestion.* Research work corresponding to the Diploma of Advanced Studies, Department of History of Art, University of Granada, 2001. [Unpublished].

Un romantico fuera de su epoca: el compositor granadino Jose Maria Guervos", *El patrimonio musical de Andahicia y sus relaciones con el contexto iberico,* ed. by F. J. Gimenez Rodriguez and J. Lopez, C. Perez, Universidad de Granada, Granada, 2009.

SADIE, Stanley (ed.), *The New Grove Dictionary of Music and Musicians*, 20 vols. Macmillan Publishers, London, 1980.

SAENZ DE LA CALZADA, Luis, "*La Barraca,* Teatro Universitario", *Revista de Occidente*, Madrid, 1976.

SALOMON, Noël, *Lo vilano en el teatro delSiglo de Oro,* Castalia, Madrid, 1985.

SANCHEZ DE ANDRES, Leticia, "Gabriel Rodriguez y su relación con Felipe Pedrell: hacia la creación de un lied hispano", *Cuadernos de musica iberoamericana,* vol. 10, 2005, pp. 97-136.

SANCHEZ MARIANA, Manuel, "Los autografos de Lope de Vega", *ManuscrtCao,* n° 10, 2011.

SANTANA GIL, Isidro, "Catalogo de las obras musicales de Bernardino Valle Chinestra conservadas en el Museo Canario de Las Palmas de Gran Canaria", in *Nasarre*, X, 1, 1994, 205-268.

SANZ GARCIA, Jose Miguel, Miguel Asins Arbo: Musica y cinematografia. Analisis musico-visual de sus composiciones en la filmografia de Luis Garcia Berlanga. Doctoral thesis. University of Valencia, Valencia, 2008. Unpublished.

SEGUI PEREZ, Salvador, La praxis armonico-contrapuntistica en la obra liederistica de Manuel Palau. Life and work of the Valencian musician. Doctoral thesis. University of Valencia, Valencia, 1994. [Microfilm].

Manuel Palau , Consell Valencia de Cultura, Valencia, 1997.

---, *Matilde Salvador*, Fundacion Autor, Madrid, 2000.

SIERRA MARTINEZ, Fermin, "Acercamiento a Lope de Vega: *El Aldegiiela,(* -anton'a o atribucion?", *Actas del X Congreso de la Asociacion Internacional de Hispanistas (*Barcelona 21-26 August 1989), Antonio Vilanova (coord.), Vol. 2, 1992, pp. 1107-11102. 1107-1120.

SIMSON, Ingrid, "Calderon as Librettist: Musical Performances in the Golden Age", in Theo Reichenberger (coord.), *Caderon: Eminent Protagonist of the European Baroque,* Edition Reichenberger, Kassel, 2000, pp. 217-43.

SOLBES, Rosa, Matilde Salvador, converses amb una compositora apassionada, Tandem, Castello, 2007.

SOPENA, Federico, *El Liedromantico,* Moneda y Credito, Madrid, 1963.

Joaqun Rodrigo, Ministry of Education and Science, Madrid, 1970.

---, El Nacionalismo musical y el "lied", Real Musical, Madrid, 1979.
Musica y Literatura , Rialp, Madrid, 1989.
STEIN, Deborah; SPILLMAN, Robert, *Poetry into song. Performance and analysis of Lieder.* Oxford University Press, New York, 1996.
STEIN, Luise K., Songs of Mortals, Dialogues of the Gods. Music and Theater in Seventh Century Spain, Oxford University Press, 1993, pp. 336-45.
STEVENS, Denis (ed.), *Historia de la cancion*, Taurus, Madrid, 1990.
SUAREZ-PAJARES, Javier, Centenario Joaquin Rodrigo. El hombre, el musico, el maestro, Sinsentido, Madrid, 2001.
TINNELL, Roger, *Federico Garcia Lorca y la musica: catalogo y discograffa anotados,* Madrid, Fundacion Juan March, 2ª edicion, Madrid, 1998.
Catalogo anotado de la musica espanola contemporanea basada en la literatura espanola, Centro de Documentation Musical de Andalucia, Granada, 2001.
TORREGO EGIDO, Luis Mariano, *Cancion de autor y educacion popular (1960-1980),* Ediciones de la Torre, 1999.
UMPIERRE, Gustavo, Songs in the Plays of Lope de Vega: A Study of their Dramatic Function, Tamesis, London, 1975.
VAZQUEZ MONTALBAN, Manuel, *Antologa de la "Nova Canco" catalana,* Ediciones de Cultura Popular, Barcelona, 1968.
VEGA SANCHEZ, Jose de la, Rafael Rodriguez Albert. Complete catalogue of his works, ONCE, Madrid, 1987.
VV. AA., *Codice 3.985,*BNE, MSS/3985. [Belonging to the Duke of Uceda. Microform reproduction, MSS.MICRO/15595].
Revista Musica , facsimile edition, Publicaciones de la Residencia de Estudiantes, Madrid, 1998.
VILLANUEVA, Carlos (ed.), *Jesus Bal y Gay: tientos y silencios 1905-1993,* Madrid, Residencia de Estudiantes, Madrid, 2005. [Catalogue of the exhibition, Residencia de Estudiantes, May 2005].
WALDE MOHENO, Lillian von der, "Amores, dineros e indianos. A proposito de la esclava de su galan", *Texto y espectaculo. Selected Proceedings of the Fifteenth International Golden Age Spanish Theater Symposium,* University of Texas, ed. by Jose Luis Suarez Garcia, Spanish Literature Publications Company, South Carolina, 1996.
WILSON, Edward M., "Imagenes y estructura en Peribanez", *El teatro de Lope de Vega,* Buenos Aires, 1962.
---Miguel de Barrios and Spanish religious poetry", *Bulletin of Hispanic Studies*, 40, 1963, p. 174-180.
ZABALA, Alejandro, "La production liederistica de Felip Pedrell", *Recerca Musicologica,* XIV-XV, 2004-2005, pp. 325-334.
ZAMORA VICENTE, Alonso, *Lope de Vega: su vida y su obra*, Gredos, Madrid, 1961.

ON LINE RESOURCES

State agency Boletin Oficial del Estado. Historical collection of the Gazette. <http://www.boe.es/aeboe/consultas/bases_datos/gazeta.php>
Biblioteca Digital Hispanica de la BNE, <http://bibliotecadigitalhispanica.bne.es>.
Miguel de Cervantes Virtual Library, <http://www.cervantesvirtual.com>.
Catalogue of Ibero-American Composers of the Fundacion Autor-SGAE, <http://www.catalogodecompositores.com>.
Catalogue of the Spanish Library of Contemporary Music and Theatre of the Juan March Foundation, <http://www.march.es/musica/contemporanea/archivo/archivo.asp>.
Catalogue of the National Library of Spain, <http://catalogo.bne.es/uhtbin/webcat>.
Corpus Diacronico del Espanol (CORDE) of the RAE, <http://corpus.rae.es/cordenet.html>.
Diccionario de la Real Academia, 22ª ed., <http://buscon.rae.es/drae>

Diccionario panhispanico de dudas, <http://buscon.rae.es/dpdl>].
ABC Newspaper Archive, <http://hemeroteca.abc.es>
Hemeroteca *La Vanguardia*, <http://hemeroteca.lavanguardia.com>
Oxford Reference Online. Oxford University Press. <http://www.oxfordreference.com>
Official website of the composer Joaquin Rodrigo, <http://www.joaquin-rodrigo.com>.
Official website of the composer Joaquin Turina, <www.joaquinturina.com>.
Theatre of the Golden Age, <http://teatrosiglodeoro.bne.es>
Teatro Espanol del Siglo de Oro (TESO), <http://teso.chadwyck.co.uk>

Annex

CATALOGUE OF THE SONGS FOR VOICE AND PIANO WITH TEXTS BY LOPE DE VEGA

This catalogue of songs for voice and piano with lyrics by Lope de Vega includes all the details of the works by Spanish composers that have been located after searching the archives, libraries and documentary collections mentioned in the following section. All the compositions are written from original texts by the poet. In some cases the text may be incomplete or abbreviated, or may contain some errors or modifications to the original, but in no case are these adaptations due to other writers. The period of data collection is from January 2008 to February 2012.
The scores were originally composed for solo voice and piano. Only two are for vocal duet. In the case of keyboard adaptations from other instrumental accompaniments, they have always been transcribed by the composer himself.
The catalogue is organised in alphabetical order of the composers. Within each one the songs are arranged in chronological order, and in the same way if they belong to cycles or groups of works. The information is organised according to "fields", whose labels are written in full to facilitate reading and to avoid the excessive use of initials or acronyms. The fields, which are omitted if there is no data to display, are presented in the following order:
Title
Subtitle
No. of Opus
Collection or cycle
Date of composition
Place of composition
It belongs to the work of Lope de Vega.
First verse
Character
Scenic notes
Duration
Shade
Tessitura
Aggressive indications
Release date
Premiere venue
Premiere singer
Premiere pianist
Location of the manuscript
Manuscript signature
Date of publication
Publisher
Place of publication
Mention of editing
Dedication
Awards
Header indications
Motivation
Remarks
The available recordings of each work, presented after the previous fields, are assigned an order number, and are organised chronologically. They include the following data:
Recording [order no.] [order no.] [order no.] [order no.] [order no.] [order no.
Year of publication
Singer
Pianist
Place of recording

Date of recording
Support
Record label
Discographical reference
Duration
Remarks

The system we follow to indicate the pitch of the notes is the so-called Franco-Belgian octave numbering system, which assigns the C3 to the one written on the first additional line below the treble clef on the second line.

ABBREVIATIONS and ACRONYMS[320]

approx.	Approximately
Bar.	Baritone
BNE	National Library of Spain
ca.	To
CD	Compact disc
CEDOA	Documentation and Archives Centre
FJM	Juan March Foundation
MS.	Manuscript
Mz.	Mezzo-soprano
Op.	Opus
Pno.	Piano
RCSMM	Royal Conservatory of Music of Madrid
RNE	Radio Nacional de Espana

SGAESociedad General de Autores
Sop. Soprano
Tenor

ARCHIVES and TEXTS CONSULTED

ARCHIVES and LIBRARIES

Emilio Reina Archive, Zaragoza
Asturias Music Archive
Family Archives of Miguel Asins Arbo, Manuel Palau, Joaquin Nin-Culmell, Vicente Miguel Peris
Personal archives of the composers: Miquel Ortega, Antoni Parera Fons, Fernando Colodro, Jose Peris Lacasa, Eduardo Rincon Garcia
Wagnerian Association of Barcelona
Valencian Library
Library of the Conservatory of Valencia
Library of Catalonia
Library of the Real Conservatorio Superior de Musica of Madrid
Juan March Foundation Library
Madrid City Council Music Library
National Library of Spain
Documentation Centre for Music and Dance
Eresbil, Basque Archive of Music
Valencia Institute of Music

[320] We have avoided as much as possible the use of abbreviations for a smoother handling of the data and comments. We do not include in this list the abbreviations of library and archive symbols, publishers, record labels and references.

Canarian Museum of Las Palmas
Radio Nacional de Espana
Royal Academy of Fine Arts of San Fernando
Student Residence
General Society of Authors and Publishers
Spanish Musical Union

EDITED SCORES

ALONSO, Celsa (ed.), Manuel Garcia (1775-1832). Canciones y caprichos liricos, ICCMU/SGAE, Madrid, 1994.
ALTISENT, Joan, Seis canciones inspiradas sobre poesias espanolas de la Edad Media y del Renacimiento, A. Boileau y Bernasconi, Barcelona, 1951.
BARRERA, Antonio, *Canciones del Siglo de Oro*, Real Musical, Madrid, 1986.
CAROL, Mercedes [Mercedes Garcia Lopez], *Cnco canciones,* Union Musical Espanola, Madrid, 1964.
CASAL CHAPI, Enrique, *Dos fragmentos del caballero de Olmedo,* Ediciones del Consejo Central de la Musica, Barcelona, 1938.
Tres cantares de Lope de Vega , Ediciones del Consejo Central de la Musica, Barcelona, 1938.
ESCUDERO, Francisco, *Al entierro de Cristo*, Alpuerto, Madrid, 1975.
GARCIA DE LA PARRA y TELLEZ, Benito, *Cancionero espanol, cuaderno primero,* Juan Bta. Pujol Editores, Barcelona, [1943].
GRANADOS, Enric, *Obra completa para voz y piano,* ed. by Manuel Garcia Morante, Trito, Barcelona, 1996.
GUERVOS y MIRA, Jose Maria, *Cnco canciones,* Union Musical Espanola, Madrid, 1936.
LARROCA, Angel, *Plegaria a Cristo crucrficado,* Jaime Piles, Valencia, [1940].
LAVILLA, Felix, *Ay, amargas soledades*, Real Musical, Madrid, 1988.
LLONGUERES BADIA, Joan, *Seis villancicos de Lope de Vega*, DINSIC, 2002.
MENENDEZ ALEYXANDRE, Arturo, *Madre, unos ojuelos vi*, Barcelona, Talleres Jose Mora, Barcelona, 1944.
MORENO TORROBA, Federico, *Copla de antano*, Copla de antano, Union Musical Espanola, Madrid, 1923.
PALAU, Manuel, *Seis Lieder (Six Lieder,* Institute). Valenciano de Musicologia, Institucion Alfonso el Magnanimo, Piles, Valencia, 1953.
— --, *Villancico*, Piles, Valencia, 1974.
PEREZ AGUIRRE, Julio, *Los ojos verdes,* Sociedad Anonima Casa Dotesio, Barcelona, [1901-1914].
RODRIGO, Joaquin, *Album centenario canto y piano,* Ediciones Joaquin Rodrigo, Madrid, 1999.
SALVADOR, Matilde, *Cancion de vela,* Piles, Valencia, 1947.
THOMAS, Juan Maria, *Canciones espanolas de instrumentos,* Ediciones Capella Classica, Mallorca, 1944.
TOLDRA, Eduard, *Seis canciones,* Union Musical Espanola, Madrid, 1992.
TURINA, Joaquin, *Homenaje a Lope de Vega,* Union Musical Espanola, Madrid, 1992.

HANDWRITTEN SCORES

CAMPO y ZABALETA, Conrado del, *Una dama se vende a quien la quiera*, manuscript score, SGAE, Box 8.51.
GOMEZ GARCIA, Julio, *Cuatro poesias liricas de Lope de Vega,* manuscript, Biblioteca Nacional de Espana, sig. MP/5352/1.
(Que tengo yo que mi amistad procuras?) , manuscript, Biblioteca Fundacion Juan March, sig. M-766-A.
— --, *La Verdad*, manuscript, Biblioteca Fundacion Juan March, sig. M-767-A.

— --, *Villancico*, manuscript, Biblioteca Fundacion Juan March, sig. M-771-A.
— --, *Villancico*, manuscript, Biblioteca Fundacion Juan March, sig. M-772-A.
Celos, que no me matais, manuscript, Biblioteca Fundacion Juan March, sig. M-768-A.
— --, *Celos, que no me matais*, manuscript, Biblioteca Fundacion Juan March, sig. M-769-A.
— --, *Celos, que no me matais*, manuscript, Biblioteca Fundacion Juan March, sig. M-770-A.
MINGOTE, Angel, *Canciones espanolas con textos de Lope de Vega*, manuscript, Archivo Emilio Reina, Zaragoza, sig. ERG 88 A1.
MORALEDA, Fernando, *Cuatro canciones con textos de Lope de Vega*, manuscript score, Biblioteca Nacional de Espana, sig. M.MORALEDA/9.

TEXTS

ACKER, Yolanda; Alfonso, Mª de los Angeles; ORTEGA, Judith; Perez Castillo, Belen (eds.) *Archivo historico de la Union Musical Espanola, partituras, metodos, librettos y libros*, Instituto Complutense de Ciencias Musicales (ICCMU), Madrid, 2000.
CASARES RODICIO, Emilio (dir. and coord.); FERNANDEZ DE LA CUESTA, Ismael; Lopez-Calo, Jose (eds.) *Diccionario de la Musica Espanola e Hispanoamericana*, 10 vols., Fundacion Autor-Sociedad General de Autores y Editores, Madrid, 2002.
FERNANDEZ-CID, Antonio, Lieder y canciones de Espana. Pequena historia contemporanea de la musica nacional 1900-1963, Editora National, Madrid, 1963.
GOMEZ RODRIGUEZ, Jose Antonio, *Catalogo de musica: autores y temas asturianos*. Oviedo: Fundacion Principe de Asturias, 1995.
GOSALVEZ LARA, Carlos Jose, *La edicion musical espanola hasta 1936*, AEDOM, Madrid, 1995.
GUTIERREZ DORADO, Pilar; MARCOS PATINO, Cristina (coords.): *20 anos de estrenos de musica: 1985-2004 (*CD-ROM), Centro de Documentacion de Musica y Danza, Madrid, 2004.
IGLESIAS, Nieves (ed.), La musica en el Boletin de la Propiedad Intelectual 1847-1915. Biblioteca Nacional, Madrid, 1997.
LIANO PEDREIRA, Maria Dolores, Catalogo de partituras del Archivo Canuto Berea en la Biblioteca de la Diputacion de A Coruna, Diputacion Provincial de La Coruna, La Coruna, 1998.
MARTINEZ DEL FRESNO, Beatriz, *Julio Gomez, Una epoca de la musica espanola*, ICCMU, Madrid, 1999.
MUNOZ TUNON, Adelaida; ARCE BUENO, Julio; SUAREZ-PAJARES, Javier, *et al.*, *Musica instrumental y vocal. Partituras y materiales del archivo sinfonico*. SGAE, Madrid, 1995.
PERIS LACASA, Jose, Catalogo del Archivo de Musica del Palacio Real de Madrid, Patrimonio Nacional, Madrid, 1993.
RODERO, Leopoldo, *Enrique Truan: vida y obra musical*, Trea, Gijon, 1996.
SANTANA GIL, Isidro, "Catalogo de las obras musicales de Bernardino Valle Chinestra conservadas en el Museo Canario de Las Palmas de Gran Canaria", in *Nasarre*, X, 1, 1994, 205-268.
SANZ GARCIA. Jose Miguel, Miguel Asins Arbo: Music and cinematography. Analisis musico-visual de sus composiciones en la filmografia de Luis Garcia Berlanga. Doctoral thesis. University of Valencia, Valencia, 2008. Unpublished.
SEGUI PEREZ, Salvador, La praxis armonico-contrapuntistica en la obra liederistica de Manuel Palau. Life and work of the Valencian musician. Doctoral thesis. Universitat de Valencia, Valencia, 1994.
TINNELL, Roger, Catalogo anotado de la musica espanola contemporanea basada en la literatura espanola, Centro de Documentacion Musical de Andalucia, Granada, 2001.
VV.AA. "El lied, una important parcel.la de la musica catalana" [Dossier]. El lied, una importante parcela de la musica catalana [Lied, an important parcel of Catalan music], *Catalunya Musica/Revista Musical Catalana*, vol. 9, n° 90 (Apr. 1992), pp. 25-39.

CATALOGUES OF COMPOSERS

ACKER, Yolanda; Suarez-Pajares, Javier, *Miguel Asins Arbo,* SGAE, Madrid, 1995.

ALONSO, Miguel, *Catalogo de obras de Conrado del Campo,* Fundacion Juan March, Centro de Documentacion de la Musica Espanola Contemporanea, Madrid, 1986.

CALMELL, Cesar, *Eduard Toldra,* SGAE, Madrid, 1995.

GARCIA ESTEFANIA, Alvaro, *Francisco Escudero,* SGAE, Madrid, 1995.

GONZALEZ LAPUENTE, Alberto, *Joaquin Rodngo,* SGAE, Madrid, 1997.

HEINE, Christiane, *Catalogo de obras de Salvador Bacarisse,* Fundacion Juan March, Madrid, 1990.

MARTINEZ DEL FRESNO, Beatriz, *Catalogo de obras de Julio Gomez,* Fundacion Juan March, Centro de Documentacion de la Musica Espanola Contemporanea, Madrid, 1987.

MORAN, Alfredo, *Joaqun Turina,* SGAE, Madrid, 1993.

REINA GONZALEZ, Emilio, *Catalogo de obras de Angel Mingote,* Institucion Fernando el Catolico-Centro de Estudios Darocenses, Daroca, 1997.

SEGUI, Salvador, *Manuel Palau,* Consell Valencia de Cultura, Valencia, 1997.

---, *Matilde Salvador*, Fundacion Autor, Madrid, 2000.

CATALOGUE

ALDAVE RODR^GUEZ, PASCUAL (1924-2013)

Title: "Romance de Fuenteovejuna".

Date of composition: 1949

It belongs to the play by Lope de Vega: *Fuente Ovejuna.*

First verse: "Al val de Fuente ovejuna".

Character: Musicians

Scenic notes: [John: Come, taned and sing, for they are for one].

Duration: 2' approx.

Key: D minor

Tessitura: D3-A4

Aggressive indications: Slow

Location of the manuscript: Eresbil-Basque Music Archive

Manuscript symbol: EP1/226

remarks: Autograph manuscript signed.

Title: "Verbena de San Juan".

Date of composition: June 1952 /revision March 1960

Place of composition: Lesaca /Parigue-le-Polin

It belongs to the play by Lope de Vega: La burgalesa de Lerma.

First verse: "Ya no cogert verbena".

Character: Iii('-s and Tristan

Scenic notes: Leonarda and Clavela dance, Int'-s and Tristan sing

Length: 2' 46"

Key: F minor

Tessitura: E3 flat-G4

Aggressive indications: *Calm*

Location of the manuscript: Eresbil-Basque Music Archive

Manuscript symbol: EP1/222

Title notes: Songs for voice and piano

Remarks: Autograph manuscript dated and signed at the end of the score: "Lesaca, Junio 1952 / Revision en Parigue-le-Polin, Marzo 1960". With the same call number, EP1/222, there are two songs for song and piano: Alta, with verses by Salinas, and Verbena de San Juan.

Recording 1
Year: 1992
Singer: Belaza, Fernando (Bar.)
Pianist: Zabala, Alejandro
Place: Church of the Capuchins, Renteria
Date: 21-5-1992
Support: Radio
Length: 2:46
Observations: Musical Week of Renteria. Recorded by RNE.
Recording 2
Year: 2003
Singer: Fresan, Inaki (Bar.)
Pianist: Alvarez Parejo, Juan Antonio
Venue: Chillida Museum, San Sebastian
Date: 22-8-2003
Support: Radio
Duration: Unspecified
Observations: San Sebastian Musical Fortnight. Recorded by RNE. Not allowed to broadcast without the permission of the performers.

ALTISENT CEARDI, JUAN (1891-1971)

Title: " jTrebole!"

Collection or cycle: Six songs inspired by Spanish poems of the Middle Ages and the Renaissance, n° 6
Date of composition: 1951
It belongs to Lope de Vega's play: Peribanez y el comendador de Ocana.
First verse: "Trebole, jay Jesus, como guele!"
Character: Llorente
Scenic notes: Sing with the guitars (Cantan)
Duration: 2' 10"
Key: G major
Tessitura: F3 sharp-G4
Aggonic indications: *Allegretto*
Date of publication: 1951
Publisher: A. Boileau and Bernasconi
Editing mention: Copyright by Juan Altisent Ceardi
Place of publication: Barcelona
Remarks: Year of composition based on date of publication. The collection "Seis canciones" also includes: Enamorado vengo (anonimo s. XV), Tres morillas me enamoran (anonimo s. XV), Quiero dormir y no puedo (anonimo s. XVI), ((Por que me beso Perico? (anonimo s. XVI), Dicen que me casë yo (Gil Vicente).

Title: "Por el montecico sola..." (On the mountain alone...)

Date of composition: 1955
It belongs to Lope de Vega's play: El villano en su rincon (The villain in his corner).
First verse: "Por el montecico sola" (On the mountain alone)
Character: Musicians
Scenic notes: Lisarda goes out dancing
Duration: 2' approx.
Key: C major
Tessitura: C3-C5 (optional, or A4 flat)

Agaggic indications: *Allegretto moderato*
Date of publication: 1955
Publisher: A. Boileau and Bernasconi
Editing mention: Copyright Juan Altisent Ceardi
Place of publication: Barcelona
Title page: Poesia de Lope de Vega, Adaptacion de J. A.
Remarks: Year of composition based on date of publication. The second letter is not by Lope.

ASINS ARBO, MIGUEL (1918-1996)

Title: "The straws of the manger".

Date of composition: 1963
It belongs to Lope de Vega's play: *Shepherds of Bethlehem.*
First verse: "The straws of the manger".
Character: Tebandra
Scenic notes: [It was not necessary to beg the other shepherds to sing, for they all came forward and joyfully began as follows].
Duration: 2' approx.
Key: A minor
Tessitura: E3-MI4
Agaggic indications: *Andantino*
Location of the manuscript: Valencian Library
Manuscript symbol: AMAA/376
Observations: The date of composition is unknown, it does not appear in the SGAE catalogue.

Title: "Mananicas floridas".

Collection or series: Four carols on ancient texts, n° 4
Date of composition: 1963
It belongs to Lope de Vega's play: *El cardenal de Belen.*
First verse: "Mananicas floridas".
Character: Musica, Pascual (Anton, Bras)
Scenic notes: Singing
Duration: 2' 40" approx.
Key: G minor
Tessitura: D3-E4 flat
Aggonic indications: *Allegretto*
Location of the manuscript: Valencian Library
Manuscript symbol: AMAA/437
Remarks: The Cuatro villancicos sobre textos antiguos includes: I. Alegres mudanzas (text by Joaquin de Hinojosa), II. Alegres pastores (Lope de Vega), III. Este nino se lleva la flor (text by Josë de Valdivieso), IV. Mananicas floridas (Lope de Vega). The SGAE catalogue indicates a total duration of the four songs of 6'. With the same title this song is included in Once villancicos, from 1974, Nos. 4, 7 and 8 with text by Lope de Vega *(Mananicas foridas, Las pajas delpesebre* and *Marianita de diciembre),* the other songs on anonymous texts, by Juan de Avila, Gongora and populares. Of the whole group there is a recording by RNE with a duration of 23'. Another song entitled Mananitas floridas, from 1991, is a version of the original for three equal voices, of which there is another version for 4 voices, included in Tres villancicos diferentes sobre una misma letra by Lope de Vega, duration 9'.

Title: "(Where are you going, Maria?"

Subtitle: Christmas carol
Date of composition: 1968

It belongs to Lope de Vega's play: *Shepherds of Bethlehem.*
First verse: "Where are you going, zagala".
Character: Aminadab
Scenic annotations: [he said to him in song:]
Duration: 2' Duration: 2' Duration: 2' Duration: 2' Duration: 2' Duration: 2' Duration: 2
Key: A minor
Tessitura: C3-E4
Aggico indications: *Moderato*
Location of the manuscript: Valencian Library
Manuscript symbol: AMAA/535
Heading notes: Christmas carol

Title: "('Where are you going, what is Irio doing?"

Subtitle: Christmas carol
Date of composition: 1970
It belongs to Lope de Vega's play: *Shepherds of Bethlehem.*
First verse: "Zagalejo de perlas".
Character: Aminadab and Palmira
Scenic notes: [Aminadab [...] verna with his beloved Palmyra [...], and his wife accompanying him with voice and instrument, said the two asft].
Duration: 1'45".
Key: A minor
Tessitura: D3-E4
Aging indications: *Allegro*
Location of the manuscript: Valencian Library
Manuscript symbol: AMAA/523
Remarks: Date of composition taken from the SGAE catalogue. The score notes at the end the lyrics of the second and third stanzas to be sung to the same music as the first. Asins omits the refrain of this poem: "Zagalejo de perlas / hijo del alba".

BACARISSE CHINORIA, SALVADOR (1898-1963)

Title: "Soneto de Lope de Vega".

Subtitle: Who doesn't know about love
Opus No.: Op. 35
Date of composition: 23 July 1943
Place of composition: Pans
It belongs to Lope de Vega's play: jSi no vieran las mujeres!....
First verse: "He who does not know love, lives among wild beasts".
Character: Emperor [Oton]
Duration: 2' 30".
Key: B-flat major *
Tessitura: C3 flat-La4 flat
Agaggic indications: Andantino quasi allegretto
Location of the manuscript: Biblioteca Fundacion Juan March
Manuscript symbol: M-76-A/M-77-A/M-79-A/M-80-A
Title notes: For voice and piano
Observations: There is a version for song and orchestra: *Soneto de Lope de Vega. Quien no sabe de amor*. Op. 35, pour chant et orchestre / Salvador Bacarisse, 23-7-1943; Andantino; Lento (M-212-A). M-76-A has annotations of dynamics in pencil, which are included in the other handwritten copies, so it is assumed to be earlier.M-77-A includes *partcella* of the voice. Only M-

80-A has as a lilule 'ОШЙП (sic) no sabe de amor_".

Title: "Que de noche le mataron" (He was killed at night)

Opus No.: Op. 39, n° 1

Collection or series: Dos cantares de Lope de Vega, n° 1

Date of composition: 27 August 1944

Place of composition: Paris

It belongs to the play by Lope de Vega: El caballero de Olmedo.

First verse: "That at night they killed him".

Character: The Voice

Scenic notes: Sing from a distance in the dressing room, and come closer with your voice, as if you were walking.

Duration: 3' Duration: 3' Duration: 3' Duration: 3' Duration: 3' Duration: 3' Duration: 3'

Key: F minor

Tessitura: C3-Flat A-4

Location of the manuscript: Biblioteca Fundacion Juan March

Manuscript symbol: M-83-A / M-84-A

Dedication: To Amparito Peris

Remarks: M-83-A: handwritten annotation at the end of the song: Paris 27 August. M-84-A: handwritten annotation by the author at the end of the two songs: 25-27 August 1944 (this copy is later than manuscript M-83-A). Manuscript M-83-A is entitled "Dos canciones de Lope de Vega", M-84-A, "Dos cantares de Lope de Vega". There are transcriptions for voice and harp (M-81, 328-A), mixed *a cappella* choir (M-35-A, M-166-A and M-165-A), voice and orchestra (M-214-A).

Recording 1

Singer: Peris, Amparito (Sop.)

Pianist: Grimand, Yvette

Support: Cassette

Remarks: Copy on cassette from the original on open cassette tape from a French Radio Television recording. Available at the FJM Library, call number: MC-927.

Title: "Por el montecico sola" (On the mountain alone)

Opus No.: Op. 39, n° 2

Collection or series: Dos cantares de Lope de Vega, n° 2

Date of composition: 25 August 1944

Place of composition: Paris

It belongs to Lope de Vega's play: El villano en su rincon (The villain in his corner).

First verse: "Por el montecico sola" (On the mountain alone)

Character: Musicians

Scenic notes: The musicians sing and Bruno sings alone / Lisarda comes out to dance.

Duration: 1' 30".

Key: C sharp minor

Tessitura: C3 sharp - A4

Agaggic indications: *Andantino*

Location of the manuscript: Biblioteca Fundacion Juan March

Manuscript symbol: M-83-A / M-84-A

Dedication: To Amparito Peris

Title notes: For voice and piano

Remarks: M-83-A: handwritten annotation at the end of the song: "Paris, 25 August 1944. Day of the Nazi liberation'. M-84-A: handwritten annotation by the author at the end of the two songs: "25-27 August 1944" (this copy is later than manuscript M-83-A). Manuscript M-83-A is entitled "Dos canciones de Lope de Vega", M-84-A, "Dos cantares de Lope de Vega". There are

transcriptions for voice and harp (M-81, 328-A), mixed *a cappella* choir (M-35-A, M-166-A and M-165-A), voice and orchestra (M-214-A).
Recording 1
Singer: Peris, Amparito (Sop.)
Pianist: Grimand, Yvette
Support: Cassette
Remarks: Copy on cassette from the original on open cassette tape from a French Radio Television recording. Available at the FJM Library, call number: MC-927.

Title: "Coplas" (couplets)

Opus No.: Op. 52, n° 2
Collection or series: Deux chansons classiques espagnoles pour deux voix et piano, n° 2
Date of composition: 1950
Place of composition: Paris
It belongs to the work of Lope de Vega: *La Dorotea.*
First verse: "Mother, I saw some eyelets".
Character: Dorotea
Scenic notes: [Here, Celia, take the harp; it obliges me to make a lot of this reply].
Duration: 2' Duration: 2' Duration: 2' Duration: 2' Duration: 2' Duration: 2' Duration: 2
Key: G minor
Tessitura: C3-G4/G2-E4 flat
Aggonic indications: *Allegretto*
Location of the manuscript: Biblioteca Fundacion Juan March
Manuscript symbol: M-92-A
Head notes: Pour deux voix et piano
Remarks: *Deux chansons classiques espagnoles* includes: I. Madrigal, with text by Gutiërrez Cetrina, and II. *Coplas.* The manuscript bears registration stamp at the Societë des Auteurs, Compositeurs et Editeurs de Musique, Paris, 11-3-1959. Year of composition taken from the FJM.

BARRERA, ANTONIO ALVAREZ (1928-1991)

Title: "Cancion de siega" (Harvest Song)

Collection or series: Songs of the Golden Age, n° 1
Date of composition: 1986
It belongs to Lope de Vega's play: El gran duque de Moscovia (The Grand Duke of Muscovy).
First verse: "Blanca me era yo".
Character: Musicians
Scene notes: The reaper musicians come out, and with them Lucinda, Demetrio, Rufino, Belardo and Febo. They sing
Duration: 1' 30" approx.
Key: D Phrygian
Tessitura: C3-E4 flat
Date of publication: 1986
Publisher: Real Musical
Place of publication: Madrid
observations: Date of composition and publication taken from registration at the office of the Deposito Legal de Madrid (M 9498-1986).

Title: "Legend".

Collection or series: Songs of the Golden Age, n° 2
Date of composition: 1986
It belongs to the play by Lope de Vega: El caballero de Olmedo.

First verse: "That they killed him at night".
Character: The Voice
Scenic notes: Sing from far away in the dressing room, and vëngase approaching the voice, as if walking.
Duration: 1' 20" approx.
Key: A minor
Tessitura: E3-Mi4
Date of publication: 1986
Publisher: Real Musical
Place of publication: Madrid
Remarks: Date of composition and publication taken from registration at the Legal Deposit Office in Madrid (M 9498-1986).

Title: "Seguidillas".

Collection or series: Songs of the Golden Age, n° 3
Date of composition: 1986
It belongs to the work of Lope de Vega: La buena guarda or La encomienda bien guardada.
First verse: "Wash me in the Tajo".
Character: Musicians
Scenic notes: Shout of music and dance, ladies and gallants, and a waiter with a tabaque as a snack.
Duration: 2' approx.
Key: A minor
Tessitura: E3-Fa4
Date of publication: 1986
Publisher: Real Musical
Place of publication: Madrid
Remarks: Date of composition and publication taken from registration at the Oficina del Deposito Legal de Madrid (M 9498-1986). The score changes the order of the stanzas with respect to the original text of the comedy: the musicians intervene alternating the three stanzas, beginning with the stanza "Lavareme en el Tajo..." (third stanza in the song), followed by the interventions of D~ Clara, Damas 1ª and 2~, Galan 1° and 2°, and then the other two stanzas in the same order as the song.

Title: "Love song".

Collection or series: Songs of the Golden Age, n° 4
Date of composition: 1986
It belongs to Lope de Vega's play: El ruisenor de Sevilla.
First verse: "Si os panicredes al alba".
Character: Musicians
Scenic notes: [FATHER: sit down and sing].
Duration: 1' 40" approx.
Key: F sharp minor
Tessitura: C3 sharp - F4 sharp
Date of publication: 1986
Publisher: Real Musical
Place of publication: Madrid
Remarks: Date of composition and publication taken from registration at the Legal Deposit Office in Madrid (M 9498-1986).

Title: "Dance".

Collection or series: Songs of the Golden Age, n° 5

Date of composition: 1986
It belongs to the play by Lope de Vega: *La villana de Getafe.*
First verse: "A lady sent me".
Character: Ruiz, In's
Stage directions: They sing and dance
Duration: 2' approx.
Key: A minor
Tessitura: D3-Fa4 sharp
Date of publication: 1986
Publisher: Real Musical
Place of publication: Madrid
Remarks: Date of composition and publication taken from the register at the Office of the Deposito Legal de Madrid (M 9498-1986).

BENAVENTE MARTINEZ, JOSE MARIA (1929-)

Title: "The vanquished sun".

Collection or series: Christmas triptych by Lope de Vega, n° 1
Date of composition: 1956
It belongs to Lope de Vega's play: *Shepherds of Bethlehem.*
First verse: "Of a beautiful Virgin".
Character: Joran
Scenic notes: [It was not necessary to beg the other shepherds to sing, for they all came forward and joyfully began as follows].
Duration: 1' 10" approx.
Key: G major
Tessitura: G3-G4
Agaggic indications: *Andantino*
Date of release: 18-5-1956
Premiere venue: Conservatorio de Madrid
Remarks: The triptych includes: I. *El sol vencido,* II. *No lloreis mis ojos,* III. *Danza gitana.* Photocopy of the cycle together with other choral compositions and compositions for voice and organ given by the composer to the library of the RCSMM, with autographed dedication: "For the library of the Real Conservatorio de Musica de Madrid..." Josë Mª Benavente, Madrid, 1995. No date of edition or mention of the publisher. The title page indicates the place and date of premiere. Year of composition taken from the date of premiere.

Title: "Don't cry my eyes out".

Collection or series: Christmas triptych by Lope de Vega, n° 2
Date of composition: 1956
It belongs to Lope de Vega's play: *Shepherds of Bethlehem.*
First verse: "Do not weep, my eyes".
Character: Finarda
Scenic annotations: [...temple an instrument and singing and crying, he said thus':]
Duration: 1' 40" approx.
Key: C minor
Tessitura: G3-G4
Aggico indications: *Moderato*
Date of release: 18-5-1956
Premiere venue: Conservatorio de Madrid
Motivation: Academic work of the subject of composition at the Conservatory of Madrid, being a student of Julio Gomez.

Remarks: The triptych includes: I. *El sol vencido,* II. *No lloreis mis ojos,* III. *Danza gitana.* Photocopy of the cycle together with other choral compositions and compositions for voice and organ given by the composer to the library of the RCSMM, with autographed dedication: "For the library of the Real Conservatorio de Musica de Madrid..." Josë Mª Benavente, Madrid, 1995. No date of edition or mention of the publisher. The title page indicates the place and date of premiere. Year of composition taken from the date of premiere.

Title: "Gypsy Dance".

Collection or series: Tnptico navideno de Lope de Vega, n° 3
Date of composition: 1956
It belongs to Lope de Vega's play: *Shepherds of Bethlehem.*
First verse: "A la dina dana".
Character: Elifila
Scenic notes: [Elifila, to whom the third lot was drawn, sang thus:]
Duration: 2' 30" approx.
Key: C major
Tessitura: C3-G4
Agaggic indications: *Allegretto scherzando*
Premiere date: 18-5-1956
Premiere venue: Conservatorio de Madrid
Remarks: The triptych includes: I. *El sol vencido,* II. *No lloreis mis ojos,* III. *Danza gitana.* Photocopy of the cycle together with other choral compositions and compositions for voice and organ given by the composer to the library of the RCSMM, with autographed dedication: "For the library of the Real Conservatorio de Musica de Madrid, Josë Mª Benavente, Madrid, 1995".
No edition date or publisher's mention. The title page indicates the place and date of release. Year of composition taken from the date of release.

BUENO AGUADO [BUENAGU], JOSE (1936-)

Title: "Sleep, my child".

Date of composition: June 1954
Place of composition: Madrid
It belongs to Lope de Vega's play: *Shepherds of Bethlehem.*
First verse: "Pues andais en las palmas".
Character: Elifila
Scenic notes: [that I intend to imitate you in my song, saying like this:]
Duration: 1' 50" approx.
Key: A major
Tessitura: A3-A4
Aggic indications: *Lento/Allegretto tranquillo*
Manuscript location: Juan March
Manuscript symbol: M-359-B
Title: Singing and Piano
observations: Autograph manuscript dated and signed at the end of the score: June 1954. In the manuscript the author's name appears as Jose B. Aguado. From the date of composition, written at the age of 18, probably from his time as a student at the Madrid Conservatory.

Campo Y ZABALETA, CONRADO DEL (1879-1953)

Title: "So alive it is in my soul".

Collection or series: A lady is for sale to whomever wants her, Altarpiece
Date of composition: 1935
It belongs to the work of Lope de Vega: *La Dorotea.*

First verse: "So alive is he in my soul".
Character: Fernando
Scenic notes: [La prima que se le ha puesto, y a cantar vuelve].
Duration: ca. 3' 30".
Key: A minor *
Tessitura: F2-A3
Release date: 12-12-1935
Place of the premiere: Teatro Espanol, Madrid
Opening singer: Miguel Fleta (Ten.)
Location of the manuscript: CEDOA-SGAE/RCSMM
Manuscript signature: Legado Conrado del Campo, box 8.51
Notes to the title: Letrilla from "La Dorotea".
Motivation: Composed for the participation of the tenor Miguel Fleta in the act of homage of the Conservatory of Madrid to Lope de Vega.
Observations: Composition for voice and piano independent of the altarpiece *Una dama se vende a quien la quiera*, performed in the intermission of the same, both premiered in the act of homage to Lope de Vega in the tercentenary of his death that the Conservatorio de Madrid offered on 12 December 1935 at the Teatro Espanol in Madrid. In the Library of the RCSMM are preserved the *parts of* the retablo, the pointing scripts and a manuscript of this song, in CEDOA-SGAE another manuscript copy of the same, this last one is annotated at the top with "Pte. De Aptar. [parte de apuntar], and is entitled *Intermedia.* The title of the song, taken from the first verse, is the one used by Miguel Alonso in the catalogue of the works of Conrado del Campo.

Title: "Song of the shepherdess Finarda".

Collection or cycle: *Figuras de Belen,* Evocaciones sinfonicas. Intermediate
Date of composition: 1946
It belongs to Lope de Vega's play: *Pastares de Belen.*
First verse: "Do not weep, my eyes".
Character: Finarda
Scenic annotations: [...temple an instrument and singing and crying, he said thus':|
Duration: 2'40" ca.
Key: G major
Tessitura: D3-Flat A4 (B4 optional)
Aging indications: *Andantno*
Premiere date: 1946
Place of the premiere: Teatro Romea, Murcia
Other performances: 4-12-86, presentation of the Catalogo de obras de Conrado del Campo, by Miguel Alonso. In the 2ª part Pura Mª Maiti'nez, sings the Cancion de la Pastora Finarda.
Location of the manuscript: CEDOA-SGAE
Manuscript signature: Legado Conrado del Campo, caja 8.30
Dedication: Elsa del Campo, daughter of the composer
Header indications: "Shepherds of Bethlehem. Lope de Vega" "With great tenderness and almost declaimed".
Motivation: Intermediate of Figures of Bel'n
Remarks: *Figures of Bethlehem.* Symphonic evocations inspired by Salzillo's Nativity. It consists of four numbers: I. *Poematic overture* (El ángel que anuncia, Los pastores caminan alegremente, El portal de Bel'n y Adoracion, with brief intervention of a voice of the angel-nino singing "Gloria in excelsis Deo..."), II. *La vieja hila y el gallo contempla. Intermediate Cancion de la pastora Finarda* ("No lloreis mis ojos"), for voice and piano (there is an arrangement by the author for voice, 2 oboes, 2 bassoons and violin solo), III. *The Three Wise Men. Cavalcade.* Adoration. IV.

Nocturne. Round of the shepherds (The shepherds march towards the portal (a child's voice sings "Dejate caer, Pascual"). The manuscript bears several dates: Nos. I and II 14 and 26-2-1946, III and IV 11-10-1946.

CARBAJO CADENAS, VICTOR (1970-)

Title: "Absence".

Date of composition: 25-9-1999
Place of composition: Madrid
It belongs to the work of Lope de Vega: *Rimas (Rhymes).*
First Verse: "To go and to stay, and with staying to depart", Rima LXI
Approximate duration: 4' 30".
Heading indications: for Soprano, Mezzosoprano (or Contralto) and Piano
Tessitura: C2-Do5/A2 sharp-E4 flat
Location of the manuscript: Personal archive of the composer
Observations: Original work for two voices and piano. The composer lends us an electronic copy of the score, which is unpublished. He himself informs us [e-mail, 8-3-2012] that it was premiered and several performances were given in South American countries, without specifying dates or places.

CAROL, MERCEDES [MERCEDES GARCIA LOPEZ].[321]

Title: "Cantarcillo".

Subtitle: No lloreis, ojuelos
Collection or series: *Five songs,* n° 4
Date of composition: 1964
It belongs to the work of Lope de Vega: *La Dorotea.*
First verse: "No lloreis, ojuelos".
Character: Don Fernando
Scenic notes: [I want to sing, so that they'll be quiet:]
Duration: 1' 40' approx.
Key: G minor
Tessitura: D3-E4 flat
Aggressive indications: Slow
Date of publication: 1964
Publisher: Union Musical Espanola
Place of publication: Madrid
Title notes: For voice and piano
Remarks: Year of composition taken from the date of publication. Mercedes Carol, pseudonym of Mercedes Garcia Lopez.
Recording 1
Year: 1977
Singer: Marlinez, Pura Maria (Sop.) **Pianist:** Rodriguez Gavilanes, Rogelio **Venue:** Casa de la Radio, Madrid
Date: 21-10-1977
Support: Radio
Duration: Unspecified
Comments: RNE recording.

[321] In spite of the enquiries we have made, it has been impossible to locate a relative who could provide us with the biographical details of Mercedes Garcia Lopez, a singing teacher at the Madrid Conservatory, where she had previously been a pupil. In her student days she premiered three of the *Cinco canciones* de Josë Maria Guervos in the Homenaje a Lope de Vega at the Teatro Espanol on 12 December 1935, of which she was also the dedicatee. Some of her students with whom we have been in contact have not been able to give any further information.

CASAL CHAPI, ENRIQUE (1909-1977)

Title: "Sonnet".

Collection or series: Two fragments of the Knight of Olmedo, n° 1
Date of composition: 21 September 1935
It belongs to the play by Lope de Vega: El caballero de Olmedo.
First verse: "I saw the most beautiful farm worker".
Character: In("s
Scenic notes: [Read [Alonso's letter]].
Length: 1' 34"
Key: D Phrygian *
Tessitura: C3 sharp-G4
Agragic indications: Lento, *quasi parlato*
Date of publication: 1938
Publisher: Ediciones del Consejo Central de la Musica
Mention of publication: Ministerio de Instruccion Publica, Direccion General de Bellas Artes.
Place of publication: Barcelona
Title notes: For voice and piano /On the tercentenary of Lope de Vega
Motivation: Supposedly, for the 1935 National Music Competition.
Recording 1
Year: 1998
Singer: Gragera, Elena (Mz.)
Pianist: Cardo, Anton
Venue: Centro Cultural Conde Duque, Madrid
Date: 9-3-1998
Support: Radio
Duration: Unspecified
Observations: RNE recording. Duration of the two songs of the cycle "Dos fragmentos del caballero de Olmedo" 6'15".

Title: "Romancillo".

Collection or series: Two fragments of the Knight of Olmedo, n° 2
Date of composition: 22 September 1935
It belongs to the play by Lope de Vega: El caballero de Olmedo.
First verse: "Alas, rigorous state".
Character: Alonso
Length: 3' 55"
Key: B flat major
Tessitura: C3 sharp-G4 sharp
Aging indications: *Molto tranquillo*
Date of publication: 1938
Publisher: Editions du Conseil Central de la Musique
Mention of publication: Ministerio de Instruccion Publica, Direccion General de Bellas Artes.
Place of publication: Barcelona
Title notes: For voice and piano /On the tercentenary of Lope de Vega
Motivation: Supposedly, for the 1935 National Music Competition.
Recording 1
Year: 1998
Singer: Gragera, Elena (Mz.)
Pianist: Cardo, Anton
Venue: Centro Cultural Conde Duque, Madrid

Date: 9-3-1998
Support: Radio
Duration: Unspecified
Observations: RNE recording. Duration of the two songs of the cycle "Dos fragmentos del caballero de Olmedo" 6'15".

Title: "Serrana".

Collection or series: Tres cantares de Lope de Vega, n° 1
Date of composition: 28 September 1935
It belongs to Lope de Vega's play: *El Adegiiela.*
First verse: "They skipped my eyes".
Character: Anton, Toribio, Alejo, Chamorro, Benito, Felipa, Teresa, Marfa and musicians are in the cast.
Scenic notes: Cantan
Length: 1' 38"
Key: F major *
Tessitura: E3-G4
Aggressive indications: *Mosso assai*
Date of publication: 1938
Publisher: Editions du Conseil Central de la Musique
Place of publication: Barcelona
Title notes: For voice and piano
Motivation: Supposedly, for the 1935 National Music Competition.

Title: "Harvest Song".

Collection or series: Tres cantares de Lope de Vega, n° 2
Date of composition: 29 September 1935
It belongs to Lope de Vega's play: El gran duque de Moscovia (The Grand Duke of Muscovy).
First verse: "Blanca me era yo".
Character: Musicians
Scenic notes: The reaper musicians come out, and with them Lucinda, Demetrio, Rufino, Belardo and Febo. They sing.
Length: 2' 25"
Key: A
Tessitura: G3-G4
Agragic indications: *Lento molto*
Date of publication: 1938
Publisher: Ediciones del Consejo Central de la Musica
Place of publication: Barcelona
Head notes: For voice and piano
Motivation: Supposedly for the 1935 National Music Competition.

Title: "Villancico" (Christmas carol)

Collection or series: Tres cantares de Lope de Vega, n° 3
Date of composition: 29 September 1935
It belongs to Lope de Vega's play: Peribanez y el comendador de Ocana.
First verse: "Cogiome a tu puerta el toro".
Character: Musicians
Scenic notes: Musicians sing
Duration: 0' 45"
Key: F minor
Tessitura: C3-Fa4

Agaggic indications: *Allegretto vivace*
Date of publication: 1938
Publisher: Ediciones del Consejo Central de la Musica
Place of publication: Barcelona
Motivation: Supposedly, for the 1935 National Music Competition.

CASARES Y ESPINOSA DE LOS MONTEROS, JOSE MARIA (CA. 1860) 1900)

Title: "Trova".

Date of composition: ca. 1890
It belongs to the work of Lope de Vega: *La Dorotea.*
First verse: "Mother, I saw some eyelets".
Character: Dorotea
Scenic notes: [Take, Celia, the harp; that obliges me to much this answer].
Duration: 1' 50" approx.
Key: A flat major
Tessitura: E3-Fa4
Location of the manuscript: Biblioteca Fundacion Juan March
manuscript symbol: M-480-A
Title: Singing and Piano
Observations: There is another manuscript (M-920-A) with the same music entitled *Coplas* which seems to be an earlier draft. The same composer has another work for voice and piano with the title *Trova* con poesia de H. Heine, which can be confused with this one. Dates of birth and death unknown. Emilio Casares Rodicio (in *Diccionario de la Zarzuela espanola e Hispanoamericana,* vol. 1, p. 416) notes that he was a composer from Granada active in Madrid from the 1870s onwards (he is also mentioned in *Diccionario de la musica espanola e hispanoamericana,* vol. 3, p. 298). A letter from Jorge Bĕcquer, son of G. A. Bĕcquer, dated 10-I-1891, authorising Josë Casares y Espinosa de los Monteros to set to music and publish his father's rhymes, is preserved in the FJM, together with other letters dated 1884, from which we take an approximate date of composition.

COLODRO CAMPOS, FERNANDO (1941-)

Title: "Mananicas floridas".

Date of composition: 5 February 1990
Place of composition: Martos (Jacn)
It belongs to Lope de Vega's play: *El cardenal de Belen.*
First verse: "Mananicas floridas".
Character: Musica, Pascual (Anton, Bras)
Scenic notes: Canten
Duration: 2' 15" approx.
Key: G major
Tessitura: D3-E4
Agragic indications: *Largo-Larghetto*
Release date: 5-2-1990
Place of the premiere: Colegio San Antonio, Martos Jacn)
Singer of the premiere: M- del Carmen Abolafia Martinez (Sop.)
Pianist for the premiere: Fernando Colodro
Location of the manuscript: Composer's archive **Dedication:** Dedicated to Laura Antonia Colodro Abolafia
Headline indications: Voice and piano

Observations: The composer dictated it to a niece and it is premiered by ësta's mother, soprano soloist of the Coral Tuccitana conducted by Colodro. According to the composer's own information, the date of the premiere given by the Centro de Documentacion Musica de Madrid (22 November 1988) is incorrect, the correct date is the one indicated in the score, 5 February 1990.

COTARELO ROMANOS, FRANCISCO (1884-1943)

Title: "Mother, I saw some eyelets".

Collection or series: *Cuato canciones,* n° 2
Date of composition: 1925
It belongs to the work of Lope de Vega: *La Dorotea.*
First verse: "Mother, some eyelets I saw".
Character: Dorotea
Scenic notes: [Take, Celia, the harp; that obliges me to much this answer].
Duration: 2' 50' approx.
Key: A major
Tessitura: B4-flat-La5
Location of the manuscript: Eresbil, Basque Music Archive
Manuscript code: E/COT-01/A-08
Remarks: Information on date of composition (ca. 1925) is from Isabel Diaz Morlan in *La cancion para voz y piano en el Pais Vasco ente 1870 y 1939,* doctoral thesis. The *Cuato canciones* also include: *El baratero, Los ninos en el parque* and *Capa espanola.*

DIAZ YERRO, GONZALO (1977-)

Title: "When I stop to contemplate my state".

Collection or series: *Four sonnets,* n° 1
Date of composition: 9-10-1998 Place of composition: Wien
It belongs to the work of Lope de Vega: *Rimas sacras (Sacred Rhymes)*
First verse: "When I stop to contemplate my state", First Sonnet
Duration: 2' 10" approx.
Tonality: Special modal
Tessitura: G1 sharp - G3 sharp
Aggressive indications: 60
Release date: October 1999
Place of the premiere: Universitat fur Musik und Darstellende Kunst, Wien
Opening singer: Alfredo Garcia (bar.)
Pianist for the premiere: Sonja Hubert
Location of the manuscript: CEDOA-SGAE
Manuscript symbol: Archivo Sinfonico 22.230
Dedication: to Alfredo Garcia
Head notes: Banton and piano (Bariton-Klavier)
Motivation: For the second composition course in Vienna
Remarks: In all of them annotation "Deo soli gloria" together with date and signature. Only no. 4 bears the indication of the place of composition, "Wien", the author states that they were all composed in that city.

Title: "Shepherd who with your loving whistles".

Collection or series: *Four Sonnets,* n° 2
Date of composition: 27-11-1998
Place of composition: Wien
It belongs to the work of Lope de Vega: *Rimas sacras (Sacred Rhymes)*

First Verse: "Shepherd, who with your loving whistles", Sonnet XIV
Duration: 2' ca.
Tonality: Special modal
Tessitura: A1 flat-G3
Agogic indications: ca. 60
Release date: October 1999
Place of the premiere: Universitat fur Musik und Darstellende Kunst, Wien
Opening singer: Alfredo Garcia (bar.)
Pianist for the premiere: Sonja Hubert
Location of the manuscript: CEDOA-SGAE
Signature, from manuscript: Archivo Sinfonico 22.230
Dedication: to Alfredo Garcia
Head notes: Bariton and piano (Bariton-Klavier)
Motivation: For the second composition course in Vienna
Remarks: In all of them annotation "Deo soli gloria" together with date and signature. Only no. 4 bears the indication of the place of composition, "Wien", the author states that they were all composed in that city.

Title: "('What do I have that you seek my friendship?"

Collection or series: *Four sonnets,* n° 4
Date of composition: 5-2-1999
Place of composition: Wien
It belongs to the work of Lope de Vega: *Rimas sacras (Sacred Rhymes)*
First Verse: "(Qnc have I, that thou seekest my friendship?", Sonnet XVIII
Duration: 2' 15" approx.
Tonality: Special modal
Tessitura: A1-E3
Aggregate indications: 60-72
Release date: October 1999
Place of the premiere: Universitat fur Musik und Darstellende Kunst, Wien
Opening singer: Alfredo Garcia (bar.)
Pianist for the premiere: Sonja Hubert
Location of the manuscript: CEDOA-SGAE
Manuscript symbol: Archivo Sinfonico 22.230
Dedication: to Alfredo Garcia
Head notes: Bariton and piano (Bariton-Klavier)
Motivation: For the second composition course in Vienna
Remarks: In all of them annotation "Deo soli gloria" together with date and signature. Only no. 4 bears the indication of the place of composition, "Wien", the author states that they were all composed in that city.

Title: "How often, Lord, have you called me".

Collection or series: *Four Sonnets,* n° 3
Date of composition: 27-12-1998
Place of composition: Wien
It belongs to the work of Lope de Vega: *Rimas sacras (Sacred Rhymes)*
First verse: "How often, Lord, you have called me", Sonnet XV
Duration: 2' ca.
Tonality: Special modal
Tessitura: G1 sharp - G3
Agogic indications: ca. 60

Release date: October 1999
Place of the premiere: Universitat fur Musik und Darstellende Kunst, Wien
Premiere singer: Alfredo Gai ria (bar.)
Pianist for the premiere: Sonja Hubert
Location of the manuscript: CEDOA-SGAE
Manuscript symbol: Archivo Sinfonico 22.230
Dedication: to Alfredo Garcia
Head notes: Bariton and piano (Bariton-Klavier)
Motivation: For the second composition course in Vienna
Remarks: In all of them annotation "Deo soli gloria" together with date and signature. Only no. 4 bears the indication of the place of composition, "Wien", the author states that they were all composed in that city.

DURAN MARTINEZ, GUSTAVO (1906-1969)

Title: "Seguidillas de la noche de San Juan".

Date of composition: October 1926
Place of composition: Playa de las Canteras, Island of Gran Canaria
It belongs to Lope de Vega's play: Las flores de Don Juan, y rico y pobre trocados (The flowers of Don Juan, and rich and poor exchanged).
First verse: "They leave Valencia".
Character: Musicians
Stage directions: Shout and shout inside, and sing with rattles.
Duration: 1' approx.
Key: B minor
Tessitura: E3-Mi4
Aging indications: Con una chiara allegrezza. Ma calmo e pesante
Remarks: Indications of date and place of composition on the score. Photocopy from Residencia de Estudiantes.
Recording 1
Year: 2000
Singer: Estëvez, Estrella (Sop.)
Pianist: Hervas, Francisco
Date: 2000
Media: CD
Label: Arsis
Discographical reference: ARSIS 4155
Length: 2:22

ESCUDERO GARCIA, FRANCISCO (1913-2002)

Title: "At the Burial of Christ".

Date of composition: 1974
It belongs to the work of Lope de Vega: *Rimas sacras (Sacred Rhymes)*
First Verse: "A los brazos de Maria", Rima CXXXII
Length: 4' 53"
Tonality: Atonal
Tessitura: A2-Do5
Date of release: 3-4-1974
Place of the premiere: Estudio Musica I, RNE. Madrid
Opening singer: Carmen Torrico
Pianist for the premiere: Mª Elena Barrientos

Location of the manuscript: Eresbil-Basque Music Archive
manuscript symbol: E/EsC-07/A-04
Date of publication: 1975
Publisher: Alpuerto
Place of publication: Madrid
Head notes: For soprano voice and piano
Motivation: Commissioned by Radio Nacional de Espana
Observations: According to the researcher Itziar Larrinaga the work dates from 1974, not 1947 as the SGAE and FJM catalogues state. In the only existing recording it is entitled: "Poema al entierro de Cristo: para soprano y piano", while the SGAE catalogue calls it "Romance al entierro de Cristo para soprano y piano". Here we take the title "Al entierro de Cristo" which is the one that appears in the published score.
Recording 1
Year: 1974
Singer: Carmen Torrico (Sop.)
Pianist: Maria Elena Barrientos
Venue: Estudio Musica I, RNE, Madrid
Date: 3-4-1974
Support: Radio
Remarks: Duration not specified.
Recording 2
Year: 1992
Singer: Kudo, Atsuko (Sop.)
Pianist: Zabala, Alejandro
Venue: San Sebastian Town Hall
Date: 18-8-1992
Support: Radio
Length: 4:53
Observations: San Sebastian Musical Fortnight. Recorded by RNE.
Recording 3
Year: 2002
Singer: Martinez, Pura Maria (Sop.)
Pianist: Lopez Laguna, Gerardo
Venue: Musigrama Studios, Madrid
Date: 2002
Media: CD
Record label: Fundacion Bilbao Bizkaia Kutxa
Label reference: BBK 010
Recording 4
Year: 2002
Singer: Maitfnez, Pura Maria (Sop.)
Pianist: Lopez Laguna, Gerardo
Venue: Miramar Palace, San Sebastian
Date: 27-8-2002
Support: Radio
Duration: 5:10
Observations: San Sebastian Musical Fortnight. Recorded by RNE. Not allowed to broadcast without the permission of the performers.

FRANCO BORDONS, JOSE MARIA (1894-1971)

Title: "To...you "

Collection or series: *Cuato canciones,* n° 1
Date of composition: 7 January 1917
Place of composition: Madrid
It belongs to Lope de Vega's play: La discreta enamorada (The Discreet Lover).
First verse: "When I look at you so beautifully".
Character: Musicians
Stage directions: Playing and singing
Duration: 1' approx.
Key: E flat major
Tessitura: B2 $_{flat-Re3}$
Agaggic indications: *Andante cantabile*
Location of the manuscript: Biblioteca Fundacion Juan March
Manuscript symbol: M-7171-B / M-7206-B
Title: Poetry by Lope de Vega
Remarks: Date of composition at the end of the manuscript. Below the title it notes "transcripcion para bajo" (transcription for bass). The *four songs* include three others with lyrics by Amado Nervo (no. 2), and by R. Tagore (nos. 3 and 4). There is another song with the same title, *A...i* with sig. M-7206-B, with a later date (Madrid, 2 April 1918), a transcription of the previous one, a sharp 4^{a} , with slight changes in the piano. With the data given in the manuscripts regarding the difference in dates and the indication of transposition, it is not clear which version is the original.

GARCIA, MANUEL DEL POPULO VICENTE (1775-1832)

Title: "The Love Boat".

Collection or series: Chansons espagnoles
Date of composition: ca. 1810
It belongs to Lope de Vega's play: *El arauco domado (The tamed arauco).*
First verse: "Piraguamonte, piragua".
Character: Musicians [Indians].
Scenic notes: The Indians ë Indians come out, and the musicians with their instruments. [...] All seated, Quidora and Leocoton dance, the musicians sing.
Duration: 2' 15" approx.
Key: E major
Tessitura: $_{D3-B4}$
Agaggic indications: *Vivace* with grace
Date of publication: 1994
Publisher: Instituto Complutense de Ciencias Musicales
Mention of edition: Canciones y caprichos liricos. Manuel Garcia. Critical edition by Celsa Alonso.
Place of publication: Madrid
Remarks: Belongs to the collection Chansons espagnoles par Manuel Garcia [x'rc, paroles francaises de Mr. Louis Pomey, arrangi'es avec acompagnement de piano par Mme. Pauline Viardot, Gerard, Paris, Paris, 1875. Lope uses in the songs descriptive words of the reality of the New World that have been adapted to 16th century Spanish, some from Caribbean languages (piragua) others from Quechua (tambo). Garcia uses in this song only the first of the four stanzas that make up the scene. In addition to the sensual and colourful description of Venus' boat, Lope shows his ability to unite two subjects, one classical with the other Indian. The element of union between the two worlds is the word "bow", that of Cupid and the weapon of the Indians. The same facility is shown in the relationship of the 4 parts of the song, which is composed of 4 romances framed by the "Indian" refrain that opens and closes the song and separates the 4 parts. While 1-

and 3- are related to the comedy by the "Indian" theme, 2- and 4- are united by the story of "el nino Amor" (Umpierre, p. 99). We find it interesting to interpret this song with all of Lope's complete lyrics, the four stanzas, with Garcia's music, as a strophic song.

GARCIA DE LA PARRA Y TELLEZ, BENITO (1884-1954)

Title: "Cancion de Lope de Vega".

Subtitle: Castilla la Vieja
Collection or series: Cancionero espanol, first volume, n° 12
Date of composition: [1943].
It belongs to Lope de Vega's play: *El bobo del colegio.*
First verse: "Naranjitas me tira la nina".
Character: Musicians
Scenic notes: Canten
Duration: 1' 45" approx.
Key: G major
Tessitura: Re3-Re4
Aggico indications: *Moderato*
Date of publication: [1943].
Publisher: Juan Bta. Pujol Editores
Mention of edition: Women's Section of F.E.T. and J.O.N.S.
Motivation: Women's Section assignment
Remarks: Year of composition deduced from the date of edition. Copy of the edition dedicated to Julio Gomez: autograph dedication of the author on the first page: "To my good friend Julio Gomez, illustrious Spanish composer. The author, 8-7-1943". In the accompaniment part, pedals and apagar pedales are indicated, from which it can be deduced that it is for piano. The first verse does not coincide with Lope.

GARCIA FERNANDEZ, VORO (1970-)

Title: "Into the night".

Collection or series: *From the soul,* n° 2
Date of composition: 2011
It belongs to the work of Lope de Vega: *Rimas (Rhymes).*
First line of verse: "Night, maker of tricks", Rima CXXXVII
Duration: 2' 30" approx.
Tonality: Atonal
Tessitura: F2 sharp-Fa4
Aging indications: *Dolce, piu intmo,* 54
Location of the manuscript: Personal archive of the composer
Release date: 12-5-2011
Premiere venue: Valencia, Ensems Festival
Debut singer: Jose Hernandez Pastor (countertenor)
Pianist for the premiere: Bartomeu Jaume
Other performances: Auditorium of Cuenca, Auditorio 400 MNCARS of Madrid and Teatro Arriga of Bilbao [April 2011].
Dedication: To my wife
Motivation: Commissioned by the Festival Festclasica in commemoration of the 400th anniversary of the death of T. L. De Victoria.
Leading indications: Once the baritone has left the stage, the countertenor enters the stage silently. [refers to the baritone who performs the previous song of the group].
Remarks: Originally written for countertenor and piano. The pianist recites some short texts by

San Juan de la Cruz as a transition between the pieces of the group. The score includes various percussion effects with various materials that are manipulated by both the singer and the pianist.

Title: "To my solitudes I go".

Collection or series: *From the soul,* n° 4

Date of composition: 2011

It belongs to the work of Lope de Vega: *La Dorotea.*

First verse: "To my solitudes I go".

Character: Don Fernando

Stage directions: Sing

Duration: 5' approx.

Tonality: Atonal

Tessitura: F2 sharp-Re3

Aging indications: *Dolce, piu intimo*, 54

Location of the manuscript: Personal archive of the composer

Release date: 12-5-2011

Premiere venue: Valencia, Ensems Festival

Debut singer: Josë Hernandez Pastor (countertenor)

Pianist for the premiere: Bartomeu Jaume

Other performances: Auditorium of Cuenca, Auditorio 400 MNCARS of Madrid and Teatro Arriga of Bilbao [April 2011].

Dedication: To my wife

Motivation: Commissioned by the Festival Festclasica in commemoration of the 400th anniversary of the death of T. L. De Victoria.

Leading indications: Once the bari'lono has left the stage, the countertenor enters silently. Taking the spazzola jazz for the script. [refers to the bantono playing the previous song of the group].

Remarks: Originally written for countertenor and piano. The pianist recites some short texts by San Juan de la Cruz as a transition between the pieces of the group. The score includes various percussion effects with various materials that are manipulated by both the singer and the pianist.

GOMEZ GARCIA, JULIO (1886-1973)

Title: "('What do I have that you seek my friendship?"

Collection or series: Cuatro poesias liricas de Lope de Vega, n° 1

Date of composition: 25 August 1935

Place of composition: Yunquera de Henares (Guadalajara)

It belongs to the work of Lope de Vega: *Rimas sacras (Sacred Rhymes)*

First Verse: "(What have I, that you seek my friendship?", Sonnet XVIII

Duration: 2' 10"

Key: A flat major

Tessitura: D2-Fa3

Agaggic indications: *Andante*

Location of the manuscript: Biblioteca Fundacion Juan March / BN

Manuscript symbol: JM: M-766-A and BN: MP/5352/1

Head notes: Bantono and piano / from the Rimas Sacras (Sacred Rhymes)

Awards: Prize at the National Music Competition in 1935

Motivation: National Music Competition 1935

Remarks: Manuscript signed and dated: "Yunquera 25 agosto 1935" (refers to Yunquera de Henares, Guadalajara). A draft is preserved (FJM, call number M-766- A). An original manuscript (MP / 5352/1) of the 4 songs is preserved in the BN, with the title on a title page: *Cuato poesias liricas de Lope de Vega,* with the songs cleaned up and corrections in the dynamic and expressive indications.

Title: "The Truth".

Collection or series: Cuatro poesias liricas de Lope de Vega, n° 2
Date of composition: 26 August 1935
Place of composition: Yunquera de Henares (Guadalajara)
It belongs to the work of Lope de Vega: *Rimas (Rhymes).*
First verse: "Daughter of time, who in the golden century", Sonnet CLIX
Duration: 1' 50".
Key: C major
Tessitura: C2-E3
Aggressive indications: Slow, severe
Location of the manuscript: Juan March Foundation Library /BN
Manuscript symbol: FJM: M-767-A and BN: MP / 5352/1
Header indications: Bantono and piano / from the Rimas humanas, 1ª part
Awards: Prize at the National Music Competition in 1935
Motivation: National Music Competition 1935
Observations: M-767-A is a manuscript draft, on a landscape sheet, dated: "Yunquera 26 agosto 935" (sic). An original manuscript (MP / 5352/1) of the 4 songs is preserved in the BN with the title on a title page: *Cuato poesias liricas de Lope de Vega,* with the songs cleaned up and corrections in the dynamic and expressive indications.

Title: "Villancico" (Christmas carol)

Collection or series: Cuatro poesias liricas de Lope de Vega, n° 3
Date of composition: September 1935
It belongs to Lope de Vega's play: *Shepherds of Bethlehem.*
First verse: "The straws of the manger".
Character: Tebandra
Scenic notes: [It was not necessary to beg the other shepherds to sing, for they all joined in, and joyfully began like this.
Duration: 3' 30".
Key: D minor
Tessitura: D3-Fa4
Agaggic indications: *Andante*, with simplicity
Location of the manuscript: Biblioteca Fundacion Juan March / BN
Manuscript symbol: JM: M-771-A, M-772-A -BN: MP / 5352/1
Head notes: Tiple and piano / Shepherds of Bethlehem, book 3°.
Awards: Prize at the National Music Competition in 1935
Motivation: National Music Competition 1935
Remarks: M-772-A is a handwritten draft, on landscape sheet, dated: "setembre 935" (sic). M-771-A only signed. An original manuscript (MP / 5352/1) of the 4 songs is preserved in the BN with the title on a title page: *Cuatopoesias liiicas de Lope de Vega*, with the songs cleaned up and corrections in the dynamic and expressive indications.
Recording 1
Year: 2011
Singer: Anna Tonna (Mz.)
Pianist: Jorge Robaina
Venue: Real Conservatorio Superior de Madrid
Date: 2011
Media: CD
Label: Verso
Discographical reference: VRS 2106

Length: 3:52
Remarks: Included in the album "Las canciones de Julio Gomez".

Title: "Jealousy, don't kill me".

Collection or series: Cuatro poesi'as li'ricas de Lope de Vega, n° 4
Date of composition: 29 September 1935
It belongs to the work of Lope de Vega: Codice Duran.
First verse: "Jealousy that does not kill me".
Length: 2' 35"
Key: D Phrygian
Tessitura: F2 sharp - A3
Aggressive indications: Slowly
Opening singer: Enrique de la Vara (Ten.)
Location of the manuscript: Biblioteca Fundacion Juan March / BN
Manuscript symbol: JM: M-768-A/M-769-A/M-769-A/M-770-A and BN: MP / 5352/1
Head notes: Tenor and piano / From the codex by D. Agiislin Duran
Awards: Prize at the National Music Competition in 1935
Motivation: National Music Competition 1935
Remarks: A draft on landscape paper is preserved in FJM, M-770-A, signed and dated: "29 sebre 935" (sic.), plus two manuscript copies signed: M-768-A and M-769-A. An original manuscript (MP / 5352/1) of the 4 songs is preserved in the BN, with the title on a title page: *Cuato poesias liricas de Lope de Vega,* with the songs cleaned and corrections in the dynamic and expressive indications.

GRANADOS Y CAMPINA, ENRIQUE (1867-1916)

Title: "No lloreis, ojuelos".

Collection or series: *Canciones amatoiias,* n° 5
Date of composition: 1914
It belongs to the work of Lope de Vega: *La Dorotea.*
First verse: "No lloreis, ojuelos".
Character: Don Fernando
Stage directions: [I want to sing, so that they'll be quiet:]
Duration: 1' 15"
Key: F major
Tessitura: F3-Do5
Aggregate indications: *Alive*
Date of publication: 1962/1996
Publisher: UME/Trito
Remarks: There are two versions published in two different keys, the modern one by Trito, in the original key, F major, in an edition by Manuel Garcia Morante (1996). The first edition by UME, revised by Rafael Ferrer (1962), is in a lower key, E flat major.
Recording 1
Year: 1998
Singer: Maria Lluisa Muntada (Sop.)
Pianist: Surinyac, Josep
Date: 1998
Media: CD
Label: LA MA DE GUIDO
Label reference: LMG 2024
Length: 1:16
Observations: Included in the album "Enric Granados: Integral de l'obra per a veu i piano".

Recorded in 1997.
Recording 2
Year: 1998
Singer: Angeles, Victoria de los (Sop.)
Pianist: Larrocha, Alicia de
Date: 1998
Media: CD
Label: EMI Classics
Discography reference: 724356694125
Length: 1:06
Remarks: "Songs of Spain", 4CD, vol. 4: "Granados and Falla", Live recording in New York, 1971.
Recording 3
Year: 2001
Singer: Bayo, Maria (Sop.)
Pianist: Zeger, Brian
Venue: Gran teatro del Liceo, Barcelona
Date: 21-5-2001
Support: Radio
Length: 1:08
Comments: Recorded by RNE, not allowed to broadcast without authorisation from the inmates.
Recording 4
Year: 2002
Singer: Pucrlolas, Sabina (Sop.)
Pianist: Estrada, Ricardo
Place: Corte Ingle's L'illa Diagonal, Barcelona
Date: 24-10-2002
Support: Radio
Diracion: Unspecified
Comments: RNE recording. No permission to broadcast without aitorizacion of the performers.
Recording 5
Year: 2003
Singer: Lorengar, Pilar (Sop.)
Pianist: Larrocha, Alicia de
Date: 2003
Media: CD
Record label: DECCA
Discography reference: 4733192
Diracion: 1:17
Remarks: Engraved in 1978.
Recording 6
Year: 2003
Singer: Fink, Bernarda (Mz.)
Pianist: Spencer, Charles
Ligar: Hospital Real, Granada
Date: 22-6-2003
Support: Radio
Diracion: Unspecified
Observations: International Festival of Music and Dance of Granada. RNE recording. No permission to broadcast without aitorizacion of the performers.

Recording 7
Year: 2003
Singer: Prieto, Maria Jesus (Sop.)
Pianist: Azizova, Karina
Venue: Auditorio de la Fundacion Canal, Madrid
Date: 30-3-2003
Support: Radio
Duration: Unspecified
Comments: RNE recording.
Recording 8
Year: 2004
Singer: Schwartz, Sylvia (Sop.)
Pianist: Munoz, Julio Alexis
Place: Capilla de los Estudiantes, Seville
Date: 11-11-2004
Support: Radio
Duration: 1:00
Observations: Cycle "Clasicos en Ruta". Recorded by RNE.
Recording 9
Year: 2004
Singer: Wagner, Virginia Lorena (Sop.)
Pianist: Lamazares, Madalit
Venue: Real Academia de Bellas Artes de San Fernando, Madrid
Date: 5-6-2004
Support: Radio
Duration: 1:10
Remarks: The concerts of Radio Clasica. Recorded by RNE.
Recording 10
Year: 2004
Singer: Folco, Maria (Mz.)
Pianist: Viribay, Aurelio
Place: San Julian and Santa Basilisa Church, Isla (Cantabria)
Date: 5-8-2004
Support: Radio
Length: 1:18
Observations: Santander International Festival. RNE recording. Not allowed to broadcast without permission of the intërpreters.
Recording 11
Year: 2006
Singer: Hendricks, Barbara (Sop.)
Pianist: Derwinger, Love
Date: 2006
Media: CD
Label: Arte Verum
Discographic reference: AVR 001
Length: 1:09
Observations: Included in the album "Canciones espanolas". Recorded in Stockholm in 2003 and 2005.
Recording 12
Year: 2006

Singer: Donato, Joyce di (Mz.)
Pianist: Drake, Julius
Date: 2006
Media: CD
Label: Eloquentia
Discography reference: 0608
Length: 1:43
Recording 13
Year: 2007
Singer: Donato, Joyce di (Mz.)
Pianist: Drake, Julius
Venue: Teatro de la Zarzuela, Madrid
Date: 09-04-2007
Support: Radio
Length: 1:23
Observations: Lied Cycle. Teatro de la Zarzuela, Madrid. Recorded by RNE. No permission to broadcast without authorisation of the intërpretes.

GUERVOS Y MIRA, JOSE MAMA (1870-1944)

Title: "The pretended true".

Collection or series: *Five songs,* n° 1
Date of composition: 1935
It belongs to Lope de Vega's play: *Lo fingido verdadero.*
First verse: "Not to be, Lucinda, your belles".
Character: Musicians
Scenic notes: Come out the MUSICIANS
Duration: 2' 20".
Key: C minor
Tessitura: D3 flat-Fa4
Release date: 12-12-1935
Premiere venue: Teatro Espanol
Opening singer: Mercedes Garcia Lopez
Pianist of the premiere: Jose Maria Guervos
Date of publication: 1936
Publisher: Union Musical Espanola
Place of publication: Madrid
Dedication: Dedicated to Antonio F. Bordas
Awards: Prize at the National Music Competition in 1935
Motivation: National Music Competition 1935

Title: "White Lucinda catches the lilies".

Collection or series: *Five songs,* n° 2
Date of composition: 1935
It belongs to the play by Lopc de Vega: El caballero de Illescas.
First verse: "Blancas coge Lucinda".
Character: Belardo, Tirreno and Riselo
Scenic notes: Belardo, Tirreno and Riselo sing.
Length: 1' 48"
Key: G minor
Tessitura: D3-Fa4 or SoL (optional)
Release date: 12-12-1935

Premiere venue: Teatro Espanol
Opening singer: Mercedes Garaa Lopez
Pianist of the premiere: Josë Maria Guervos
Date of publication: 1936
Publisher: Union Musical Espanola
Place of publication: Madrid
Dedication: Dedicated to Mercedes Garaa Lopez
Awards: Prize at the National Music Competition in 1935
Motivation: National Music Competition 1935

Title: "Harvest Song".

Collection or series: *Five songs,* n° 3
Date of composition: 1935
It belongs to Lope de Vega's play: El gran duque de Moscovia (The Grand Duke of Muscovy).
First verse: "Blanca me era yo".
Character: Musicians
Scëuic notes: The reaper musicians come out, and with them Lucinda, Demetrio, Rufino, Belardo and Febo. They sing.
Duration: 1' Duration: 1' Duration: 1' Duration: 1' Duration: 1' Duration: 1' Duration: 1'
Key: A minor
Tessitura: E3-Fa4
Release date: 12-12-1935
Premiere venue: Teatro Espanol
Opening singer: Mercedes Garaa Lopez
Pianist of the premiere: Josë Maria Guervos
Date of publication: 1936
Publisher: Union Musical Espanola
Place of publication: Madrid
Dedication: Dedicated to my sister Carmen
Awards: Prize at the National Music Competition in 1935
Motivation: National Music Competition 1935

Title: "Riberitas hermosas".

Collection or series: *Five songs,* n° 4
Date of composition: 1935
Belongs to the work of Lope de Vega: *Pedro Carbonero*
First verse: "Riberitas hermosas".
Character: Moros
Scenic notes: Some masked Moors come out, and dance a zambra,...They sing.
Duration: 1' 50".
Key: E Phrygian
Tessitura: E3- F4 sharp
Date of publication: 1936
Publisher: Union Musical Espanola
Place of publication: Madrid
Dedication: Dedicated to my niece Florinda
Awards: Prize at the National Music Competition in 1935
Motivation: National Music Competition 1935
Observations: The first interpretation of which we have evidence is that of Joan Cabero.
Recording 1
Year: 1990

Singer: Cabero, Joan (Ten.)
Pianist: Cabero, Manuel
Venue: Caja Postal, Madrid
Date: 12-3-1990
Support: Radio
Duration: 2:30
Observations: RNE recording. Not available in RNE due to sound or performance deficiencies.

Title: "Trebole".

Collection or series: *Five songs,* n° 5
Date of composition: 1935
It belongs to Lope de Vega's play: Peribanez y el comendador de Ocana.
First verse: "Trebole, jay Jesus, como guele!"
Character: Llorente [Helipe, Mendo, Lujan, Chaparro, Bartolo and Llorente].
Stage directions: Sing with the guitars
Length: 1' 36"
Key: E minor
Tessitura: E3-Fa4 sharp
Date of publication: 1936
Publisher: Union Musical Espanola
Place of publication: Madrid
Dedication: Dedicated to Benito Garcia de la Parra
Awards: Prize at the National Music Competition in 1935
Motivation: National Music Competition 1935
Observations: It has a choir part, although it can be sung, as the composer himself indicates, with only one voice.

ITURRALDE PEREZ, JOSE LUIS (1908-1985)

Title: "At the death of Jesus".

Collection or series: *Passion Scenes,* n° 3
Date of composition: 1980
It belongs to the work of Lope de Vega: *Rimas sacras (Sacred Rhymes)*
First line of verse: "The evening is swinging", Rhyme CXXXIV
Duration: 3' 15" approx.
Key: F major
Tessitura: Do3-La4
Agaggic indications: Lento lastimoso */Andante*
Location of the manuscript: Eresbil-Basque Music Archive
manuscript symbol: E/ITu-07/R-02
Heading indications: soprano
Remarks: *Escenas de la pasion* consists of 3 numbers: n° 1 *Via Crucis* (Ofrenda), with text by Gerardo Diego, n° 2 *A Maria* (Plegaria), text Josë Zorrilla y Moral, and n° 3 *A la muerte de Jesus,* text by Lope de Vega.
Recording 1
Year: 1980
Singer: Melero, Beatriz (sop.)
Pianist: Turina, Fernando
Venue: Casa de la Radio, Madrid
Date: 17-3-1980
Support: Radio
Duration: Unspecified

Comments: RNE recording.

LARROCA RECH, ANGEL (1880-1947)

Title: "Plea to Christ crucified".

Date of composition: ca. 1940

It belongs to the work of Lope de Vega: *Rimas sacras (Sacred Rhymes)*

First Verse: "Shepherd, who with your loving whistles", Sonnet XIV

Duration: 6' approx.

Key: G minor / C minor

Tessitura: E3 flat-G4

Aggressive indications: Slowly

Date of publication: 1940 ca.

Editor: Jaime Piles

Place of publication: Valencia

Dedication: To my good friend Enrique Dominguez

Head notes: A solo for treble or tenor, with accompaniment.

Remarks: Approximate year of composition deduced from the year of foundation of the Piles publishing house, 1934, and the composer's date of death, 1947.

Title: "The prayer of Christ in the Garden".

Date of composition: 1945

It belongs to the work of Lope de Vega: *Rimas sacras (Sacred Rhymes)*

First line of verse: "Hincado esta de rodillas", Rima CXX

Duration: 18' Duration: 18' Duration: 18' Duration: 18' Duration: 18' Duration: 18' Duration: 18

Key: G minor / F major

Tessitura: F3-Flat A-4

Agaggic indications: *Andante*

Date of release: 27-3-1945

Place of the premiere: Catedral de Murcia

Opening singer: Carmen Andujar

Pianist for the premiere: Eduardo Lopez-Chavarri

Location of the manuscript: Valencian Library

Manuscript code: AELCH/pro 352

Title page: Poesia de Lope de Vega (siglo XVI [sic]) Melodi'a para tiple o tenor / con acompanamiento por Angel Larroca Pbro.

Motivation: Lesson-concert on Holy Tuesday in the Cathedral of Murcia.

Remarks: Date of the premiere taken from the letters sent by Manuel Massotti Escuder to Eduardo Lopez-Chavarri and Carmen Andujar, where this work, the date of the concert and the conditions of the concert are quoted. The author made an arrangement for sextet, it is not known what instrumental combination (Eduardo Lopez-Chavarri Marco: correspondencia, Conselleria de Cultura, Educacio i Ciencia, 1996, p. 372-373). Only the autographed vocal part of this piece of music has been preserved. The instrumental accompaniment part is missing.

LAVILLA MUNARRIZ, FELIX (1928- 2013)

Title: "Oh, bitter loneliness".

Date of composition: 1988

It belongs to the work of Lope de Vega: Poesia suelta published in the *Romancero General.*

First verse: "Alas, bitter solitudes".

Length: 1' 54"

Key: F sharp minor

Tessitura: C3 sharp - E4

agogic indications: *Andantino-Allegretto*
Release date: 1988
Premiere venue: Teatro Espanol
Opening singer: Manuel Cid (Ten.)
Pianist for the premiere: Miguel Zanetti
Date of publication: 1988
Publisher: Real Musical
Dedication: To Manuel Cid
Header indications: On an anonymous melody / Voice and piano
Motivation: Homage to Lope de Vega in the Spanish Theatre
Remarks: Year of composition taken from the date of edition. Antonio Gallego, in the introduction, states that the song is an arrangement for voice and piano of a renaissance melody from the Cancionero de Turin.
Recording 1
Year: 2009
Singer: Higueras, Ana (Sop.)
Pianist: Val, Jaime del
Date: 2009
Media: CD
Record label: Exclusive distribution on the Internet
Length: 3'12"
Remarks: Included in the album "Nine centuries of song. 88 vocal works from the 13th to the 21st centuries".
Recording 2
Year: 2009
Singer: Lavilla, Cecilia (Sop.)
Pianist: Okinena, Josu
Date: 2009
Media: CD
Label: Prion
Discographic reference: PRION 1259
Length: 1:54
Observations: Included in the album 'Felix Lavilla: Canciones".

LLONGUERES BADIA, JOAN (1880-1953)

Title: "Let yourself fall Pascual".

Collection or series: Seis villancicos de Lope de Vega, n° 1
Date of composition: 1942
It belongs to the work by Lope de Vega: Rimas divinas y humanas del licenciado Torë de Burguillos.
First Verse: "Let him fall, Pascual", Rima CLXXI
Duration: 2' 10" approx.
Key: E flat major
Tessitura: C3-E4
Aggico indications: *Moderato*
Date of publication: 2002
Publisher: DINSIC
Place of publication: Barcelona
Header indications: Per a veu i piano [in 5 languages].
Observations: Date of composition taken from BNC, it indicates: "Inscripcio al Registro de la

Propiedad Intelectual: Barcelona 8 d'agost de 1942" (inventari Fons Joan Llongueres). There are four different editions: Barcelona (Paseo de Gracia, 54): Union Musical, Casa Werner, between 1926 and 1934 (BNC dates it 1953); Madrid: Union Musical Espanola, D.L. 1962; Barcelona: Dinsic, 2001, 1ª ed.; Barcelona: Dinsic, D.L. 2002, 1ª reprint (data taken from the BNE).

Title: "Cry for love".

Collection or series: Six Christmas carols by Lope de Vega, n° 2
Date of composition: 1942
It belongs to Lope de Vega's play: *Shepherds of Bethlehem.*
First verse: "Today the ice is born".
Character: Lucela
Scenic notes: [It was not necessary to beg the other shepherds to sing, for they all came forward and joyfully began as follows].
Duration: 2' 10" approx.
Key: G major
Tessitura: E3-Mi4
Aggadogic indications: *Moderato*
Date of publication: 2002
Publisher: DINSIC
Place of publication: Barcelona
Header indications: Per a veu i piano [in 5 languages].
Observations: Date of composition taken from BNC, it indicates: "Inscripcio al Registro de la propiedad intelectual: Barcelona 8 d'agost de 1942" (inventari Fons Joan Llongueres). There are four different editions: Barcelona (Paseo de Gracia, 54): Union Musical, Casa Werner, between 1926 and 1934 (BNC dates it 1953); Madrid: Union Musical Espanola, D.L. 1962; Barcelona: Dinsic, 2001, 1ª ed.; Barcelona: Dinsic, D.L. 2002, 1ª reprint (data taken from the BNE).

Title: "A la gala del zagal".

Collection or series: Six Christmas carols by Lope de Vega, n° 3
Date of composition: 1942
It belongs to Lope de Vega's play: *Shepherds of Bethlehem.*
First verse: "Let's go to Bethlehem, Paschal".
Character: Lorente
Scenic notes: [Llorente with a pious soul, although with a rustic wit, playing him a flute Pascual, his cousin, began to sing like this, and the others with their voices, with their hands and with joyful leaps to answer him:].
Duration: 1' approx.
Key: G minor
Tessitura: E3-E4 flat
Agrochemical indications: *Ayroso*
Date of publication: 2002
Publisher: DINSIC
Place of publication: Barcelona
Header indications: Per a veu i piano [in 5 languages].
Observations: Date of composition taken from BNC, it indicates: "Inscripcio al Registro de la propiedad intelectual: Barcelona 8 d'agost de 1942" (inventari Fons Joan Llongueres). There are four different editions: Barcelona (Paseo de Gracia, 54): Union Musical, Casa Werner, between 1926 and 1934 (BNC dates it 1953); Madrid: Union Musical Espanola, D.L. 1962; Barcelona: Dinsic, 2001, 1ª ed.; Barcelona: Dinsic, D.L. 2002, 1ª reprint (data taken from the BNE).

Title: "The vanquished sun".

Collection or cycle: Seis villancicos de Lope de Vega, n° 4

Date of composition: 1942
It belongs to Lope de Vega's play: *Shepherds of Bethlehem.*
First verse: "Of a beautiful Virgin".
Character: Joran
Scenic notes: [It was not necessary to beg the other shepherds to sing, for they all came forward and joyfully began like this.
Duration: 1' 20" approx.
Key: A major
Tessitura: E3-Fa4 sharp
Aggical indications: *Allegretto-amabile*
Date of publication: 2002
Publisher: DINSIC
Place of publication: Barcelona
Header indications: Per a veu i piano [in 5 languages|
Observations: Date of composition taken from BNC, it indicates: "Inscripcio al Registro de la propiedad intelectual: Barcelona 8 d'agost de 1942" (inventari Fons Joan Llongueres). There are four different editions: Barcelona (Paseo de Gracia, 54): Union Musical, Casa Werner, between 1926 and 1934 (BNC dates it 1953); Madrid: Union Musical Espanola, D.L. 1962; Barcelona: Dinsic, 2001, 1ª ed.; Barcelona: Dinsic, D.L. 2002, 1ª reprint (data taken from the BNE).

Title: "The straws in the manger".

Collection or series: Six Christmas carols by Lope de Vega, n° 5
Date of composition: 1942
It belongs to Lope de Vega's play: *Shepherds of Bethlehem.*
First verse: "The straws of the manger".
Character: Tebandra
Scenic notes: [It was not necessary to beg the other shepherds to sing, for they all came forward and joyfully began like this.
Duration: 2' 05" approx.
Key: E major
Tessitura: B2-M4
Agaggic indications: *Andante amoroso*
Date of publication: 2002
Publisher: DINSIC
Place of publication: Barcelona
Header indications: Per a veu i piano [in 5 languages].
Observations: Date of composition taken from BNC, it indicates: "Inscripcio al Registro de la propiedad intelectual: Barcelona 8 d'agost de 1942" (inventari Fons Joan Llongueres). There are four different editions: Barcelona (Paseo de Gracia, 54): Union Musical, Casa Werner, between 1926 and 1934 (BNC dates it 1953); Madrid: Union Musical Espanola, D.L. 1962; Barcelona: Dinsic, 2001, 1ª ed.; Barcelona: Dinsic, D.L. 2002, 1ª reprint (data taken from the BNE).

Title: " ^Where are you going?"

Collection or series: Seis villancicos de Lope de Vega, n° 6
Date of composition: 1942
It belongs to Lope de Vega's play: *Shepherds of Bethlehem.*
First verse: "Zagalejo de perlas".
Character: Aminadab and Palmira
Scenic annotations: [Aminadab [...] came with his beloved Palmyra [...], and his wife accompanying him with voice and instrument, they both said thus:]
Duration: 1' approx.

Key: C major
Tessitura: C3-E4
Aging indications: Moved gracefully
Date of publication: 2002
Publisher: DINSIC
Place of publication: Barcelona
Header indications: Per a veu i piano [in 5 languages].
Observations: Date of composition taken from BNC, it indicates: "Inscripcio al Registro de la propiedad intelectual: Barcelona 8 d'agost de 1942" (inventari Fons Joan Llongueres). There are four different editions: Barcelona (Paseo de Gracia, 54): Union Musical, Casa Werner, between 1926 and 1934 (BNC dates it 1953); Madrid: Union Musical Espanola, D.L. 1962; Barcelona: Dinsic, 2001, 1ª ed.; Barcelona: Dinsic, D.L. 2002, 1ª reprint (data taken from the BNE).

MARTO POMPEY, ANGEL (1902-2001)

Title: "Sleep my child".

Subtitle: Song
Date of composition: 20 August 1952
Place of composition: Robledo de Chavela (Madrid)
It belongs to Lope de Vega's play: *Pastores de belen (Shepherds of Bethlehem).*
First verse: "Pues andais en las palmas".
Character: Elifila
Stage directions: [that I intend to imitate you in my song, saying thus:]
Duration: 1' 50" approx.
Key: E minor
Tessitura: D3-A4
Agaggic indications: *Andantino*
Location of the manuscript: Biblioteca Fundacion Juan March
Manuscript symbol: M-1311-A
Headline indications: Voice and piano
Remarks: Place of composition, date and signature at the end of the manuscript, which states: "it is original". It also states: "The poetry of this song is taken from the famous one by Lope entitled "Cancion de la Virgen a su Nino" (from "Los pastores de Belen" 1612)".

MENENDEZ ALEYXANDRE, ARTURO (1899-1984)

Title: "Lucinda".

No. of Opus: Ob. 175
Date of composition: 12 May 1932
It belongs to the work of Lope de Vega: *Rimas (Rhymes).*
First Verse: "I gave sustenance to a little bird one day", Sonnet CLXXIV
Duration: 3' approx.
Tonality: Various tonal centres
Tessitura: F3-B4
Location of the manuscript: Associació Wagneriana de Barcelona
Observations: Manuscript signed and dated. Also indicates: "Ref. Aug. 1943. Rev. 15-3-1982". The opus no. (Ob. 175) is indicated on the title page. Photocopy of the manuscript provided by the Associacio Wagneriana de Barcelona.

Title: "Mother, I saw some eyelets".

Date of composition: 1944
It belongs to the work of Lope de Vega: *La Dorotea.*
First verse: "Mother, I saw some eyelets".

Character: Dorotea
Scenic notes: [Take, Celia, the harp; that obliges me to much this answer].
Duration: 2' 40" approx.
Key: G minor
Tessitura: D3-G4
Date of publication: 1944
Publication note: Printed at Talleres Josë Mora, Barcelona, 2 May 1944/property of the author.
Place of publication: Barcelona
Headings: Voice and piano /soprano or tenor
Remarks: The score bears a note at the head: "For a poem there is only one music; all others are false. The difficult thing is to find it". Date of composition taken from the date of publication.

MIGUEL PERIS, VICENTE (1929-2010)

Title: "Mananicas de mayo".

Subtitle: Spanish Tonadilla
Collection or cycle: Three Spanish songs for baritone and piano
Date of composition: 2009
It belongs to the play by Lope de Vega: *El robo de Dina* **First verse:** "En las mananicas".
Character:
Scenic notes: MUSIC, and those who can with a bouquet of garlands and a gypsy dance.
Duration: 2' 30" approx.
Key: F major / F minor *.
Tessitura: C2-Fa3
Aggonic indications: *Allegretto*
Location of the manuscript: Family archive

Title: "Tonadilla navidena".

Date of composition: 2009
It belongs to Lope de Vega's play: *Shepherds of Bethlehem.*
First verse: "The straws of the manger".
Character: Tebandra
Scenic notes: [It was not necessary to beg the other shepherds to sing, for they were all forewarned, and so they joyfully began].
Duration: 3' approx.
Key: C minor *
Tessitura: C2-E3
Aging indications: Serenely
Location of the manuscript: Family archive
Dedication: To His Holiness Benedict XVI
Head notes: For bantone and piano.

MINGOTE LORENTE, ANGEL (1891-1960)

Title: "To the Child God in Bethlehem".

Opus No: ERG 88 A1, n° 1
Collection or series: Canciones espanolas con textos de Lope de Vega, n° 1
Date of composition: 1935
It belongs to Lope de Vega's play: *Shepherds of Bethlehem.*
First verse: "The straws of the manger".
Character: Tebandra
Scenic notes: [It was not necessary to beg the other shepherds to sing, for they all came forward and joyfully began like this.

Duration: 3' 30".
Key: A major
Tessitura: E3-Re4
Agaggiatura indications: *Andante moderato*
Location of the manuscript: Archivo Emilio Reina, Zaragoza
Title: Song and piano /Awarded at the National Music Competition of 1935 - Tercentenary of the Fenix de los Ingenios
Awards: Prize at the National Music Competition in 1935
Motivation: National Music Competition 1935
Remarks: The catalogue entry is: Canciones espanolas [VI|, for voice and piano (with texts by Lope de Vega), ERG 88 A1 (Reina Gonzalez, Emilio, Catalogo de obras de Angel Mingote, Centro de Estudios Darocenses, Daroca (Zaragoza) 1995, p. 58.) The music is written for the 1ª stanza, the 2~ and 3ª only indicate the lyrics.

Title: "Copla".

Opus No: ERG 88 A1, n° 2
Collection or series: Spanish Songs with texts by Lope de Vega, n° 2
Date of composition: 1935
It belongs to the work of Lope de Vega: *La Dorotea.*
First verse: "Mother, some eyelets I saw".
Character: Dorotea
Scenic notes: [Here, Celia, take the harp; it obliges me to much this answer.
Duration: 2' 30".
Key: B minor
Tessitura: F3 sharp-E4
Agaggic indications: *Andante mosso*
Location of the manuscript: Archivo Emilio Reina, Zaragoza
Title: Song and piano /Awarded in the National Music Competition of 1935 - Tercentenary of the Fenix de los Ingenios
Awards: Prize at the National Music Competition in 1935
Motivation: National Music Competition 1935
Remarks: The catalogue entry is: Canciones espanolas [VI], for voice and piano (with texts by Lope de Vega), ERG 88 A1 (Reina Gonzalez, Emilio, Catalogo de obras de Angel Mingote, Centro de Estudios Darocenses, Daroca (Zaragoza) 1995, p. 58.) The music is written for the refrain (which is not repeated) and the 1st verse (ª), for the 2nd verse only the lyrics are indicated. Mingote inverts the order of the two stanzas with respect to Lope's text.

Title: "Cantar moreno de siega" (Brown harvest song)

Opus No: ERG 88 A1, n° 3
Collection or series: Spanish songs with texts by Lope de Vega, n° 3
Date of composition: 1935
It belongs to Lope de Vega's play: El gran duque de Moscovia (The Grand Duke of Muscovy).
First verse: "Blanca me era yo".
Character: Musicians
Scene notes: The reaper musicians come out, and with them Lucinda, Demetrio, Rufino, Belardo and Febo. They sing.
Duration: 1' 20".
Key: E minor
Tessitura: F3 sharp-E4
Aging indications: Somewhat bumpy
Location of the manuscript: Archivo Emilio Reina, Zaragoza

Title: Song and piano /Awarded in the National Music Competition of 1935 - Tercentenary of the Fenix de los Ingenios
Awards: Prize at the National Music Competition in 1935
Motivation: National Music Competition 1935
Remarks: The catalogue entry is: Canciones espanolas [VI], for voice and piano (with texts by Lope de Vega), ERG 88 A1 (Reina Gonzalez, Emilio, Catalogo de obras de Angel Mingote, Centro de Estudios Darocenses, Daroca (Zaragoza) 1995, p. 58.)

Title: "Canto de un mal nacer" (Song of an unborn child)

Opus No: ERG 88 A1, n° 4
Collection or series: Canciones espanolas con textos de Lope de Vega, n° 4
Date of composition: 1935
It belongs to the play by Lope de Vega: Las famosas asturianas.
First verse: "Pariome mi madre" (My mother, my mother)
Character: Musicians
Scenic notes: [Sing, let's see if the cruel one shows up].
Duration: 1' 15"
Key: E flat minor
Tessitura: E3 flat - E4 flat
Aggressive indications: Moderately
Location of the manuscript: Archivo Emilio Reina, Zaragoza
Title: Song and piano /Awarded in the National Music Competition of 1935 - Tercentenary of the Fenix de los Ingenios
Awards: Prize at the National Music Competition in 1935
Motivation: National Music Competition 1935
Remarks: The catalogue entry is: Canciones espanolas [VI], for voice and piano (with texts by Lope de Vega), ERG 88 A1 (Reina Gonzalez, Emilio, Catalogo de obras de Angel Mingote, Centro de Estudios Darocenses, Daroca (Zaragoza) 1995, p. 58.)

Title: "Folia y Parabien a unos recién casados".

Opus No: ERG 88 A1, n° 5
Collection or series: Canciones espanolas con textos de Lope de Vega, n° 5
Date of composition: 1935
It belongs to Lope de Vega's play: Peribanez y el comendador de Ocana.
First verse: "Dente parabienes".
Character: Musicians
Stage directions: Playing and singing
Duration: 2' 20".
Key: A major
Tessitura: D3-E4
Aggonic indications: *Allegretto*
Location of the manuscript: Archivo Emilio Reina, Zaragoza
Title: Song and piano /Awarded in the National Music Competition of 1935 - Tercentenary of the Fenix de los Ingenios
Awards: Prize at the National Music Competition in 1935
Motivation: National Music Competition 1935
Remarks: The cataloguing entry is: Canciones espanolas [VI], for voice and piano (with texts by Lope de Vega), ERG 88 A1 (Reina Gonzalez, Emilio, Catalogo de obras de Angel
Mingote, Centro de Estudios Darocenses, Daroca (Zaragoza) 1995, p. 58.) For the 2nd stanza only the lyrics are indicated.

Title: "La Morenica".

Opus No: ERG 88 A1, n° 6
Collection or series: Canciones espanolas con textos de Lope de Vega, no. 6
Date of composition: 1935
It belongs to Lope de Vega's play: Los Porceles de Murcia.
First verse: "Morenica me adoran".
Character: Musicians
Scenic notes: Other musicians and Lucrecia de Vera, lady, don Lope, her husband and servants come out. They sing.
Duration: 1' 25"
Key: G major
Tessitura: E3-Fa4 sharp
Agrological indications: Tpo. de Seguidillas
Location of the manuscript: Archivo Emilio Reina, Zaragoza
Title: Song and piano /Awarded at the National Music Competition of 1935 - Tercentenary of the Fënix of the Ingenuity
Awards: Prize at the National Music Competition in 1935
Motivation: National Music Competition 1935
Remarks: The catalogue entry is: Canciones espanolas [VI], for voice and piano (with texts by Lope de Vega), ERG 88 A1 (Reina Gonzalez, Emilio, Catalogo de obras de Angel Mingote, Centro de Estudios Darocenses, Daroca (Zaragoza) 1995, p. 58.)

MORALEDA BELLVER, FERNANDO (1911-1981)

Title: "Chanzoneta".

Collection or series: Cuatro canciones con textos de Lope de Vega, n° 1
Date of composition: September 1935
Place of composition: Madrid
Belongs to the work of Lope de Vega: Manuscript MSS/3985
First verse: "Oh, my fellows! What I see".
Duration: 4' approx.
Key: D minor
Tessitura: E3-Fa4 sharp
Agagic indications: Allegro/Andantino/Allegro vivo
Location of the manuscript: BNE
Headline marking: At the top of the title page, in Roman numerals: MDCXXXV-MCMXXXV
Motivation: Supposedly, for the 1935 National Music Competition.
Observations: The group of Cuatro canciones con textos de Lope de Vega is made up of *Chanzoneta, Dicha, Soneto* and *Pobre barquila mla, it* has a title page on which, in addition to the title, the dates of the tercentenary and the name of the author, it notes the title and order of the songs. No. 3, *Soneto,* is missing and cannot be found in the BNE collections. The BNE manuscript MSS/3985 comes from the library of the Duque de Uceda. The only edition in which this poem appears is *Poesias ineditas de Herrera el Divino, Quevedo, Lope de Vega, Argensola (Lupercio), Gongora, Marques de Urena y Samaniego, Marla Gertrudis Hore, Alvaro Cubilo de Aragon, Juan de Matos Fragoso, Cristobal del Castillejo, Luis Galvez de Montalvo, Zaida (Moorish poetess), Tirso de Molina, Baltasar de Alcazar,* Madrid, Editorial Amërica, 1917.

Title: "Dicha".

Collection or series: Four songs with texts by Lope de Vega, n° 2
Date of composition: September 1935
Place of composition: Madrid
It belongs to Lope de Vega's play: La esclava de su galan.
First verse: "How short-lived are the joys".

Character: Elena
Scenic notes: [Sola].
Duration: 1' 20" approx.
Key: E minor
Tessitura: C3 sharp - F4 sharp
Agaggic indications: *Andante*
Location of the manuscript: BNE
Manuscript symbol: M.MORALEDA/9
Headline marking: At the top of the title page, in Roman numerals: MDCXXXV-MCMXXXV
Motivation: Supposedly for the 1935 National Music Competition.
Observations: The group of Cuatro canciones con textos de Lope de Vega is made up of *Chanzoneta, Dicha, Soneto* and *Pobre barquilla mia, it has* a title page on which, in addition to the title page, the dates of the tercentenary and the name of the author, the title and order of the songs are noted. No. 3, *Soneto,* is missing and cannot be found in the BNE collections. Moraleda sets to music the first 13 of the 19 verses of Elena's monologue.

Tltuio: "Pobre barquilla mia" (Poor littlc boat of mine)

Collection or series: Cuatro canciones con textos de Lope de Vega, n° 4
Date of composition: September 1935
Place of composition: Madrid
It belongs to the work of Lope de Vega: *La Dorotea.*
First verse: "Pobre barquilla mi'a".
Character: Don Fernando
Scëmca annotations: [Sing, sing, for you have been tempered].
Duration: 1' 40" approx.
Key: E major
Tessitura: A3-Fa4 sharp
Aggonic indications: *Allegretto*
Location of the manuscript: BNE
Manuscript symbol: M.MORALEDA/9
Headline marking: At the top of the title page, in Roman numerals: MDCXXXV-MCMXXXV
Motivation: Supposedly for the 1935 National Music Competition.
Observations: The group of Cuatro canciones con textos de Lope de Vega is made up of *Chanzoneta, Dicha, Soneto* and *Pobre barquilla mia, it has* a title page on which, in addition to the title, the dates of the tercentenary and the name of the author, it notes the title and order of the songs. No. 3, *Soneto,* is missing and cannot be found in the BNE collections. Moraleda sets music to stanzas 1, 2, 4 and 5 of the 32 stanzas of the poem. The title of this song no. 4, unlike the others, is written in brackets, both on the title page and in the heading of the collection.

MORENO TORROBA, FEDERICO (1891-1982)

Title: "Copla de antano".

Date of composition: 1923
It belongs to the work of Lope de Vega: *La Dorotea.*
First verse: "Mother, some eyelets I saw".
Character: Dorotea
Notes евсёшсзБ: [Take, Celia, the harp; it obliges me to much this answer].
Duration: 2' 10" approx.
Key: A major
Tessitura: E3-G4
Auggian indications: *Allegro moderato*
Opening date: 19-5-1923

Place of the premiere: Teatro de la Comedia, Madrid
Debut singer: Dagmara Renina (Sop.)
Pianist of the premiere: Joaquin Turina
Date of publication: 1923
Publisher: Union Musical Espanola
Place of publication: Madrid
Dedication: To Dagmara Renina
Header notes: Lyrics by Lope de Vega
Remarks: Details of the premiere in Martinez del Fresno, pp. 204-205.

NIN-CULMELL, JOAQUIN (1908-2004)

Title: "Welcome".

Collection or series: *Songs of La Baraca,* n° 3
Date of composition: June 1997
Place of composition: Sarria
It belongs to the play by Lope de Vega: *Fuente Ovejuna.*
First verse: "Be welcome".
Character: All [Musicians]
Scenic notes: Cantan
Length: 1' 44"
Key: G minor
Tessitura: A3-G4
Heading indications: Chant-piano
Motivation: Music from a notebook kept by Luis Saenz de la Calzada and Angel Barja with pieces sung in the performances of the theatre company "La Barraca" directed by Federico Garcia Lorca.
Remarks: Copy on loan from Gayle Nin Rosenkranz. The edition was prepared for 1998 but Editions Max Eschig did not publish it. This edition included a French version of each text by Jean-Charles Godoy. Date of composition at the end of the score.
Recording 1
Year: 1998
Singer: Gragera, Elena (Mz.)
Pianist: Cardo, Anton
Venue: Centro Cultural Conde Duque, Madrid
Date: 9-3-1998
Support: Radio
Duration: 2:00
Observations: Premiere of Canciones de La Barraca. Cycle Lunes musicales at the Conde Duque. Recorded by RNE.
Recording 2
Year: 1999
Singer: Gragera, Elena (Mz.)
Pianist: Cardo, Anton
Date: 1999
Media: CD
Label: Columna Musica
Discographic reference: CM 0053
Length: 1:44
Remarks: Included in the album "Obra para canto y piano".

Title: "Wash me in the Tagus".

Collection or series: *Songs of La Baraca,* n° 4
Date of composition: June 1997
Place of composition: Sama
It belongs to the work by Lope de Vega: La buena guarda or La encomienda bien guardada **First verse:** "Lavareme en el Tajo" Character: Musicos
Scenic notes: Shout of music and dance, ladies and gallants, and a waiter with a tabaque as a snack.
Length: 1' 47"
Key: G major
Tessitura: D3-G4 sharp
Date of publication: 1998
Publisher: Editions Max Eschig
Place of publication: Paris
Heading indications: Chant-piano
Motivation: Putting to music of a notebook preserved by Luis Saenz de la Calzada and Angel Baija with pieces sung in the performances of the theatrical group "La Barraca" directed by Federico Garcia Lorca.
Remarks: Copy on loan from Gayle Nin Rosenkranz. The edition was prepared for 1998 but Editions Max Eschig did not publish it. This edition includes a French version of each text by Jean-Charles Godoy. Date of composition at the end of the score.
Recording 1
Year: 1998
Singer: Gragera, Elena (Mz.)
Pianist: Cardo, Anton
Venue: Centro Cultural Conde Duque, Madrid
Date: 9-3-1998
Support: Radio
Length: 2:36
Observations: Premiere of Canciones de La Barraca. Cycle Lunes musicales at the Conde Duque. Recorded by RNE.
Recording 2
Year: 1999
Singer: Gragera, Elena (Mz.)
Pianist: Cardo, Anton
Date: 1999
Media: CD
Label: Columna Musica
Discography reference: CM 0053
Length: 1:47
Remarks: Included in the album "Obra para canto y piano".
Recording 3
Year: 2005
Singer: Gragera, Elena (Mz.)
Pianist: Cardo, Anton
Place: Real Balneario Solan de Cabras, Beteta (Cuenca)
Date: 9-9-2005
Support: Radio
Length: 2:08
Observations: Cycle "Music in the Water". Recorded by RNE. No permission to broadcast without the permission of the performers.

Recording 4
Year: 2007
Singer: Gragera, Elena (Mz.)
Pianist: Cardo, Anton
Venue: Centro Cultural Conde Duque, Madrid
Date: 6-3-2007
Support: Radio
Length: 1:54
Remarks: RNE recording. Not allowed to broadcast without the permission of the performers.

ORTEGA I PUJOL, MIQUEL (1963-)

Title: "Sonnet".

Date of composition: 29 October 2005
Place of composition: Barcelona
It belongs to the work of Lope de Vega: *Rimas (Rhymes).*
First verse: "These the willows are and ësta the fountain".
Duration: 2' 40" approx.
Key: D Phrygian *
Tessitura: D2-Fa3 sharp
Agaggiatura indications: *Andante moderato*
Location of the manuscript: Personal archive of the composer
Dedication: To Federico Gallar
Headline indications: Baritone and piano
Remarks: The composer himself has a transposed version, for bass, a descending 3~m.
Recording 1
Year: 2006
Singer: Latorre, Fernando (Bar.)
Pianist: Barredo, Itziar
Date: 2006
Media: CD
Label: Arsis
Discographical reference: ARSIS 4198
Length: 3:17
Observations: Included in the album "Cantar del alma, La poesia del Siglo de Oro en la musica del siglo XX".

PALAU BOIX, MANUEL (1893-1967)

Title: "Villancico" (Christmas carol)

Date of composition: 1947
It belongs to Lope de Vega's play: *Shepherds of Bethlehem.*
First verse: "The straws of the manger".
Character: Tebandra
Scenic notes: [It was not necessary to beg the other shepherds to sing, for they all began cheerfully and joyfully as follows
Duration: 2' 15"
Key: B minor
Tessitura: C3 sharp - E4
Aggregate indications: Semplice ma teneramente
Release date: 1-6-1952
Place of the premiere: Conservatorio de Musica, Valencia

Debut singer: Emilia Munoz (Sop.)
Pianist for the premiere: Manuel Palau
Date of publication: 1974
Publisher: Piles
Ed. under the care of Salvador Segui, Institute Valenciano de Musicologi'a, Institucion Alfonso el Magnanimo
Place of publication: Valencia
Header notes: Poetry by Lope de Vega

Title: "Por el montecico sola" (On the mountain alone)

Collection or cycle: *Six Lieder,* n° 1
Date of composition: 1950
It belongs to Lope de Vega's play: El villano en su rincon (The villain in his corner).
First verse: "Por el montecico sola" (On the mountain alone)
Character: Musicians
Scenic notes: The musicians sing and Bruno sings alone.
Duration: 1' 15" approx.
Key: E major
Tessitura: D3-G4
Aggonic indications: *Allegretto*
Date of release: 19-4-1953
Premiere venue: Ateneo, Madrid
Opening singer: Tony Rosado (Sop.)
Pianist for the premiere: Felix Lavilla
Date of publication: 1953
Publisher: Piles
Publication mention: Institute Valenciano de Musicologfa, Institucion Alfonso el Magnanimo
Place of publication: Valencia
Head notes: Soprano and piano
Recording 1
Year: 1988
Singer: Fabuel, Gloria (Sop.)
Pianist: Pastor, Ramon
Venue: Caja de Ahorros de Valencia, Valencia
Date: 21-6-1988
Support: Radio
Length: 2:25
Remarks: RNE recording.

Title: "E-legia para el caballero de Olmedo".

Date of composition: 1951
It belongs to the play by Lope de Vega: El caballero de Olmedo.
First verse: "That at night they killed him".
Character: The Voice
Scenic notes: Sing from afar in the dressing room, and come closer with your voice, as if you were walking.
Duration: 3' Duration: 3' Duration: 3' Duration: 3' Duration: 3' Duration: 3' Duration: 3'
Key: D minor *
Tessitura: G3-A4
Auggian indications: *Allegro moderato*
Location of the manuscript: Manuel Palau Family Archives

Comments: Version for voice and piano of the original for voice and orchestra by the composer himself. This orchestral version was premiered by Mary Jordan (Sop.) and the Orquesta Municipal de Valencia (OMV), conducted by Manuel Palau, on 2 December 1951, at the Teatro Principal, Valencia. Date of composition taken from the date of the orchestral premiere.

PARERA FONS, ANTONI (1943-)

Title: "Palmas de Belen".

Date of composition: 2006

It belongs to Lope de Vega's play: *Shepherds of Bethlehem.*

First verse: "Pues andais en las palmas".

Character: Elifila

Scenic notes: [that I intend to imitate you in my song, saying like this:]

Duration: 2' approx.

Key: D major

Tessitura: A2-E3

Location of the manuscript: Composer's archive

Remarks: Copy on loan from the composer himself. The score for voice and piano is followed by two pages of an arrangement for a finale with soloist, choir and orchestra in G major, with the text of the first stanza. It does not use the refrain of the poem, but only sets the stanzas to music, in a different order than usual (second for third and vice versa). On the title page, above the title, it indicates "II", which suggests that it is the second piece of a group.

PEREZ AGUIRRE, JULIO (-1916)

Title: "Green Eyes".

Subtitle: Spanish song

Date of composition: ca. 1900-1914

It belongs to the work of Lope de Vega: *La Dorotea.*

First verse: "Mother, I saw some eyelets".

Character: Dorotea

Scenic notes: [Here, Celia, take the harp; that obliges me to answer a lot].

Duration: 2' 20" approx.

Key: G minor

Tessitura: D3-G4

Aggico indications: *Moderato*

Date of publication: between 1901-1914

Publisher: Sociedad Anonima Casa Dotesio (sic.)

Dedication: To the eminent artist Ramon Blanchart

Indications of the heading: Cancion espanola letra de Lope de Vega

Remarks: The year of birth is unknown. The year of death is taken from the *Diccionario de la Zarzuela Espanola e Hispanoamericana (*Emilio Casares Rodicio (coord.), ICCMU, Madrid, 2003, vol. 2, p. 513). Publication date taken from the cataloguing card of the Biblioteca de Catalunya. It is known that he published the score of his operetta *Los amores de un veneciano* in 1985. The dedicatee, Ramon Blanchart (Barcelona, 1860 - San Salvador, 1934), was a bantono who developed his career at the Liceu in Barcelona, the Teatro Real in Madrid and various Italian theatres.

PERIS LACASA, JOSE (1924-2017)

Title: "Mananicas floridas".

Subtitle: Christmas carol

Date of composition: 1955

Place of composition: Madrid
It belongs to Lope de Vega's play: *El cardenal de Belen.*
First verse: "Mananicas floridas".
Character: Musica, Pascual (Anton, Bras)
Stage directions: Sing
Duration: 3' Duration: 3' Duration: 3' Duration: 3' Duration: 3' Duration: 3' Duration: 3'
Key: A minor *
Tessitura: B2-G4
Aggressive indications: *Calm*
Release date: 1955
Premiere venue: Conservatorio de Madrid
Premiere Singer: Teresa Berganza
Pianist for the premiere: Esteban Sanchez
Location of the manuscript: Personal archive of the composer
Motivation: Academic work from Julio Gomez's composition class.
Remarks: The composer lends for this work a copy of the digitalised score, at the end of which a handwritten annotation reads: "Clase de composicion (1955) Conservatorio de Madrid".
Recording 1
Year: 1994
Singer: Egido, Inmaculada (Sop.)
Pianist: Arner, Lucy
Venue: Auditorio Nacional, Sala de Camara, Madrid
Date: 7-10-1994
Support: Radio
Length: 2:13
Remarks: Autumn Festival. Recorded by RNE.

RINCON GARCIA, EDUARDO (1924-)

Title: "Sweet Lord, I was blind".

Collection or series: *Three relgious poems,* n° 1
Date of composition: 1-7 June 2004
It belongs to the play by Lope de Vega: *El serafn humano*
First verse: "Sweet Jesus, I was blind".
Character: Francisco
Duration: 2' 40" approx.
Key: D minor *
Tessitura: B2 or A2 (optional)-G4
Release date: 21-3-2005
Place of the premiere: Festival de Musica Religiosa, Cuenca
Opening singer: Elena Grajera (Mz.)
Pianist of the premiere: Anton Cardo
Head notes: Mezzo-soprano and piano **Remarks:** Copy on loan from the composer himself.
Recording 1
Year: 2005
Singer: Gragera, Elena (Mz.)
Pianist: Cardo, Anton
Place: Iglesia Monasterio de la Concepcion Franciscana, Cuenca
Date: 21-3-2005
Support: Radio
Length: 4:19

Observations: RNE recording. Absolute premiere.

Title: "Mananicas floridas".

Collection or series: *Three religious poems,* n° 2
Date of composition: 1-7 June 2004
It belongs to Lope de Vega's play: *El cardenal de Belen.*
First verse: "Mananicas floridas".
Character: Musica, Pascual (Anton, Bras) Stage directions: Canten
Duration: 2' 10" approx.
Key: D major *
Tessitura: D3-G4
Agaggic indications: *Andante*
Release date: 21-3-2005
Place of the premiere: Festival de Musica Religiosa, Cuenca
Opening singer: Elena Grajera (Mz.)
Pianist of the premiere: Anton Cardo
Head notes: Mezzo-soprano and piano **Remarks:** Copy on loan from the composer himself.
Recording 1
Year: 2005
Singer: Gragera, Elena (Mz.)
Pianist: Cardo, Anton
Place: Iglesia Monasterio de la Concepcion Franciscana, Cuenca
Date: 21-3-2005
Support: Radio
Length: 3:05
Observations: RNE recording. Absolute premiere.

Title: "('What do I have that you seek my friendship?"

Collection or series: *Three religious poems,* n° 3
Date of composition: 1-7 June 2004
It belongs to the work of Lope de Vega: *Rimas sacras (Sacred Rhymes)*
First Verse: "(What have I, that thou seekest my friendship?", Sonnet XVIII
Duration: 2' 35" approx.
Key: B minor *
Tessitura: A2 flat-Fa3
Release date: 21-3-2005
Place of the premiere: Festival de Musica Religiosa, Cuenca
Opening singer: Elena Grajera (Mz.)
Pianist of the premiere: Anton Cardo
Headline indications: Mezzo-soprano and piano
Remarks: Copy on loan from the composer himself.
Recording 1
Year: 2005
Singer: Gragera, Elena (Mz.)
Pianist: Cardo, Anton
Place: Iglesia Monasterio de la Concepcion Franciscana, Cuenca
Date: 21-3-2005
Support: Radio
Length: 4:53
Observations: RNE recording. Absolute premiere.

RODRIGO VIDRE, JOAQUIN (1901-1999)

Title: "Coplas del pastor enamorado" ("Shepherd's couplets in love")
Date of composition: 1935
It belongs to the work of Lope de Vega: La buena guarda or La encomienda bien guardada.
First verse: "Green pleasant shores".
Character: Pastor
Duration: 3' 30".
Key: A
Tessitura: B2-G4
Agaggic indications: *Andantino*
Premiere date: 1936
Premiere venue: Paris
Opening singer: Maria Cid (Sop.)
Pianist of the premiere: Joaquin Rodrigo
Date of publication: 1980
Publisher: Edicion del autor
Mention of edition: Songs for voice and piano
Place of publication: Madrid
Dedication: To Aurelio Vinas
Observations: Published by Ediciones Joaquin Rodrigo in compilation albums: Album Centenario (EJR 190195, 2000) and Album de canciones (EJR 19015a). There is a version by the composer himself for voice and guitar.
Recording 1
Year: 1965
Singer: Cabals, Montserrat (Sop.)
Pianist: Zanetti, Miguel
Date: 1965
Media: CD
Label: EMI Classics
Discographical reference: CDC 724355720221
Length: 4:12
Remarks: Produced in 1965. Commemorative edition of the centenary of Joaquin Rodrigo, Grabaciones historicas I, vol. I. 11 CD. CDS album reference 724355723727
Recording 2
Year: 1966
Singer: Higueras, Ana (Sop.)
Pianist: Zanetti, Miguel
Date: 1966
Support: LP
Record label: Discos Tempo
Discographical reference: T2L-001 S Discos Tempo
Observations: Included in the album "Recital de canciones de Joaquin Rodrigo por Ana Higueras Aragon". There is another publication of the same recording on the Marfer label, 1981.
Recording 3
Year: 1979
Singer: Peters, Maria Angeles (Sop.)
Pianist: Garcia Chornet, Perfecto
Venue: Casa de la Radio, Madrid
Date: 8-5-1979
Support: Radio

Length: 3:50
Comments: RNE recording.
Recording 4
Year: 1981
Singer: Higueras, Ana (Sop.)
Pianist: Lavilla, Fëlix
Venue: Philharmonic Society, Bilbao
Date: 12-10-1981
Support: Radio
Length: 3:48
Observations: Cycle Lunes musicales de RNE. Recorded by RNE. Tribute to Joaquin Rodrigo on his 80th anniversary.
Recording 5
Year: 1981
Singer: Higueras, Ana (Sop.)
Pianist: Zanetti, Miguel
Date: 1981
Support: LP
Label: Marfer
Discographic reference: M 55015 S Marfer
Observations: Included in the album "Recital de canciones de Joaqum Rodrigo por Ana Higueras Aragon".
Recording 6
Year: 1986
Singer: Cid, Manuel (Ten.)
Pianist: Lavilla, Fëlix
Date: 1986
Support: LP
Label: Fundacion Banco Exterior
Discographical reference: D.L. M- 4670
Observations: Included in the album "Compositores Espanoles del siglo XX. Concert Songs".
Recording 7
Year: 1989
Singer: Kudo, Atsuko (Sop.)
Pianist: Zabala, Alejandro
Venue: Real Academia de Bellas Artes San Fernando, Madrid
Date: 1-12-1989
Support: Radio
Length: 3:33
Remarks: Radio 2 concerts. RNE recording.
Recording 8
Year: 1992
Singer: Manuel Cid (t)
Pianist: Miguel Zanetti
Venue: Juan March Foundation
Date: 25-5-1992
Backing: Magnetic tape
Length: 3' 49"
Observations: Concert of the Juan March Foundation. Concert in memory of Federico Sopena.
Recording 9

Year: 1994
Singer: Fresan, Inaki (Bar.)
Pianist: Alvarez Parejo, Juan Antonio
Venue: Real Academia de Bellas Artes de San Fernando, Madrid
Date: 5-2-1994
Support: Radio
Length: 3:08
Remarks: The radio concerts 2. RNE recording.
Recording 10
Year: 1997
Singer: Higueras, Ana (Sop.)
Pianist: Turina, Fernando
Date: 1997
Media: CD
Label: Higueras Arte
Discographical reference: EK CD 106
Observations: Included in the album "Cancion espanola, primera mitad del siglo XX".
Recording 11
Year: 1997
Singer: Kudo, Atsuko (Sop.)
Pianist: Zabala, Alejandro
Place: Fundacion Juan March, Madrid
Date: 8-1-1997
Support: Radio
Length: 3:25
Observations: Cycle "Integral de las canciones de Joaqum Rodrigo". Recorded by RNE.
Recording 12
Year: 1999
Singer: Cabals, Montserrat (Sop.)
Pianist: Zanetti, Miguel
Date: 1999
Media: CD
Label: EMI Classics
Discographical reference: CDM 724356721821
Length: 4:11
Comments: Recorded in 1964.
Recording 13
Year: 2000
Singer: Garrigosa, Francesc (Ten.)
Pianist: Cardo, Anton
Venue: Centro Cultural Conde Duque, Madrid
Date: 4-12-2000
Support: Radio
Length: 3:05
Observations: Musical Mondays at the Conde Duque. Recorded by RNE.
Recording 14
Year: 2001
Singer: Gragera, Elena (Mz.)
Pianist: Cardo, Anton
Venue: Zuloaga Museum, San Juan de los Caballeros (Segovia)

Date: 13-9-2001
Support: Radio
Length: 3:08
Remarks: Festivals of Segovia, Recording of RNE, No permission to broadcast without authorisation of the intërpretes.
Recording 15
Year: 2001
Singer: Maravella, Consol (Sop.)
Pianist: Rubën Parejo
Date: 2001
Media: CD
Record label: PM Produccions
Discographic reference: P.M. / CD-22
Remarks: Paco Munoz Produccions. Sponsored by the Ajuntament de Monserrat (Valencia).
Recording 16
Year: 2001
Singer: Masino, Fabiola (Sop.)
Pianist: Turina, Fernando
Date: 2001
Media: CD
Label: Blue Moon
Discographical reference: BMCD 2071
Recording 17
Year: 2002
Singer: Mailinez, Ana Marfa (Sop.)
Pianist: Guinovart, Albert
Date: 2002
Media: CD
Label: EMI Classics
Recording reference: CDS 724356783324
Length: 3:41
Remarks: Commemorative edition of the centenary of Joaquin Rodrigo, 12 CD, vol. 2.
Recording 18
Year: 2002
Singer: Mailinez, Ana Maria (Sop.)
Pianist: Guinovart, Albert
Date: 2002
Media: CD
Label: EMI Classics
Discographic reference: PE02001
Length: 3'43"
Remarks: Included in the album "Joaquin Rodrigo, 100 anos", vol. 2.
Recording 19
Year: 2005
Singer: Gragera, Elena (Mz.)
Pianist: Cardo, Anton
Place: Real Balneario Solan de Cabras, Beteta (Cuenca)
Date: 9-9-2005
Support: Radio
Length: 3:07

Observations: Cycle "Music in the Water". Recorded by RNE. No permission to broadcast without the permission of the performers.

Title: "Pastorcito Santo

Collection or cycle: *Three carols,* n° 1
Date of composition: 1952
It belongs to Lope de Vega's play: *Shepherds of Bethlehem.*
First verse: "Zagalejo de perlas".
Character: Aminadab and Palmira
Scenic annotations: [Aminadab [...] came with his beloved Palmyra [...], and his wife accompanying him with voice and instrument, they both said thus:]
Duration: 2' 40"
Key: E minor
Tessitura: D3 sharp-Do4
Agaggic indications: *Andante*
Release date: January 1954
Place of the premiere: Real Conservatorio de Musica de Madrid
Date of publication: 1953
Publisher: Joaquin Rodrigo
Mention of edition: Grafispania
Place of publication: Madrid
Dedication: To Dr. Schermant
Remarks: Several later editions: UME (1968), Joaquin Rodrigo-Grafispania (1970), EJR (2000). There is a version by the composer himself for voice and guitar from 1959.
Recording 1
Year: 1967
Singer: Angeles, Victoria de los (Sop.)
Pianist: Soriano, Gonzalo
Date: 1961.12.04/08
Support: LP
Label: Angel
Discographical reference: Reference 35775
Length: 3'59".
Remarks: Included in the album "Siglo 20°. Spanish Songs".
Recording 2
Year: 1976
Singer: Martm, Fuencisla (Sop.)
Pianist: Elcoro, Valentm
Venue: Casa de la Radio, Madrid
Date: 24-11-1976
Support: Radio
Duration: Unspecified
Comments: RNE recording.
Recording 3
Year: 1978
Singer: Diaz, Ana Amelia (Sop.)
Pianist: Perera, Julian
Venue: Casa de la Radio, Madrid
Date: 13-12-1978
Support: Radio

Length: 2:55
Comments: RNE recording.
Recording 4
Year: 1981
Singer: Higueras, Ana (Sop.)
Pianist: Lavilla, Fëlix
Venue: Philharmonic Society, Bilbao
Date: 12-10-1981
Support: Radio
Length: 4:04
Observations: Cycle Lunes musicales de RNE. Recorded by RNE. Tribute to Joaquin Rodrigo on its 80th anniversary.
Recording 5
Year: 1981
Singer: Higueras, Ana (Sop.)
Pianist: Zanetti, Miguel
Date: 1981
Support: LP
Label: Marfer
Discographic reference: M 55015 S Marfer
Observations: Included in the album "Recital de canciones de Joaquin Rodrigo por Ana Higueras Aragon".
Recording 6
Year: 1993
Singer: Angeles, Victoria de los (Sop.)
Pianist: Soriano, Gonzalo
Date: 1993
Media: CD
Label: EMI Classics
Discographic reference: 5650642 CMS 5650612
Length: 2:31
Comments: 4 CDs. Recorded in 1962.
Recording 7
Year: 1994
Singer: Chaves, Soraya (Sop.)
Pianist: Pares, Xavier
Venue: Real Conservatorio Superior de Musica, Madrid
Date: 15-4-1994
Support: Radio
Length: 2:38
Observations: Jacinto e Inocencio Guerrero Foundation, International Singing Prize of the Guerrero Foundation, final audition, first prize, prize for the best interpretation of Spanish music. Recorded by RNE.
Recording 8
Year: 1994
Singer: Fresan, Inaki (Bar.)
Pianist: Alvarez Parejo, Juan Antonio
Venue: Real Academia de Bellas Artes de San Fernando, Madrid
Date: 5-2-1994
Support: Radio

Length: 2:47
Remarks: The radio concerts 2. RNE recording.
Recording 9
Year: 1995
Singer: Alcedo, Celia (Sop.)
Pianist: Tamayo, Celsa
Place: Iglesia de San Josë, Madrid
Date: 23-12-1995
Support: Radio
Length: 3:11
Observations: Certamen de Musica Vocal en Navidad, closing concert. Not available on RNE due to sound or performance deficiencies.
Recording 10
Year: 1995
Singer: Montiel, Maria Josë (Sop.)
Pianist: Zanetti, Miguel
Venue: Real Academia de Bellas Artes San Fernando, Madrid
Date: 4-3-1995
Support: Radio
Duration: Unspecified
Comments: RNE recording.
Recording 11
Year: 1996
Singer: Higueras, Ana (Sop.)
Pianist: Zanetti, Miguel
Date: 1966
Support: LP
Record label: Discos Tempo
Discographical reference: T2L-001 S Discos Tempo
Observations: Included in the album "Recital de canciones de Joaqum Rodrigo por Ana Higueras Aragon". There is another publication of the same recording on the Marfer label, 1981.
Recording 12
Year: 1996
Singer: Aragon, Mana (Mz.)
Pianist: Turina, Fernando
Venue: Theatre of the Hotel Alhambra Palace, Granada
Date: 27-6-1996
Support: Radio
Length: 2:40
Observations: International Festival of Music and Dance of Granada. Not allowed to broadcast without the permission of the performers.
Recording 13
Year: 1996
Singer: Fresan, Inaki (Bar.)
Pianist: Alvarez Parejo, Juan Antonio
Venue: Headquarters of the Orfeon Donostiarra, San Sebastian
Date: 29-8-1996
Support: Radio
Length: 2:40
Observations: San Sebastian Musical Fortnight. Recorded by RNE. No permission to broadcast

without the permission of the performers.
Recording 14
Year: 1997
Singer: Higueras, Ana (Sop.)
Pianist: Turina, Fernando
Date: 1997
Media: CD
Label: Higueras Arte
Discographical reference: EK CD 106
Observations: Included in the album "Cancion espanola, primera mitad del siglo XX".
Recording 15
Year: 1997
Singer: Kudo, Atsuko (Sop.)
Pianist: Zabala, Alejandro
Place: Fundacion Juan March, Madrid
Date: 22-1-1997
Support: Radio
Duration: Unspecified
Observations: Cycle "Integral de las canciones de Joaqum Rodrigo". Recorded by RNE.
Recording 16
Year: 1998
Singer: Bustamante, Carmen (Sop.)
Pianist: Garcia Chornet, Perfecto
Date: 1998
Media: CD
Label: Arcobaleno
Discographical reference: Arcobaleno 9426
Length: 2'52"
Remarks: Included in the album "Spanish Festival".
Recording 17
Year: 1998
Singer: Montiel, Maria Josë (Sop.)
Pianist: Zanetti, Miguel
Venue: Casa de la Radio, Madrid
Date: January-April 1998
Support: Radio
Length: 2:57
Comments: Recording for RTVE MUSICA 619682, La casa de la Radio, Madrid.
Recording 18
Year: 1999
Singer: Ostolaza, Euken (Ten.)
Pianist: Urcola, Ana Maria
Venue: San Sebastian Town Hall
Date: 18-12-1999
Support: Radio
Duration: 4:30
Observations: Guipuzcoan Athenaeum. Recorded by RNE. Not allowed to broadcast without the permission of the performers.
Recording 19
Year: 1999

Singer: Castro-Alberty, Margarita (Sop.)
Pianist: Cebro, Carlos
Date: 1999
Media: CD
Label: LYS
Observations: Included in the album "Joaquin Rodrigo: Integral de canciones. Premiere mondiale", vol. 1.
Recording 20
Year: 1999
Singer: Montiel, Mana Josë (Sop.)
Pianist: Zanetti, Miguel
Date: 1999
Media: CD
Record label: RTVE Musica
Discography reference: 65115
Length: 4:25
Remarks: Recorded in 1998, Casa de la Radio, Madrid.
Recording 21
Year: 2000
Singer: Gragera, Elena (Mz.)
Pianist: Cardo, Anton
Place: Church of Santa Marfa del Puerto, Santona (Santander)
Date: 19-8-2000
Support: Radio
Length: 2:23
Observations: Santander International Festival. RNE recording. Not allowed to broadcast without permission of the intërpreters.
Recording 22
Year: 2000
Singer: Gragera, Elena (Mz.)
Pianist: Cardo, Anton
Venue: Centro Cultural Conde Duque, Madrid
Date: 27-11-2000
Support: Radio
Length: 2:24
Observations: Musical Mondays at the Conde Duque. Recorded by RNE.
Recording 23
Year: 2001
Singer: Montiel, Mana Josë (Sop.)
Pianist: Turina, Fernando
Place: Fundacion Juan March, Madrid
Date: 10-1-2001
Support: Radio
Length: 4:46
Remarks: RNE recording.
Recording 24
Year: 2001
Singer: Martos, Maria Josë (Sop.)
Pianist: Blanes, Marisa
Venue: Auditorio Nacional de Musica, Sala de Camara, Madrid

Date: 13-6-2001
Support: Radio
Length: 2:24
Remarks: RNE recording, not allowed to broadcast without permission of the intërpretes.
Recording 25
Year: 2001
Singer: Gragera, Elena (Mz.)
Pianist: Cardo, Anton
Venue: Zuloaga Museum, San Juan de los Caballeros (Segovia)
Date: 13-9-2001
Support: Radio
Duration: 2:30
Remarks: Festivals of Segovia, Recording of RNE, No permission to broadcast without authorisation of the intërpretes.
Recording 26
Year: 2001
Singer: Maravella, Consol (Sop.)
Pianist: Parejo, Rubën
Date: 2001
Media: CD
Record label: PM Produccions
Discographical reference: P.M. / CD-22
Remarks: Paco Munoz Produccions. Sponsored by the Ajuntament de Monserrat (Valencia).
Recording 27
Year: 2002
Singer: Gragera, Elena (Mz.)
Pianist: Cardo, Anton
Venue: Centro Cultural Conde Duque, Madrid
Date: 16-12-2002
Support: Radio
Length: 2:27
Observations: Musical Mondays at the Conde Duque. Recorded by RNE. Not allowed to broadcast without authorisation of the intërpretes.
Recording 28
Year: 2002
Singer: Martmez, Ana Maria (Sop.)
Pianist: Guinovart, Albert
Date: 2002
Media: CD
Label: EMI Classics
Discography reference: PE02001
Length: 2'55"
Remarks: Included in the album "Joaquin Rodrigo, 100 anos", vol. 2.
Recording 29
Year: 2002
Singer: Marlinez, Ana Maria (Sop.)
Pianist: Guinovart, Albert
Date: 2002
Media: CD
Label: EMI Classics

Recording reference: CDS 724356783324
Length: 2:53
Remarks: Commemorative edition of the centenary of Joaquin Rodrigo, 12 CD, vol. 2.
Recording 30
Year: 2002
Singer: Fink, Bernarda (Mz.)
Pianist: Vignoles, Roger
Date: 2002
Media: CD
Label: Hyperion
Discographic reference: HYP 67186
Recording 31
Year: 2002
Singer: Monar, Isabel (Sop.)
Pianist: McClure, Mac
Date: 2002
Media: CD
Label: Columna Musica
Discographic reference: CM 0077
Recording 32
Year: 2003
Singer: Gragera, Elena (Mz.)
Pianist: Cardo, Anton
Venue: Centro Cultural Conde Duque, Madrid
Date: 13-1-2003
Support: Radio
Length: 2:36
Observations: Musical Mondays at the Conde Duque. Recorded by RNE. Not allowed to broadcast without the permission of the performers.
Recording 33
Year: 2003
Singer: Rey, Isabel (Sop.)
Pianist: Zabala, Alejandro
Date: 2003
Media: CD
Label: Edicions Albert Moraleda
Discography reference: Edicions Albert Moraleda: 0155
Remarks: Included in the album "Songs for Christmas".
Recording 34
Year: 2003
Singer: Darijo, Conchm (Sop.)
Pianist: Monasterio, Aida
Date: 2003
Media: CD
Label: EGT
Discographical reference: EGT 911
Length: 2:42
Comments: Recorded in 2002.
Recording 35
Year: 2004

Singer: Sanchez, Ana Maria (Sop.)
Pianist: Moretti, Kennedy
Venue: Palau de la Musica, Valencia
Date: 13-3-2004
Support: Radio
Duration: Unspecified
Comments: RNE recording. Not allowed to broadcast without authorisation from the inlc'rpreles.
Recording 36
Year: 2006
Singer: Latorre, Fernando (Bar.)
Pianist: Barredo, Itziar
Date: 2006
Media: CD
Label: Arsis
Discographical reference: ARSIS 4198
Length: 2:45
Observations: Included in the album "Cantar del alma, La poesi'a del Siglo de Oro en la musica del siglo XX".
Recording 37
Year: 2009
Singer: Vundru, Franziska (Sop.)
Pianist: Ickert, Bernd
Date: 2009
Media: CD
Label: Musicaphon
Discographic reference: M56844
Remarks: Included in the album "Herz, stirb, oder singe!".

SALVADOR SEGARRA, MATILDE (1918-2007)

Title: "Castellana".

Collection or series: *Six Spanish songs,* n° 1
Date of composition: 1 June 1939
It belongs to Lope de Vega's play: El gran duque de Moscovia (The Grand Duke of Muscovy).
First verse: "Blanca me era yo".
Character: Musicians
Scene notes: The reaper musicians come out, and with them Lucinda, Demetrio, Rufino, Belardo and Febo. They sing.
Duration: 1' 15" approx.
Key: B minor *
Tessitura: E3-Fa4 sharp
Aggressive indications: Tranquilo-72
Manuscript location: Institute Valencia de la Musica
Manuscript symbol: Provisional inventory
Dedication: To Manuel de Falla
Title: Singing and Piano
Observations: Of the *Seis canciones espanolas,* one copy says soprano and piano (inside one song it says voz media), and another copy says voz media and piano. The tonalities and tessituras are identical. The song cycle obtained Honourable Mention in the Concurso de Composicion de la Jefatura de Propaganda de Vizcaya, in January 1940.

Title: "Gallega".

Collection or series: *Six Spanish songs,* n° 2
Date of composition: 10 June 1939
It belongs to Lope de Vega's play: El villano en su rincon (The villain in his corner).
First verse: "Por el montecico sola" (On the mountain alone)
Character: Musicians
Scenic notes: The musicians sing and Bruno sings alone.
Duration: 1' 30" approx.
Key: A minor *
Tessitura: E3-G4
Agaggic indications: *Allegro ma mon* molto-120
Location of the manuscript: Instituto Valencia de la Musica
Manuscript symbol: Provisional inventory
Dedication: To Manuel de Falla
Title: Singing and Piano
Observations: There is another copy with Galician text (it is titled *Galeica* (sic.) and another copy that says: "2- version with anonymous Galician text and slight variants in the harmony". Of the *Seis canciones espanolas*, one copy says soprano and piano (inside one song it says voz media), and another copy says voz media and piano. The tonalities and tessituras are identical.
The song cycle obtained Honourable Mention in the Composition Competition of the Propaganda Headquarters of Vizcaya, in January 1940.

Title: "Levantina".

Subtitle: Valenciana
Collection or series: *Seis canciones espanolas,* n° 6
Date of composition: 30 July 1939
It belongs to Lope de Vega's play: *El bobo del colegio.*
First verse: "Naranjitas me tira la nina".
Character: Musicians
Scenic notes: Canten
Duration: 1' 45" approx.
Key: E major *
Tessitura: E3-A4
Aggressive indications: Moderate-72
Location of manuscript: Institute Valencia de la Musica
Manuscript symbol: Provisional inventory
Dedication: To Manuel de Falla
Title notes: Singing and Piano
Remarks: *Valenciana*, from the suite *Seis canciones espanolas* for voice and orchestra, not titled *Levantna* like the original for voice and piano. Annotation in pencil on the title page "Versio de l'any del rey Pepet" (sic.). The orchestration of the song is for woodwinds, trumpets in F and C2, harp and strings. The voice does not have the lyrics written down, it includes parts. Of the *Seis canciones espanolas*, one copy says soprano and piano (inside one song it says medium voice), and another copy says medium voice and piano. The tonalities and tessituras are identical. The song cycle obtained an Honourable Mention in the Composition Competition of the Propaganda Headquarters of Vizcaya, in January 1940.

Title: "Cancion de vela" (Sailing Song)

Date of composition: 1946
It belongs to Lope de Vega's play: *Las almenas de Toro.*
First verse: "Watchman that the castle candles".
Character: Flores and Layn

Scenic notes: they both sing
Duration: 1'45
Key: D minor
Tessitura: D3-E4
Aggressive indications: Slowly
Date of publication: 1947
Publisher: Piles
Place of publication: Valencia
Dedication: To Victoria de los Angeles
Head notes: For medium voice and piano
Remarks: Date of composition taken from the SGAE catalogue. Publication date taken from the copy of the edition, which bears a handwritten dedication on the title page: "A la gran liederista Carmen Andujar, amb la meva gratitud per les interpretacions de les meves cancons, molt cordialment, Matilde Salvador. Valencia, 1947". Premiere of the orchestral version: Emilia Munoz (Sop.) and Orquesta Municipal de Valencia, conductor Hans von Benda, 6 May 1951, Teatro Principal, Valencia.

THOMAS SABATER, JUAN MARIA (1896-1966)

Title: "Guitar".

Collection or series: Spanish Instrumental Songs, n° 1
Date of composition: 1944
It belongs to Lope de Vega's play: Peribanez y el comendador de Ocana.
First verse: "Cogiome a tu puerta el toro".
Character: Musicians
Scenic notes: sing
Duration: 1' 30" approx.
Key: E flat major
Tessitura: B2 flat - E4 flat
Agaggic indications: *Allegro ma non troppo*
Date of publication: 1944
Publisher: Ediciones Capella Classica
Place of publication: Mallorca
Recording 1
Year: 2001
Singer: Cordon, Carmelo (Bar.)
Pianist: Celebon, Monica
Venue: Teatro Monumental, Madrid
Date: 7-4-2001
Support: Radio
Duration: Unspecified
Remarks: The Classical Radio Concerts. Recorded by RNE.

Title: "Gaita".

Collection or series: Spanish Instrumental Songs, n° 5
Date of composition: 1944
It belongs to Lope de Vega's play: Peribanez y el comendador de Ocana.
First verse: "Dente parabienes".
Character: Musicians
Scenic notes: they play and sing
Duration: 2' 40" approx.
Key: C major

Tessitura: F3-G4

Aggico indications: *Moderato*

Date of publication: 1944

Publisher: Ediciones Capella Classica

Place of publication: Mallorca

Remarks: Date of composition taken from the date of publication.

TOLDRA I SOLER, EDUARD (1885-1962)

Title: "Cantarcillo".

Subtitle: Well, you're clapping your hands.

Collection or series: *Six songs,* n° 5

Date of composition: 1941

It belongs to Lope de Vega's play: *Shepherds of Bethlehem.*

First verse: "Pues andais en las palmas".

Character: Elifila

Scenic notes: [that I intend to imitate in my song, saying thus:]

Length: 3' 15

Key: C sharp minor / D flat major

Tessitura: F3-Fa4

Agaggic indications: Andante, non troppo lento

Date of release: 29-3-1941-29

Place of the premiere: Palau de la Musica de Barcelona

Opening singer: Mercedes Plantada

Pianist of the premiere: Blay - Net

Date of publication: 1942/1992

Publisher: Josë Porter/Union Musical Espanola

Place of publication: Barcelona/Madrid

Title: Singing and Piano

Remarks: There is a version for orchestra by the composer himself. The manuscript orchestral materials are preserved in the archive of the Orquestra Simfonica de Barcelona i Nacional de Catalunya (OBC).

Recording 1

Year: 1978

Singer: Callao, Francesca (Sop.)

Pianist: Panella, Juli

Venue: Casa de la Radio, Madrid

Date: 13-2-1978

Support: Radio

Length: 1:55

Comments: RNE recording.

Recording 2

Year: 1987

Singer: Berganza, Teresa (Mz.)

Pianist: Alvarez Parejo, Juan Antonio

Date: 1987

Media: CD

Label: Claves

Discographic reference: CD508704

Length: 1:55

Observations: Included in the album "Teresa Berganza: Canciones espanolas". Recorded in 1977.

Recording 3
Year: 1989
Singer: Blanco, Carmen (Sop.)
Pianist: Quero, Raquel
Date: 1989
Support: LP
Record label: Caja Provincial de Ahorros de Cordoba
Discographic reference: CPAD 1056
Duration: Unspecified
Comments: 2 LP. Live recording Palacio de Viana, Cordoba.
Recording 4
Year: 1992
Singer: Bustamante, Carmen (Sop.)
Pianist: Garcia Morante, Manuel
Date: 1992
Media: CD
Record label: Audiovisuals de Sama
Discography reference: 251516
Duration: 4:00
Recording 5
Year: 1994
Singer: Casariego, Lola (Mz.)
Pianist: Zanetti, Miguel
Venue: Real Academia de Bellas Artes de San Fernando, Madrid
Date: 26-3-1994
Support: Radio
Duration: Unspecified
Remarks: Radio 2 concerts. RNE recording.
Recording 6
Year: 1995
Singer: Gragera, Elena (Mz.)
Pianist: Cardo, Anton
Venue: Fundacion Carlos de Amberes, Madrid
Date: 14-12-1995
Support: Radio
Duration: Unspecified
Observations: Cycle "La canco de concert a Catalunya", Generalitat de Catalunya, Fundació Carlos de Amberes. Recorded by RNE.
Recording 7
Year: 1995
Singer: Montiel, Maria Josë (Sop.)
Pianist: Zanetti, Miguel
Place: Fundacion Juan March, Madrid
Date: 17-5-1995
Support: Radio
Length: 2:17
Remarks: RNE recording.
Recording 8
Year: 1997
Singer: Lorengar, Pilar (Sop.)

Pianist: Lavilla, Fëlix
Date: 1997
Media: CD
Label: RCA Classics
Label reference: BMG 74321397692
Duration: 3:30
Observations: Included in the album "Pilar Lorengar: Canciones", 2CD. Recorded by 1959.
Recording 9
Year: 1997
Singer: Higueras, Ana (Sop.)
Pianist: Turina, Fernando
Date: 1997
Media: CD
Label: Higueras Arte
Discographical reference: EK CD 106
Remarks: Included in the album "Cancion espanola, primera mitad del siglo XX".
Recording 10
Year: 1997
Singer: Montiel, Marfa Josë (Sop.)
Pianist: Zanetti, Miguel
Date: 1997
Media: CD
Label: Dial Discos-Doblon
Discography reference: 96984
Length: 2:17
Observations: Live recording by RNE. Juan March Foundation Hall, 17-5-95.
Recording 11
Year: 1998
Singer: Bayo, Mana (Sop.)
Pianist: Zeger, Brian
Venue: Teatro de la Zarzuela, Madrid
Date: 23-3-98
Support: Radio
Duration: 1:45
Observations: Lied Cycle. Teatro de la Zarzuela, Madrid. Recorded by RNE. No permission to broadcast without authorisation of the intërpretes.
Recording 12
Year: 2001
Singer: Bayo, Mana (Sop.)
Pianist: Werkle, Veronique
Venue: Teatro de la Zarzuela, Madrid
Date: 12-11-2001
Support: Radio
Duration: Unspecified
Observations: Lied Cycle. Teatro de la Zarzuela, Madrid. Teatro de la Zarzuela, Madrid. RNE recording. No permission to broadcast without authorisation from the inlc'ipreles.
Recording 13
Year: 2001
Canlanle: Ricci, Anna (Mz.)

Pianist: Soler, Angel
Date: 2001
Soporle: CD
Label: Edicions Albert Moraleda
Discography reference: 741
Length: 3:38
Recording 14
Year: 2001
Singer: Muntada, Maria Lluisa (Sop.)
Pianisla: Surinyac, Josep
Place: Parroquia de la Purisima Concepcion, Los Molinos (Madrid)
Date: 28-7-2001
Support: Radio
Length: 3:10
Comments: RNE recording
Recording 15
Year: 2001
Singer: Bordoy, Teresa (Sop.)
Pianist: Celebon, Monica
Venue: Teatro Monumental, Madrid
Date: 7-4-2001
Support: Radio
Duration: Unspecified
Remarks: The Classical Radio Concerts. Recorded by RNE.
Year: 2005
Singer: Londono, Gloria (Sop.)
Pianist: Lamazares, Madalit
Venue: Principe Felipe Auditorium, Oviedo
Date: 14-12-2005
Support: Radio
Length: 3:09
Remarks: RNE recording. Not allowed to broadcast without the permission of the intërpreters.
Recording 17
Year: 2005
Singer: Schwartz, Sylvia (Sop.)
Pianist: Turina, Fernando
Place: Fundacion Marcelino Botin, Santander
Date: 15-2-2005
Support: Radio
Length: 3:09
Remarks: RNE recording. Not allowed to broadcast without the permission of the performers.
Recording 18
Year: 2005
Singer: Londono, Gloria (Sop.)
Pianist: Lamazares, Madalit
Venue: Real Academia de Bellas Artes de San Fernando, Madrid
Date: 28-05-2005
Support: Radio
Length: 3:04
Comments: RNE recording.

Recording 19
Year: 2006
Singer: Genicio, Bek'n (Sop.)
Pianist: Segura, Juan Carlos
Date: 2006
Media: CD
Label: Coda Out
Discography reference: COUT 2025
Length: 3:11
Title: "Mother, I saw some eyelets".
Collection or series: *Six songs,* n° 2
Date of composition: 1941
It belongs to the work of Lope de Vega: *La Dorotea.*
First verse: "Mother, I saw some eyelets".
Character: Dorotea
Scenic notes: [Take, Celia, the harp; that obliges me to much this answer].
Duration: 3' 10"
Key: E minor
Tessitura: D3 sharp-E4
Aggonic indications: *Allegretto*
Date of publication: 1942/1992
Publisher: Jose Porter/Union Musical Espanola
Place of publication: Barcelona/Madrid
Dedication: To Mercedes Plantada
Title: Singing and Piano
Remarks: There is a version for orchestra by the composer himself. The manuscript orchestral materials are preserved in the archive of the Orquestra Simfonica de Barcelona i Nacional de Catalunya (OBC).
Recording 1
Year: 1978
Singer: Diaz, Ana Amelia (Sop.)
Pianist: Perera, Julian
Venue: Casa de la Radio, Madrid
Date: 13-12-1978
Support: Radio
Length: 2:35
Comments: RNE recording.
Recording 2
Year: 1978
Singer: Callao, Francesca (Sop.)
Pianist: Panella, Juli
Venue: Casa de la Radio, Madrid
Date: 13-2-1978
Support: Radio
Length: 2:38
Comments: RNE recording.
Recording 3
Year: 1979
Singer: Ruival, Amelia (Sop.)

Pianist: Gorostiaga, Ana Maria
Venue: Casa de la Radio, Madrid
Date: 30-4-1979
Support: Radio
Length: 3:45
Comments: RNE recording.
Recording 4
Year: 1987
Singer: Berganza, Teresa (Mz.)
Pianist: Alvarez Parejo, Juan Antonio
Date: 1987
Media: CD
Label: Claves
Discographic reference: CD508704
Length: 2:41
Remarks: Included in the album "Teresa Berganza: Canciones espanolas". Recorded at 1977.
Recording 5
Year: 1987
Singer: Kudo, Atsuko (Sop.)
Pianist: Pares, Xavier
Venue: Casa de la Radio, Madrid

Date: 20-2-1987
Support: Radio
Length: 2:45
Comments: RNE recording.
Recording 6
Year: 1990
Singer: Poblador, Milagros (Sop.)
Pianist: Penalver, Juana
Venue: International Institute of Spain, Madrid
Date: 14-12-1990
Support: Radio
Length: 2:18
Comments: RNE recording.
Recording 7
Year: 1990
Singer: Belmonte, Elisa (Sop.)
Pianist: Parc's, Xavier
Venue: Caja Postal, Madrid
Date: 2-4-1990
Support: Radio
Duration: Unspecified
Comments: RNE recording.
Recording 8
Year: 1992
Singer: Bustamante, Carmen (Sop.)
Pianist: Garria Morante, Manuel
Date: 1992
Media: CD
Record label: Audiovisuals de Sarria
Discography reference: 251516
Length: 3:01
Year: 1993
Singer: Berganza, Teresa (Mz.)
Pianist: Alvarez Parejo, Juan Antonio
Venue: Manuel de Falla Auditorium, Granada
Date: 20-6-1993
Support: Radio
Duration: Unspecified
Observations: International Festival of Music and Dance of Granada. Recorded by RNE. No permission to broadcast without authorisation from the
Recording 10
Year: 1994
Singer: Casariego, Lola (Mz.)
Pianist: Zanetti, Miguel
Venue: Real Academia de Bellas Artes de San Fernando, Madrid
Date: 26-3-1994
Support: Radio
Duration: Unspecified
Remarks: Radio 2 concerts. RNE recording.
Recording 11

Year: 1995
Singer: Gragera, Elena (Mz.)
Pianist: Cardo, Anton
Venue: Fundacion Carlos de Amberes, Madrid
Date: 14-12-1995
Support: Radio
Duration: Unspecified
Observations: Cycle "La canco de concert a Catalunya", Generalitat de Catalunya, Fundació Carlos de Amberes. Recorded by RNE.
Recording 12
Year: 1995
Singer: Montiel, Maria Josë (Sop.)
Pianist: Zanetti, Miguel
Place: Fundacion Juan March, Madrid
Date: 17-5-1995
Support: Radio
Duration: 3:00
Comments: RNE recording.
Recording 13
Year: 1996
Singer: Angeles, Victoria de los (Sop.)
Pianist: Moore, Gerald
Date: 1996
Media: CD
Label: Testament
Discographical reference: SBT 1087 MO
Length: 3:13
Remarks: Included in the album "Victoria de los Angeles: The early recordings, 19421953". Recorded in 1950.
Recording 14
Year: 1996
Singer: Brito, Augusto (Bar.)
Pianist: Garcia Gutiërrez, Angeles
Venue: Casino de Tenerife
Date: 27-6-1996
Support: Radio
Length: 2:23
Remarks: RNE recording. Not allowed to broadcast without the permission of the intërpreters.
Recording 15
Year: 1997
Singer: Rinon, Marfa Josë (Sop.)
Pianist: Moretti, Kennedy
Venue: Academia de Bellas Artes de San Fernando, Madrid
Date: 12-4-1997
Support: Radio
Length: 3:34

Remarks: Cycle Los conciertos de Radio Clasica. Recorded by RNE.
Recording 16
Year: 1997
Singer: Montiel, Maria Josë (Sop.)
Pianist: Zanetti, Miguel
Date: 1997
Media: CD
Label: Dial Discos-Doblon
Discography reference: 96984
Duration: 3:00
Observations: Live recording by RNE. Juan March Foundation Hall, 17-5-95.
Recording 17
Year: 1997
Singer: Lorengar, Pilar (Sop.)
Pianist: Lavilla, Fëlix
Date: 1997
Media: CD
Label: RCA Classics
Label reference: BMG 74321397692
Length: 2:56
Observations: Included in the album "Pilar Lorengar: Canciones", 2CD. Recorded in 1959.
Recording 18
Year: 1997
Singer: Higueras, Ana (Sop.)
Pianist: Turina, Fernando
Date: 1997
Media: CD
Label: Higueras Arte
Discographical reference: EK CD 106
Remarks: Included in the album "Cancion espanola, primera mitad del siglo XX".
Year: 1997
Singer: Serrano, Carmen (Sop.)
Pianist: Lopez, Antonio
Place: Palacio de Viana, Cordoba
Date: 31-1-1997
Support: Radio
Duration: Unspecified
Comments: RNE recording. Not allowed to broadcast without authorisation from the inlc'ipreles.
Recording 20
Year: 1997
Singer: Genicio, Be1ëп (Sop.)
Pianisla: Albala Agundo, Pilar
Venue: Centro Cultural Conde Duque, Madrid
Date: 3-3-1997
Support: Radio
Length: 2:33
Remarks: RNE recording.
Recording 21
Year: 1998
Singer: Bayo, Maria (Sop.)

Pianist: Zeger, Brian
Venue: Teatro de la Zarzuela, Madrid
Date: 23-3-98
Support: Radio
Duration: 3:30
Observations: Lied Cycle. Teatro de la Zarzuela, Madrid. Recorded by RNE. No permission to broadcast without authorisation of the intërpretes.
Recording 22
Year: 1998
Singer: Galiano Cepad, Sandra (Sop.)
Pianist: Gallo, Pilar
Venue: Real Conservatorio de Musica, Madrid
Date: 23-4-1998
Support: Radio
Length: 2:57
Observations: Jacinto e Inocencio Guerrero Foundation, Acisclo Fernandez International Prize, final test. Recorded by RNE.
Recording 23
Year: 2000
Singer: Gragera, Elena (Mz.)
Pianist: Cardo, Anton
Place: Church of Santa Maiia del Puerto, Santona (Santander)
Date: 19-8-2000
Support: Radio
Length: 2:25
Observations: Santander International Festival. RNE recording. Not allowed to broadcast without permission of the performers.
Recording 24
Year: 2000
Singer: Genicio, Bek'n (Sop.)
Pianist: Albala Agundo, Pilar
Place: Auditorio Casa de la Cultura Alfonso X el Sabio, Guadarrama (Madrid)
Date: 26-8-2000
Support: Radio
Length: 2:33
Comments: RNE recording.
Recording 25
Year: 2001
Singer: Montiel, Maria Josë (Sop.)
Pianist: Turina, Fernando
Place: Fundacion Juan March, Madrid
Date: 10-1-2001
Support: Radio
Length: 2:45
Comments: RNE recording.
Recording 26
Year: 2001
Singer: Bayo, Mana (Sop.)
Pianist: Werkle, Veronique
Venue: Teatro de la Zarzuela, Madrid

Date: 12-11-2001
Support: Radio
Duration: Unspecified
Observations: Lied Cycle. Teatro de la Zarzuela, Madrid. Recorded by RNE. No permission to broadcast without the permission of the performers.
Recording 27
Year: 2001
Singer: Montiel, Mana Jose (Sop.)
Pianist: Martin, Chiki
Venue: Teatro Real, Madrid
Date: 15-6-2001
Support: Radio
Length: 2:58
Observations: Recording of RNE. Extraordinary concert for the benefit of AFANIAS
Recording 28
Year: 2001
Singer: Mateu, Assumpta (Sop.)
Pianist: Poyato, Francisco
Venue: Auditori, Barcelona
Date: 27-10-2001
Support: Radio
Duration: Unspecified
Remarks: RNE recording. Not allowed to broadcast without the permission of the performers.
Recording 29
Year: 2001
Singer: Muntada, Maria Lluisa (Sop.)
Pianist: Surinyac, Josep
Place: Parroquia de la Punsima Concepcion, Los Molinos (Madrid)
Date: 28-7-2001
Support: Radio
Length: 2:38
Comments: RNE recording
Recording 30
Year: 2001
Singer: Cordon, Carmelo (Bar.)
Pianist: Celebon, Monica
Venue: Teatro Monumental, Madrid
Date: 7-4-2001
Support: Radio
Duration: Unspecified
Remarks: The Classical Radio Concerts. Recorded by RNE.
Recording 31
Year: 2002
Singer: Gragera, Elena (Mz.)
Pianist: Cardo, Anton
Venue: Centro Cultural Conde Duque, Madrid
Date: 16-12-2002
Support: Radio
Length: 2:35
Observations: Musical Mondays at the Conde Duque. Recorded by RNE. Not allowed to

broadcast without the permission of the performers.
Recording 32
Year: 2002
Singer: Angeles, Victoria de los (Sop.)
Pianist: Wilmotte, Madge
Date: 2002
Media: CD
Label: Institut National de l'Audiovisuel
Discographical reference: IMV (sic) 2002
Length: 2:57
Remarks: Memorie Vive series. Recorded in 1950.
Recording 33
Year: 2004
Singer: Sanchez, Ana Mana (Sop.)
Pianist: Përez de Guzman, Enrique
Venue: Gran Teatre del Liceu, Barcelona
Date: 23-3-2004
Support: Radio
Length: 2:45
Remarks: RNE recording.
Recording 34
Year: 2005
Singer: Villoria, Mario (Bar.)
Pianist: Lamazares, Madalit
Venue: Principe Felipe Auditorium, Oviedo
Date: 14-12-2005
Support: Radio
Length: 2:46
Remarks: RNE recording. Not allowed to broadcast without the permission of the performers.
Recording 35
Year: 2005
Singer: Schwartz, Sylvia (Sop.)
Pianist: Turina, Fernando
Place: Fundacion Marcelino Bolin, Santander
Date: 15-2-2005
Support: Radio
Length: 1:56
Comments: RNE recording. Not allowed to broadcast without authorisation from the inlc'iprclcs.
Recording 36
Year: 2005
Singer: Villoria, Mario (Bar.)
Pianist: Lamazares, Madalit
Venue: Real Academia de Bellas Artes de San Fernando, Madrid
Date: 28-05-2005
Support: Radio
Length: 2:46
Comments: RNE recording.
Recording 37
Year: 2006
Singer: Bayo, Mana (Sop.)

Pianist: Vignoles, Roger
Venue: Teatro Gayarre, Pamplona
Date: 07-11-2006
Support: Radio
Duration: Unspecified
Comments: Recorded by RNE. Not allowed to broadcast without the authorisation of the inslcrprclcs.
Recording 38
Year: 2006
Singer: Latorre, Fernando (Bar.)
Pianist: Barredo, Itziar
Date: 2006
Media: CD
Label: Arsis
Discographical reference: ARSIS 4198
Length: 2:58
Observations: Included in the album "Cantar del alma, La poesi'a del Siglo de Oro en la musica del siglo XX".
Recording 39
Year: 2006
Singer: Genicio, Bek'n (Sop.)
Pianist: Segura, Juan Carlos
Date: 2006
Media: CD
Label: Coda Out
Discography reference: COUT 2025
Length: 2:41

TRUAN ALVAREZ, ENRIQUE (1905-1995)

Title: "Mananicas floridas".

No. of Opus: Op. 12
Collection or series: Three carols by Lope de Vega, n° 1
Date of composition: May 1947
Place of composition: Gijon
It belongs to Lope de Vega's play: *El cardenal de Belen.*
First verse: "Mananicas floridas".
Character: Musica, Pascual [Anton, Bras].
Scenic notes: Canten
Duration: 2' approx.
Key: F major
Tessitura: F3-Fa4
Aggonic indications: *Allegretto*
Release date: 23-7-1947
Premiere venue: Gijon
Singer of the premiere: Yudita de la Vina (Sop.)
Location of the manuscript: Archivo de Musica de Asturias
Manuscript symbol: AMA C 23-29
Title notes: For voice and piano
Observations: The AMA does not provide a copy of the manuscript but a digitised copy of the original made by L. Rodero in 2004, with collation and revision by Vicente Cueva. The grouping

of the three songs, *Mananicas foridas, No Iloreis mis ojos* and *Zagalejo,* seems to be subsequent to the composition, given the dates and opus numbers.
Recording 1
Year: [ca. 1970-1980].
Singer: Alvarez Blanco, Celia (Sop.)
Pianist: Truan, Enrique
Media: CD
Record label: [Leopoldo Rodero, Gijon].
Remarks: Included in the album "Veinte canciones de Enrique Truan".

Title: "Don't cry my eyes".

Opus No.: Op. 28
Collection or series: Three carols by Lope de Vega, n° 2
Date of composition: August 1960
Place of composition: Gijon
It belongs to Lope de Vega's play: *Shepherds of Bethlehem.*
First verse: "Do not weep, my eyes".
Character: Finarda
Scenic notes: [...temple an instrument and singing and weeping, he said thus:]
Duration: 2' 30" approx.
Key: G major
Tessitura: G3-E4
Agaggic indications: Molto andante con tenereza
Release date: 10-2-1978
Premiere venue: Gijon
Opening singer: Celia Alvarez Blanco (Sop.)
Location of the manuscript: Archivo de Musica de Asturias
Manuscript symbol: AMA C 23-26
Title notes: For voice and piano
Observations: The AMA does not provide a copy of the manuscript but a digitised copy of the original made by L. Rodero in 2004, with collation and revision by Vicente Cueva. The grouping of the three songs, *Mananicas foridas, No lloreis mis ojos* and *Zagalejo,* seems to be subsequent to the composition, given the dates and opus numbers.

Title: "Zagalejo".

Opus No.: Op. 70
Collection or series: Tres villancicos de Lope de Vega, n° 3
Date of composition: December 1959
Place of composition: Gijon
It belongs to Lope de Vega's play: *Shepherds of Bethlehem.*
First verse: "Zagalejo de perlas".
Character: Aminadab and Palmira
Scenic notes: [Aminadab [...] verna with his beloved Palmira [...], and his wife accompanying him with voice and instrument, said the two ash].
Duration: 1' 20" approx.
Key: C minor
Tessitura: F3-Fa4
Aggressive indications: *Arioso*
Release date: 7-1-1976
Premiere venue: Gijon
Opening singer: Celia Alvarez Blanco (Sop.)

Location of the manuscript: Archivo de Musica de Asturias
Manuscript symbol: AMA C 23-27
Title notes: For voice and piano
Observations: The AMA does not provide a copy of the manuscript but a digitised copy of the original made by L. Rodero in 2004, with collation and revision by Vicente Cueva. The grouping of the three songs, *Mananicas foridas, No lloreis mis ojos* and *Zagalejo,* seems to be subsequent to the composition, given the dates and opus numbers.

TURINA PEREZ, JOAQUIN (1882-1949)

Title: "When I look at you so beautifully".

Opus No.: Op. 90, n° 1
Collection or series: *Homage to Lope de Vega,* n° 1
Date of composition: 1935
It belongs to Lope de Vega's play: La discreta enamorada (The Discreet Lover).
First verse: "When I look at you so beautifully".
Character: Musicians
Stage directions: Playing and singing
Duration: 2' Duration: 2' Duration: 2' Duration: 2' Duration: 2' Duration: 2' Duration: 2
Key: D minor
Tessitura: G3 sharp-B4 flat
Aggico indications: *Moderato*
Release date: 12-12-1935
Place of the premiere: Teatro Espanol, Madrid
Singer of the premiere: Rosita Hermosilla (Sop.)
Pianist of the premiere: Joaqum Turina
Manuscript location: FJM
Manuscript symbol: LJT-P-A-33
Date of publication: 1936 / 1983
Publisher: Union Musical Espanola
Place of publication: Madrid
Dedication: To Rosita Hermosilla
Head notes: For voice and piano / from "La discreta enamorada".
Motivation: Tribute to Lope de Vega by the Conservatorio de Madrid in the Spanish Theatre
Remarks: The manuscript bears on the last leaf the date 13 November 1935.
There is another Union Musical Espanola edition from 1992.
Recording 1
Singer: Anton, Jorge (Ten.)
Pianist: Acebes, M.~ Jesus
Support: Cassette
Observations: Original support deposited in the FJM Library, call number: MC-387.
Recording 2
Year: 1990
Singer: Kraus, Alfredo (Ten.)
Pianist: Arnaltes, Edelmiro
Date: 1990
Media: CD
Label: Amadeo
Discography reference: 429 556 2
Observations: Total duration of the cycle "Tribute to Lope de Vega" 6'56".
Recording 3

Year: 1990
Singer: Belmonte, Elisa (Sop.)
Pianist: Parc's, Xavier
Venue: Caja Postal, Madrid
Date: 2-4-1990
Support: Radio
Duration: Unspecified
Comments: RNE recording.
Recording 4
Year: 1990
Singer: Lorengar, Pilar (Sop.)
Pianist: Zanetti, Miguel
Venue: Teatro de la Zarzuela, Madrid
Date: 8-4-1990
Support: Radio
Length: 2:17
Remarks: RNE recording. Not allowed to broadcast without the permission of the performers.
Recording 5
Year: 1991
Singer: Kraus, Alfredo (Ten.)
Pianist: Zanetti, Miguel
Date: 1991
Media: CD
Label: Diapason
Label reference: CAL 101
Observations: Total duration of the cycle "Tribute to Lope de Vega" 6' 06".
Recording 6
Year: 1991
Singer: Lorengar, Pilar (Sop.)
Pianist: Zanetti, Miguel
Venue: Campoamor Theatre, Oviedo
Date: 22-10-1991
Support: Radio
Length: 2:20
Remarks: Farewell concert by Pilar Lorengar. Recorded by RNE.
Recording 7
Year: 1992
Singer: Lorengar, Pilar (Sop.)
Pianist: Zanetti, Miguel
Date: 1992
Media: CD
Record label: RTVE Musica
Discography reference: 65010
Length: 2:18
Observations: Included in the album "Pilar Lorengar: los adioses", 2 CD. Recorded by RNE in Teatro de la Zarzuela on 8-4-1990.
Recording 8
Year: 1997
Singer: Cid, Manuel (Ten.)
Pianist: Requejo, Ricardo

Date: 1997
Media: CD
Label: Claves Records
Discographical reference: CD 509602
Length: 2:21
Recording 9
Year: 1998
Singer: Resnik, Regina (Sop.)
Pianist: Wiotach, Richard
Date: 1998
Media: CD
Label: Sony Classical
Discographic reference: SMK 60784
Length: 2:37
Remarks: Vocal Masterworks series. Recorded in 1967 or 1968.
Recording 10
Year: 2000
Singer: Lorengar, Pilar (Sop.)
Pianist: Zanetti, Miguel
Date: 2000
Media: CD
Record label: RTVE Musica
Discography reference: 65130
Length: 2:16
Observations: Live recording at the Teatro de la Zarzuela on 8-4-1990. Farewell concert by Pilar Lorengar. 2 CDS.
Recording 11
Year: 2001
Singer: Jordi, Ismael (Ten.)
Pianist: Munoz, Julio Alexis
Venue: Teatro Monumental, Madrid
Date: 26-5-2001
Support: Radio
Duration: Unspecified
Remarks: The Classical Radio Concerts. Recorded by RNE. Total duration Homenaje a Joaqum Turina: 6:08.
Recording 12
Year: 2005
Singer: Schwartz, Sylvia (Sop.)
Pianist: Turina, Fernando
Place: Fundacion Marcelino Bolin, Santander
Date: 15-2-2005
Support: Radio
Length: 1:56
Remarks: RNE recording. Not allowed to broadcast without the permission of the intërpreters.
Recording 13
Year: 2006
Singer: Latorre, Fernando (Bar.)
Pianist: Barredo, Itziar
Date: 2006

Media: CD
Label: Arsis
Discographical reference: ARSIS 4198
Length: 2:07
Observations: Included in the album "Cantar del alma, La poesia del Siglo de Oro en la musica del siglo XX".

Title: "Yes with my wishes".

Opus No.: Op. 90, n° 2
Collection or series: *Homage to Lope de Vega,* n° 2
Date of composition: 1935
It belongs to Lope de Vega's play: La estrella de Sevilla.
First verse: "If with my desires".
Character: Star
Length: 1' 54"
Key: D major
Tessitura: D3-E4 flat
Agaggic indications: *Andante*
Release date: 12-12-1935
Place of the premiere: Teatro Espanol, Madrid
Singer of the premiere: Rosita Hermosilla (Sop.)
Pianist of the premiere: Joaqum Turina
Manuscript location: FJM
Manuscript symbol: LJT-P-A-33
Date of publication: 1936 / 1983
Publisher: Union Musical Espanola
Place of publication: Madrid
Dedication: To Rosita Hermosilla
Head notes: For voice and piano /from "La Estrella de Sevilla".
Motivation: Tribute to Lope de Vega by the Conservatorio de Madrid in the Spanish Theatre
Remarks: The manuscript bears on the last leaf the date 13 November 1935.
There is another Union Musical Espanola edition from 1992.
Recording 1
Year: 1977
Singer: Caballë, Montserrat (Sop.)
Pianist: Zanetti, Miguel
Date: 1977
Support: LP
Label: Alhambra-Columbia
Discographical reference: SCE 981
Duration: 2'25
Observations: Included in the album "Canciones espanolas". Reissue on Columbia CD, WD 71320, in 1987.
Recording 2
Year: 1990
Singer: Kraus, Alfredo (Ten.)
Pianist: Arnaltes, Edelmiro
Date: 1990
Media: CD
Label: Amadeo

Discography reference: 429 556 2
Observations: Total duration of the cycle "Tribute to Lope de Vega" 6'56".
Recording 3
Year: 1990
Singer: Belmonte, Elisa (Sop.)
Pianist: Pares, Xavier
Venue: Caja Postal, Madrid
Date: 2-4-1990
Support: Radio
Duration: Unspecified
Comments: RNE recording.
Recording 4
Year: 1991
Singer: Kraus, Alfredo (Ten.)
Pianist: Zanetti, Miguel
Date: 1991
Media: CD
Label: Diapason
Label reference: CAL 101
Observations: Total duration of the cycle "Tribute to Lope de Vega" 6'06".
Recording 5
Year: 1997
Singer: Cid, Manuel (Ten.)
Pianist: Requejo, Ricardo
Date: 1997
Media: CD
Label: Claves Records
Discographical reference: CD 509602
Length: 2:12
Recording 6
Year: 1997
Singer: Lorengar, Pilar (Sop.)
Pianist: Lavilla, Fëlix
Date: 1997
Media: CD
Label: RCA Classics
Label reference: BMG 74321397692
Length: 2:15
Observations: Included in the album "Pilar Lorengar: Canciones", 2CD. Recorded in 1959.
Recording 7
Year: 1998
Singer: Resnik, Regina (Sop.)
Pianist: Wiotach, Richard
Date: 1998
Media: CD
Label: Sony Classical
Discographic reference: SMK 60784
Length: 2:20
Remarks: Vocal Masterworks series. Recorded in 1967 or 1968.
Recording 8

Year: 2001
Singer: Jordi, Ismael (Ten.)
Pianist: Munoz, Julio Alexis
Venue: Teatro Monumental, Madrid
Date: 26-5-2001
Support: Radio
Duration: Unspecified
Remarks: The Classical Radio Concerts. Recorded by RNE. Total duration Homenaje a Joaqum Turina: 6:08.
Recording 9
Year: 2005
Singer: Schwartz, Sylvia (Sop.)
Pianist: Turina, Fernando
Place: Fundacion Marcelino Botin, Santander
Date: 15-2-2005
Support: Radio
Duration: 2:00
Remarks: RNE recording. Not allowed to broadcast without the permission of the performers.

Title: "Al val de Fuente Ovejuna".

Opus No.: Op. 90, n° 3
Collection or series: *Homage to Lope de Vega,* n° 3
Date of composition: 1935
It belongs to the play by Lope de Vega: *Fuente Ovejuna.*
First verse: "Al val de Fuente Ovejuna".
Character: Musicians
Scenic notes: [Ea, taned y cantad, pues que para en uno son.]
Length: 2' 13"
Key: C major *
Tessitura: F3 - B4 flat
Aggonic indications: *Alegro Vivace*
Release date: 12-12-1935
Place of the premiere: Teatro Espanol, Madrid
Singer of the premiere: Rosita Hermosilla (Sop.)
Pianist of the premiere: Joaquin Turina
Manuscript location: FJM
Manuscript symbol: LJT-P-A-33
Date of publication: 1936 / 1983
Publisher: Union Musical Espanola
Place of publication: Madrid
Dedication: To Rosita Hermosilla
Head notes: For song and piano /from "Fuente Ovejuna".
Motivation: Tribute to Lope de Vega by the Conservatorio de Madrid in the Spanish Theatre
Remarks: The manuscript bears on the last leaf the date 13 November 1935.
There is another Union Musical Espanola edition from 1992.
Recording 1
Year: 1978
Singer: Diaz, Amable (Sop.)
Pianist: Gorostiaga, Ana Maria
Venue: Casa de la Radio, Madrid

Date: 17-11-1978
Support: Radio
Length: 2:25
Comments: RNE recording.
Recording 2
Year: 1990
Singer: Kraus, Alfredo (Ten.)
Pianist: Arnaltes, Edelmiro
Date: 1990
Media: CD
Label: Amadeo
Discography reference: 429 556 2
Observations: Total duration of the cycle "Tribute to Lope de Vega" 6'56".
Recording 3
Year: 1990
Singer: Belmonte, Elisa (Sop.)
Pianist: Parc's, Xavier
Venue: Caja Postal, Madrid
Date: 2-4-1990
Support: Radio
Duration: Unspecified
Comments: RNE recording.
Recording 4
Year: 1991
Singer: Kraus, Alfredo (Ten.)
Pianist: Zanetti, Miguel
Date: 1991
Media: CD
Label: Diapason
Label reference: CAL 101
Observations: Total duration of the cycle "Tribute to Lope de Vega" 6'06".
Recording 5
Year: 1997
Singer: Cid, Manuel (Ten.)
Pianist: Requejo, Ricardo
Date: 1997
Media: CD
Label: Claves Records
Discographical reference: CD 509602
Length: 2:33
Recording 6
Year: 1998
Singer: Resnik, Regina (Sop.)
Pianist: Wiotach, Richard
Date: 1998
Media: CD
Label: Sony Classical
Discographical reference: SMK 60784
Length: 1:59
Remarks: Vocal Masterworks series. Recorded in 1967 or 1968.

Recording 7
Year: 1998
Singer: Gragera, Elena (Mz.)
Pianist: Cardo, Anton
Venue: Centro Cultural Conde Duque, Madrid
Date: 9-3-1998
Support: Radio
Length: 2:07
Comments: RNE recording.
Recording 8
Year: 2001
Singer: Jordi, Ismael (Ten.)
Pianist: Munoz, Julio Alexis
Venue: Teatro Monumental, Madrid
Date: 26-5-2001
Support: Radio
Duration: Unspecified
Remarks: The Classical Radio Concerts. Recorded by RNE. Total duration Homenaje a Joaquin Turina: 6:08.
Recording 9
Year: 2005
Singer: Schwartz, Sylvia (Sop.)
Pianist: Turina, Fernando
Place: Fundacion Marcelino Botin, Santander
Date: 15-2-2005
Support: Radio
Length: 2:20
Remarks: RNE recording. Not allowed to broadcast without the permission of the interpreters.

VALLE CHINESTRA, BERNARDINO (1849-1928)

Title: "La barquilla" (The basket)

Date of composition: ca. 1900
It belongs to the work of Lope de Vega: *La Dorotea.*
First verse: "Pobre barquilla mi'a".
Character: Don Fernando
Scenic notes: [Sing, sing, for you have been tempered].
Duration: 3' 40" approx.
Key: F major
Tessitura: C3 sharp-Fa4
Location of the manuscript: Canarian Museum of Las Palmas
Manuscript symbol: EN 35001 AMC/MCC 125.046
Head notes: Cancion de Fëlix Lope de Vega (fragment). Voice and piano
Remarks: Manuscript with the text of the second stanza written on the staff of the voice.

Title: "Freedom".

Subtitle: Soliloquy
Date of composition: ca. 1900
It belongs to the work of Lope de Vega: *La Arcadia.*
First verse: "O precious freedom".
Character: Benalcio
Scenic annotations: [...the venerable old man begged him to sing, and ë! he said thus:]

Duration: 7' 45" approx.
Key: F major
Tessitura: C3-G4
Location of the manuscript: Canarian Museum of Las Palmas
Manuscript symbol: ES 35001 AMC/MCC 126.012
Header indications: (Monologue.) (Narracion de un pastor) / Poesia de Fëlix Lope de Vega (Fragmento) / Coro y solo ad libitum /Voz y piano
Observations: It has a chorus part al uni'sono included which alternates with the solo. On page 5 of the manuscript, in the entry for the chorus of the sëptimo compas, there is a footnote which reads: "When the piece is sung by a soloist in its entirety, all the words should be recited in speech rather than sung, until the solo is reached". Valle uses 6 of the 9 stanzas that make up the poem (1-4-5-7-8-9).

LIST OF SONGS BY YEAR OF COMPOSITION

ca. 1810	Garcia, Manuel	The boat of Love
ca. 1891	Casaresandlos Monteros, Jose Maria	Trova
ca. 1900	Valle Chinestra, Bernardino	The basket
		La Libertad
ca. 1900	Perez Aguirre, Julio	Green eyes
1914		
1914	Granados, Enrique	Don't cry, you little eyes
1917	Franco Bordons, Jose Maria	A...you
1923	Moreno Torroba, Federico	Copla de antano
1925	Cotarelo, Francisco	Mother, I saw some eyelets
1926	Duran, Gustavo	Seguidillas of the night of San Juan
1932	Menendez Aleyxandre, Arturo	Lucinda
1935	Campo y Zabaleta, Conrado del	So alive in my soul
	Casal Chapi, Enrique	Sonnet
	Gomez Garcia, Julio	Romancillo
	Guervos, Jose Maria	Serrana
		Mowing song
		Christmas carol
		Christmas carol
		Jealousy, don't kill me
		The Truth
		(What do I have that you seek my friendship?
		The pretended true
		Lucinda catches the lilies white
		Mowing song
		Beautiful little rivers
		Trebole
		Coplas del pastor enamorado
		Al val de Fuente Ovejuna
		When I look at you so beautiful
		If with my wishes
		Al Nino Dios in Bethlehem
	Rodrigo, Joaqrnn	Copla
	Turina, Joaquin	Cantar moreno de siega (Brown harvest song)
	Mingote, Angel	Canto de un mal nacer
	Moraleda Bellver, Fernando	Folia and Parabien to newlyweds
		La Morenica
		Chanzoneta
		This
		Poor little nacelle of mine
1939	Salvador, Matilde	Castellana
		Galician
		Levantina
ca. 1940	Larroca, Angel	Prayer to Christ crucified
1941	Toldra, Eduard	Mother, I saw some eyelets

		Cantarcillo
1942	Llongueres Badia, Joan	Drop yourself Pascual
		Cry for love
		To the gala of the zagal
		The vanquished sun
		The straws of the manger ^Where are you going?
1943	Bacarisse, Salvador	Sonnet by Lope de Vega
	Garcia de la Parra y Tellez, Benito	Song by Lope de Vega
1944	Bacarisse, Salvador	On the mountain alone
	Menendez Aleyxandre, Arturo	That he was killed at night
		Mother, I saw some eyelets
	Thomas Sabater, Juan Maria	Guitar
		Bagpipes
1945	Larroca, Angel	The prayer of Christ in the Garden
1946	Campo y Zabaleta, Conrado del	Song of the shepherdess Finarda
	Salvador, Matilde	Sailing song
1947	Palau, Manuel	Christmas carol
	Truan Alvarez, Enrique	Flowering mannikins
1949	Aldave Rodriguez, Pascual	Romance of Fuenteovejuna
1950	Bacarisse, Salvador	Coplas
	Palau, Manuel	On the mountain alone
1951	Altisent, Juan	jTrebole!
	Palau, Manuel	Elegy for the Knight of Olmedo
1952	Aldave Rodriguez, Pascual	St. John's Eve
	Martin Pompey, Angel	Sleep my child
	Rodrigo, Joaquin	Holy Shepherd
1954	Bueno Aguado [Buenagu], Jose Antonio	Sleep, my child
1955	Altisent, Juan	On the mountain alone...
	Peris Lacasa, Jose	Flowering mannikins
1956	Benavente Martinez, Jose Marla	The vanquished sun
		Don't cry my eyes out.
		Gypsy dance
1959	Truan Alvarez, Enrique	Zagalejo
1960	Truan Alvarez, Enrique	Don't cry my eyes out
1963	Asins Arbo, Miguel	Flowering mannikins
		The straws in the manger

1964 Carol, Mercedes — Cantarcillo

1968 Asins Arbo, Miguel — (Where are you going, Maria?

1970 Asins Arbo, Miguel — (Where are you going when it's cold?

1974 Escudero Garcia, Francisco — At the burial of Christ

1980 Iturralde Perez, Jose Luis — At the death of Jesus

1986 Barrera, Antonio — Mowing song
Legend
Seguidillas
Love song
Dance

1988 Lavilla, Felix — Oh, bitter loneliness

1990 Colodro Campos, Fernando — Flowering mannikins

1997 Nin Culmell, Joaquin — Welcome
Wash me in the Tagus

1998 Diaz Yerro, Gonzalo — When I stop to contemplate my state
Shepherd who with your loving whistles
How many Lord, how many times have you
called

1999 Diaz Yerro, Gonzalo — (What do I have that you seek my friendship?

1999 Carbajo Cadenas, Victor — Absence

2004 Rincon Garcia, Eduardo — Sweetest Lord, I was blind
Flowering mannikins
(What do I have that you seek my friendship?

2005 Ortega i Pujol, Miquel — Sonnet

2006 Parera Fons, Antoni — Palms of Belen

2009 Miguel Peris, Vicente — Mananicas de mayo
Christmas tune

2011Garcia Fernandez, Voro — At night
To my solitudes I go

9 786207 277032